I0095775

Gesa Mackenthun, Jörn Dosch (eds.)
Subversive Semantics in Political and Cultural Discourse

Political Science | Volume 130

Gesa Mackenthun is a professor of American studies at Universität Rostock. She initiated the DFG graduate school Cultural Encounters and the Discourses of Scholarship.

Jörn Dosch is a professor of international politics and development cooperation at Universität Rostock. He did his doctorate at Johannes Gutenberg-Universität Mainz. From 2000 to 2011 he was lecturer, senior lecturer, and professor of Asian-Pacific Studies at the University of Leeds. He spent guest professorships at Stanford University and Monash University, Malaysia.

Gesa Mackenthun, Jörn Dosch (eds.)

Subversive Semantics in Political and Cultural Discourse

The Production of Popular Knowledge

[transcript]

We would like to express our thanks to the German Research Foundation (DFG) and to Rostock University for funding this publication and the work of the graduate School "Deutungsmacht: Religion and Belief Systems in Deutungsmachtkonflikten" (Rostock, Germany) which gave rise to it.

Bibliographic information published by the Deutsche Nationalbibliothek

The Deutsche Nationalbibliothek lists this publication in the Deutsche Nationalbibliografie; detailed bibliographic data are available in the Internet at http://dnb.d-nb.de

This work is licensed under the Creative Commons Attribution-NonCommercial-NoDerivatives 4.0 (BY-NC-ND) which means that the text may be used for non-commercial purposes, provided credit is given to the author.

To create an adaptation, translation, or derivative of the original work and for commercial use, further permission is required and can be obtained by contacting rights@transcript-publishing.com

Creative Commons license terms for re-use do not apply to any content (such as graphs, figures, photos, excerpts, etc.) not original to the Open Access publication and further permission may be required from the rights holder. The obligation to research and clear permission lies solely with the party re-using the material.

First published in 2023 by transcript Verlag, Bielefeld
© Gesa Mackenthun, Jörn Dosch (eds.)

Cover layout: Maria Arndt, Bielefeld

https://doi.org/10.14361/9783839461778
Print-ISBN 978-3-8376-6177-4
PDF-ISBN 978-3-8394-6177-8
ISSN of series: 2702-9050
eISSN of series: 2702-9069

Contents

Introduction
Gesa Mackenthun and Jörn Dosch 7

Conspiracy Theories as Populist Counter-Narratives
Michael Butter 21

Populism, Populist Democracy, and the Shifting of Meanings
Subverting – Disfiguring – Transforming
Hans-Jürgen Puhle 47

Legitimizing Colonial Rule in the Twenty-First Century
Discursive Strategies of the AfD's Politics of Remembrance
Aram Ziai 71

**The Origins of Replacement Narratives and the Resemanticization
of Feminism in Two Novels of the Far Right**
Enrico Schlickeisen 99

Indignants of the World, Unite?
Mobilizations of Indignation in Alter- and Anti-Globalism
Christine Unrau 123

Right-Wing Extremism and Ecology
Denial and Appropriation of the Climate Crisis by the Far Right
Daniela Gottschlich 157

Planters of Doom and Playful Gardeners
Determinist and Possibilist Narratives of Mankind
Gesa Mackenthun 181

Contested Nationhood in the United States of America
Susanne Lachenicht 227

Contributors 253

Introduction

Gesa Mackenthun and Jörn Dosch[1]

The Pawn

© Victoria Glinka

1   We would like to thank Leonard William Olof Björk for his meticulous copy-editing.

In the early morning of February 24, 2022, Wladimir Putin gave a speech announcing the reasons for his troops' illegal invasion of Ukraine. The action was necessary, he claimed, because Ukraine was committing a "genocide" against Russians and would therefore have to be "denazified". In his reply, the Ukrainian president Wolodymyr Selenskyi mixed anger with sarcasm, wondering what his Jewish grandfather would think about such a justification of this aggressive military takeover. After all, he had fought on the side of the Sovjets against Hitler's troops which were involved in a similar act of aggression as now committed by Putin's troops. Selenskyi's suggestion to meet in Israel for negotiations was a smart follow-up to this reply. It discloses the enormousness of Putin's historical construct: a visit in Yad Vashem might refresh the memory on the issues of Nazism and genocide!

A related instance of semantic subversion by linguistic reinscription is Russian foreign minister Sergej Lawrow's assertion of March 10, 2022 that weapons of ethnic biological mass destruction were developed in Pentagon-run Ukrainian secret laboratories, which filled the politically policed information channels of the Russian media (Palmer 2022; Wion 2022). In their aggressive inversion of perpetrators and victims, the rhetorical tricks and twists used by the Kremlin in legitimizing the Russian attack on Ukraine resemble the semantic practice of right-wing groups and despotic rulers and their admirers around the world.

The idea for the present volume on the rhetorical power of "subversive semantics" was conceived long before Russia's recent imperial takeover which continues to threaten peace in Europe and food security in the world. Its object are the metaphorical and narrative strategies of semantic subversion, predominantly in populist and right-wing discourses but also in anticolonial and postcolonial struggles. It is a well-known fact by now that metaphors, tropes, and narratives, rather than being innocent speech ornaments, reflect and produce social realities (Johnson/Lakoff 1980; White 1987). These social semantics are in constant flux, interacting with ideological requirements and emotionally affected belief systems. Their various elements can form semantic clusters which, after ceasing to signify, may fall apart again – perhaps to reappear in different arrangements at some later moment. While successful stories, narratives, and images tend to migrate between historical situations, not all of them possess subversive traits, as in the particularly blatant case of the Kremlin's rhetorical contortions. Few migrating cultural stories enjoy great longevity, but some of them, as philosopher Hans Blumenberg has shown for the image of a shipwreck with spectator as a metaphor expressing various philosophical ideas, among them epistemic transgression and existential abandonment (Blumenberg 1979), can assume remarkable transhistorical potential.

It is important to understand that the migration of tropes and narratives as such is an unavoidable part of cultural signification. Exemplary historical anecdotes – say, of famous leaders crossing famous rivers or climbing famous mountains – or philosophical examples like Blumenberg's shipwreck; or literary examples adopted into political-philosophical discourse such as Fyodor Dostoyevsky's story of the diabolical grand inquisitor (Lethen 2022); can be actualized at different times and in different contexts but disappear when their explanatory power fades. Equally crucial, not all reformulation and reinterpretation in political and cultural discourses results in the subversion of concepts into their opposite meanings or aims at the production of questionable "alternative knowledge". Think, for example, of the development discourse. When US President Harry Truman pioneered the idea of development cooperation in his inaugural address of January 1949, he described development as an increase in industrial activity. This increase would then substantially raise the standards of living in underdeveloped nations (Truman 1949). Development was understood purely as an economic pathway following the experience and example of the industrialized nations of Europe and North America. The strongly normative and empirically vaguely substantiated term "underdevelopment" was also Truman's invention and by the stroke of a pen he had divided the world into two halves. "Underdevelopment" might not be in frequent use anymore, but the approach of clustering states according to their level of development still lives on in the idea of the "Global North" and the "Global South". This semantic practice has received growing criticism from within the countries expected to develop along the trodden economic path of the West (e.g. Escobar 1995). The crucial difference is that today the semantics of development go far beyond the notion of industrial output or GDP per capita. Rather, the language of development has migrated to the anthropological realm: a frequent concept now is *human* development. The human development discourse, the closely related debate on the Sustainable Development Goals (SDG) and "non-Western" approaches to development such as *Buen Vivir* in Ecuador and Bolivia, stress in a much more holistic way the importance of social, health-related, educational and cultural dimensions and even question the idea of development as a linear process altogether.

Perhaps one of the most impressive and visible examples for the semantic turn in the construction of the development narrative is the *Tropenmuseum* in Amsterdam. Founded as the Colonial Museum in 1910 and following the fashion of the day, it first reflected the mindset of colonialism as the driving force behind the "development of the colonies" in the fields of administration, economic activities in general, agriculture and export crops, in particular timber and rubber extraction as well as education and health care (Legêne 1998, 4). As the result of a decades-long "heated social debate on the nature of Dutch colonialism" (Legêne 1998, 5), today's *Tropenmuseum* is devoted to an entirely critical perspective. The museum's permanent exhibition "Our Colonial Inheritance" presents colonialism exclusively as a history of European domination, oppression and exploitation and, even more prominently, explores the resilience of the colonized peoples as they fought against a system which was exogenously forced upon them. The term development is not mentioned once in the entire exhibition; rather, the implicit *leitmotiv* is the clear message that colonialism can only be understood as an anti-development phenomenon.

Similar observations regarding evolutionary non-subversive semantic shifts apply to the term security in a political context. Narrowly defined during the Cold War as the absence of a military threat to the physical integrity of the state, the idea of security has transformed to focus mainly at the level of the individual. In the broadest understanding of human security, the state cannot be secure if its citizens face socio-economic and environmental threats, live in fear of violent crimes, are subjected to human rights violations, or lack access to education. In both cases, development and security, the – what may be called – constructive reshaping of semantics has resulted in a much-needed reconceptualization of both analytical concepts and more useful and effective political and policy responses to pressing challenges. Under the impact of political and social change, the formation of interpretive power has shifted.

However, as the 2020 Presidential and Congressional elections in the United States have demonstrated, even the most stable ideas and belief systems in political thought and practice, whose meanings have seemingly been taken for granted for decades, can show their subversive potential. Even before Joe Biden was officially declared the winner of the Presidential race, incumbent President Donald Trump started to craft a narrative of fraud and a stolen election. In the preceding months Trump had already pre-emptively voiced media-effective strategic concerns about the integrity of the electoral process.[2] When the influential, opinion-mongering Republican senator Lindsey Graham was asked why Joe Biden's election was not valid while all the Republican Congressional victories should stand, he answered: "We win because of our ideas, we lose elections because they cheat us" (quoted in Waldman 2020). Democracy is no longer the quasi-sacred highest institutional norm but becomes subjected to us v. them discourses. In other words, democracy is when we win. When the others claim to have won, it can only mean that they have cheated and thus disrespected core democratic values. Consequently, according to the favorite Republican key argument that went on for months and at least until the mid-term elections of 2022, democracy is under threat. Following this narrative, democracy is not under threat because ex-President Donald Trump and his surrogates have tried to delegitimize the legitimate result of a democratic election but because Democrats are not respecting the widely televised alternative truth claims of Mr. Trump. Dan Patrick, lieutenant governor (vice governor) of Texas, proclaimed on his official homepage after the 2020 elections: "President Trump's pursuit of voter fraud is not only essential to determine the outcome of this election, it is essential to

---

2   For a timeline of the construction of this narrative leading up to election night see, for example, Kessler and Rizzo (2020).

maintain our democracy and restore faith in future elections."[3] This is subversive semantics at its best: anti-democratic thought and action emerges as the savior of democracy. Yet, this phenomenon is certainly not restricted to the United States. As Steven Levitsky and Daniel Ziblatt note in their bestseller *How Democracies Die*, "This is how we tend to think of democracies dying: at the hands of men with guns. [...] But there is another way to break a democracy. It is less dramatic but equally destructive. Democracies may die at the hands not of generals but of elected leaders – presidents or prime ministers who subvert the very process that brought them to power" (Levitsky and Ziblatt 2018, 3).

In a broader sense, this seems to be a particular tactic of reactionary[4] discourses, as when white supremacist groups in the United States – here discussed by Enrico Schlickeisen – proclaim a conspiracy to effect the "genocide" of the white "race". More particularly they evoke an on-slaught on *white men* – in direct response to the Me Too, Black Lives Matter, and Idle No More movements. A similar near-future catastrophe is announced for the European context in response to the "Syrian migration crisis". The powerful resemanticization of human migration as a "refugee crisis" was only partly the result of the rise of far-right populists and their promotion of new meanings to replace existing words. In the wake of the substantial influx of migrants and refugees to Europe in 2015 and 2016, the idea of "crisis" in the context of migration was advanced by political decision-makers across almost the entire political-ideological spectrum, and embraced by the media. As Pedro Góis and Maria Faraone explain (2019, 140), linking migration rhetorically and discursively with crisis significantly stimulated "fears associated with financial burdens, cultural and religious differences, and the need for security from terrorists." In a narrower sense, the securitization of migration – i.e. using a rhetoric of emergency by referring to migrants as a threat and danger

---

3   https://www.danpatrick.org/, accessed November 11, 2022 (this statement is no longer online).

4   We are using this term to refer to rhetorics that react to mainstream rhetorics, usually by subverting their meanings into their opposite.

in order to justify extraordinary political measures such as new exclusionary immigration legislation – is a much older phenomenon and has been discussed in academia since the early 1990s (e.g. Waever et al. 1993; Huysmans 2000; Ibrahim 2005).

It does not take any deep analysis to discover the entirely different meaning associated with the term migration in the case of, say, the Mayflower Pilgrims who arrived on the coast of today's Massachusetts in 1620 to establish Plymouth Colony. This migration event is deeply enshrined in the DNA of the United States and a foundation stone of the national myth (Whittock 2020), which is quite literally represented by Plymouth Rock, the powerful symbol or even "fetish" of the new beginnings (Paul 2014, 149, 161). The granite bolder, inscribed with the number 1620, can still be visited at its supposedly original position on the shore of Plymouth Harbor, Massachusetts. The information board next to the Rock describes it as a "solid, steadfast and everlasting [...] icon for the birth of a nation." "What if we applied modern immigration arguments to the Pilgrims?", asks Matthew Rowley (2021, 4–5) and continues: "If governments had a right to reject immigrants – regardless of claims to be experiencing hardship or persecution (consider Hungary's closed response to the 'Migrant Crisis') – then surely the Pilgrims had no right to presume they were welcome on Native American land." As interesting and stimulating as it may be from an academic point of view to highlight the inconsistencies in the perception of migration in different historical contexts, there can be little doubt that the ship of resemanticization in the political and public spheres is in no danger of suffering shipwreck: today's most powerful connotation with migration is fear.

Narratives of world conspiracy and deep states, analyzed in this volume by Michael Butter, effectively allied themselves with other stories of fear, e.g. during the 2020–2023 pandemic. Covid's narrative existed long before the pandemic itself entered the scene: it is anticipated in numerous novels, films, and online blogs. Like the above-mentioned stories of population replacement, the pandemic conspiracy narrative is a story intended to generate fear; it is building on existing, mostly diffuse fears of the future, as well as a pervasive suspicion toward social, political, and intellectual elites. Presently, the extinction narrative seems to be particularly *en vogue*, with "extinction" acting as battlefield between re-actionary racist groups on the one hand and environmentalist groups on the other (like Extinction Rebellion and Last Generation). What seems to unite them, in spite of occupying radically opposite ends of the political spectrum, is an anthropocentric perspective largely undisturbed by con-siderations of non-human lifeforms. Thus, reactionary back-to-the-land groups are more interested in claiming ethnically "clean" territories and returning to patriarchal rural structures than in establishing environ-ments friendly for other than human species (see Daniela Gottschlich's essay in this volume).

The rising awareness of environmental deterioration and emerging discussions about the temporality of the Anthropocene have produced a rearticulation of colonial relations as well. In her critique of popular his-tories of the deep past, Gesa Mackenthun discusses the rhetorical twists displayed in quasi-scientific portrayals of the pre-Columbian past: in these recent texts, original inhabitants are represented as both savages causing a mass-slaughter of big animals during the Pleistocene era and as disastrous agriculturalists contributing to early phases of global warming. Anthropocene discourse tends to abolish the distinctions be-tween environmentally extractive colonizing societies and Indigenous societies sharing the catastrophic consequences of colonialism with the other-than-human world. In some cases, it thus lends support to exculpatory narratives of the colonial past as promoted by the new Right (see Aram Ziai's contribution in this volume).

Various essays in this book (Gottschlich, Schlickeisen, Ziai) are ded-icated to analyzing the subversive migrations of tropes and narratives in texts by German and transatlantic rightwing groups, whose conser-vatism consists in their desire to reinstall a society from an idealized past – a time of happiness and prosperity and traditional social hier-archies. Their explicit valuation of heteronormative gender structures, racial purity and an ethnopluralistic order between human groups is combined with latent and manifest variations of aggressiveness, in-cluding terrorism, an extractive economy to bolster cherished comforts, and an antihumanistic anthropology celebrating blood relations but rejecting the values of a common humanity. Some German rightwing parochialists present themselves as the true ecologists keeping both nature and the "people's" genes clean from foreign infiltration and pollution. The "people" evoked by such rhetoric differs somewhat from the "people"/"el pueblo" evoked by decolonial groups in the Global South, as Hans-Jürgen Puhle shows in this volume. This concept, together with related terms such as "Heimat" or a rootedness to emotionally important locations, can be seen as an ideological battleground between oppositional discourses, one of which dreams of reviving an imaginary halcyon past while the other emphasizes the importance of reducing carbon emissions and of practicing more organic forms of agriculture. Sometimes the real audiences of both groups overlap.

The subversive use of mythical stories and concepts is thus particularly intense in reactionary discourses whose anti-humanist matrix, due to its lack of an idea of human agency and initiative, obstructs the unfolding of creative thinking. However, anticolonial and decolonial groups are also prone to tactical uses of established mythical narratives – such as abolitionist and black civil rights groups powerfully appropriating the biblical story of Exodus, or Indigenous groups adopting the language of nationhood in their struggles for political and territorial sovereignty and self-determination (as Susanne Lachenicht shows in this volume). These cases of creative adaptation on the part of disenfranchised groups must be categorically distinguished from the uncreative, at best carnivalesque practice of reactionary discourses discussed above. The reactionary resemanticization of reform-oriented ideas and narratives – such as a right-wing group's public display of Rosa Luxemburg's remark that "Freedom is always the freedom of the dissenter" – are embedded in a general ideological framework dismissing diversity, manufacturing suspicion of scientific knowledge, and capitalizing on fears of the future. Reformist narratives, conversely, may creatively tap into traditional knowledges (see the use of Traditional Ecological Knowledge in many environment-related contexts) but they do so in order to promote practices and narratives of hope (Solnit 2016).

Conscious of the function of language in the production of social power, *Subversive Semantics* explores the phenomenon of linguistic resemanticization – of filling old rhetorical wine into new bottles, thereby frequently inverting the original meaning. It should not remain unmentioned that semantic play, pastiche, and subversiveness are quintessentially literary pursuits, practiced with great aesthetic appeal by modernist and postmodernist writers. Ironical repetition of speech acts can affirm an existing master trope or narrative but can also consist of using dominant tropes and narratives for parodistic or paradoxical purposes, aiming at irritating readers by subverting the grounds of their intellectual coordinates. Representatives of subaltern social groups have abundantly used humor and travesty, "slipping the yoke by changing the joke" in Ralph Ellison's famous pun (Ellison 1958), performing literary acts of postcolonial parody, and ironically "signifying" on classic texts of the dominant culture (Gates 1988). Rightwing and authoritarian groups, which are notoriously less capable of wit and creativity, frequently just invert the original wording, as George Orwell imagines his dictatorship to do in its invention of Newspeak in *Nineteen Eighty-four* (1948). While the subversiveness of the first group (of witty "signifying") invites the unleashing of further creative activity, that of the latter group aims at producing confusion. Appealing to the constitutionally guaranteed freedoms of speech and cultural diversity, such actors actually seek to erode the liberal democratic order on which these rights rest in order to replace it with an authoritarian, racist, and patriarchal regime. Speaking of themselves as the victims of pogroms and genocide, they prepare the intellectual ground for the persecution of everybody not assenting to their crude world picture. Their rhetoric of causing confusion resembles that of the "merchants of doubt" analyzed by Naomi Oreskes and Erik Conway (2010), working in favor of capitalist corporations by inventing scientific "proof" of the healthiness of nicotine and agrochemicals or the falsity of scientific evidence for climate change and species extinction.

Several questions are pivotal to the individual contributions: How precisely do the analyzed rhetorical maneuvers assume hermeneutic power; to what extent do they serve to establish new and powerful belief systems beyond rational and democratic control? Why is it that societies priding themselves in technological and rational excellence as well as broad and deep knowledge may fall victim to an expanding communicative cultivation of ignorance coupled with a general hostility toward life? And what exactly drives the observed semantic shifts? What is it that makes these subversions (and perversions) so powerful? Is it an aesthetic fascination with postmodern travesty and pastiche? Or is it that an in-built textual technique links such narratives (of victimization, conspiracy, ecological destruction) to an ancient psychological pattern which we may term as *Angstlust* (pleasurable fear)? Is it modernity's "fascination of the abomination", as Joseph Conrad famously writes in his ambivalent parody of empire, *Heart of Darkness* (Conrad 1902/1985, 31)? How are the shifting expressions of indignation, which Christine Unrau analyzes in her essay, linked to economic and communicative globalization? This volume is the place to document semantic subversions, not to psychologize them. We invite our readers to consider our empirical assemblage and find their own answers.

Works Cited

Blumenberg, Hans (1979). Schiffbruch mit Zuschauer: Paradigma einer Daseinsmetapher. Frankfurt/M.: Suhrkamp

Conrad, Joseph (1902/1985) Heart of Darkness. London: Penguin.

Ellison, Ralph Waldo (1958) Change the Joke and Slip the Yoke. Partisan Review 25(2), 212–22.

Escobar, Arturo (1995) Encountering Development. The Making and Unmaking of the Third World. Repr. Princeton: Princeton University Press, 2012.

Gates, Henry Louis (1988) The Signifying Monkey. A Theory of African American Literary Criticism. Oxford: Oxford University Press.

Góis, Pedro and Maria Faraone (2019) Reconstructing the migration communication discourse The call for contextual and narrative-based evidence in the deconstruction of fear. In: Stephen M. Croucher, João R. Caetano and Elsa A. Campbell (eds). The Routledge Companion to Migration, Communication, and Politics. London: Routledge.

Huysmans, Jeff (2000) The European Union and the securitization of migration. Journal of Common Market Studies 38(5), 751–777.

Ibrahim, Maggie (2005) The Securitization of Migration: A Racial Discourse. International Migration 43(5), 163–187.

Johnson, Mark and George Lakoff (1980) Metaphors We Live By. Chicago: University of Chicago Press.

Kessler, Glenn and Salvador Rizzo (2020) President Trump's false claims of vote fraud: A chronology. The Washington Post (5 November). Web: https://www.washingtonpost.com/politics/2020/11/05/presid ent-trumps-false-claims-vote-fraud-chronology/

Legêne, Susan (1998) The Tropenmuseum and the Colonial Heritage. Position paper. Amsterdam: Vrije Universiteit Amsterdam.

Lethen, Helmut (2022) Der Sommer des Großinquisitors. Hamburg: Rowohlt.

Levitsky, Steven and Daniel Ziblatt (2018) How Democracies Die. New York: Viking.

Oreskes, Naomi, and Erik M. Conway (2010) Merchants of Doubt. How a Handful of Scientists Obscured the Truth on Issues from Tobacco Smoke to Global Warming. Bloomsbury.

Orwell, George (2019) Nineteen Eighty-Four. Repr. London: Penguin, 1948.

Palmer, Ewan (2022) U.S. Biological Weapons in Ukraine—Separating the Facts From the Fiction. Newsweek (3 August). Web: https://www .newsweek.com/us-biological-weapons-ukraine-labs-germ-warfar e-1685956.

Paul, Heike (2014). The Myths That Made America. An Introduction to American Studies. Bielefeld: transcipt.

Rowley, Matthew (2021) Many Great Migrations: Colonial History and the Contest for American Identity. The Review of Faith & International Affairs 19(3), 5–19, DOI: 10.1080/15570274.2021.1954425

Solnit, Rebecca (2016) Hope in the Dark. Untold Histories, Wild Possibilities. Chicago: Haymarket.

Truman, Harry (1949) Inaugural Address. National Archives. Web: https ://www.trumanlibrary.gov/library/public-papers/19/inaugural-add ress

Waever, Ole, Barry Buzan, Morten Kelstrup and Pierre Lemaitre (1993) *Identity, Migration and the New Security Agenda in Europe.* New York: St. Martin's Press.

Waldman, Paul (2020) Opinion. Trump's strategy to have the courts swing the election lies in tatters. The Washington Post (13 November). Web: https://www.washingtonpost.com/opinions/2020/11/13/trumps-strategy-have-courts-swing-election-lies-tatters/

White, Hayden (1987) The Content of the Form. Narrative Discourse and Historical Representation. Baltimore: John Hopkins University Press.

Whittock, Martyn (2020) The 1620 Mayflower voyage and the English settlement of North America. Historian (London) 145, 10–14.

Wion (2022) Found 30 Biological Labs in Ukraine. Wion (8 March). Web: https://www.wionews.com/world/found-30-biological-labs-in-ukraine-possibly-for-bioweapons-claim-russian-forces-460189

Conspiracy Theories as Populist Counter-Narratives

Michael Butter

To say that conspiracy theories are populist counter-narratives may sound like stating the obvious. It has by now been well established by a rich body of research from literary and cultural studies, anthropology, and related disciplines that conspiracy theories are narratives (see for example, Fenster 2008; Butter 2014; Rabo 2020). Moreover, that there is a close relationship between conspiracism and populism has also been frequently observed and will be discussed in detail below. And that conspiracy theories always and necessarily challenge the official version of events is a widespread idea both among scholars and the public at large. In fact, several studies on the subject – ranging from John Fiske's classic *Media Matters* (1994) to the introduction to a recent collection of essays on conspiracy theories in central and eastern Europe (Deutschmann, Herlth and Woldan 2020) – see opposition to the official version of events as a defining feature of conspiracy theories. The position taken by media scholar Jack Bratich is even more extreme. Not only does he hold that "proving that conspiracy theories [are] disparaged by mainstream sources" amounts to "belaboring the obvious" (Bratich 2008, 7); he also argues that "conspiracy theory [is] a symptom of the discourse that *positions* it" (Bratich 2008, 16; emphasis in the original). In other words, Bratich suggests that labeling something a conspiracy theory is a strategic move by those in power to denounce certain views as illegitimate and false. Consequently, for him, conspiracy theories are by definition counter-narratives.

There is a lot of truth to Bratich's argument, but the story is more complicated. It is correct that the term "conspiracy theory" is a weapon, and it is also correct that it is often used to disqualify and ridicule unwanted ideas. But it is not true that it is impossible to define "conspiracy theory" in any other way. In fact, there is remarkable agreement among scholars from various disciplines as to how to define it, as the contributions to the *Routledge Handbook of Conspiracy Theories* show (Butter and Knight 2020).[1] Put simply, conspiracy theories assert the existence of a covertly operating group of people – the conspirators – who seek, from base motives and by underhand means, to achieve certain ends. Such theories assume that nothing happens by accident, that nothing is as it seems, and that everything is connected (Barkun 2003, 3–4). In other words, they hold that everything has been planned by the conspirators and that events unfold exactly as they intend; that these conspirators are operating in secret; and that there are links between seemingly unconnected events, organizations, and people.

If conspiracy theories are defined this way and if one assumes a historical and transcultural perspective, it quickly becomes clear that conspiracy theories are not always counter-narratives. Outside of the western world, they often constitute the official version of events until today (Gray 2010; Radnitz 2021; Boukari and Philipps, 2022); in the western world they only ceased being the official explanation of events during the late 1950s and early 1960s – a transformation that I address in the first part of this chapter. The second part addresses the relationship between populism and conspiracy theory and introduces the concept of science-related populism. It was recently proposed by Mede and Schäfer (2020) to capture how populists do not only oppose political elites but also challenge expert knowledge and common wisdom. In the third and longest

---

1   In Germany, the term "conspiracy theory" has received considerable criticism in recent years, however, mostly outside of academic discourse. Internationally, the term remains unchallenged. I have discussed the proposed alternatives and the reasons why the original term captures the phenomenon best elsewhere (see Butter 2021).

part, I apply the idea of science-related populism to the conspiracist documentaries *Plandemic: The Hidden Agenda Behind Covid-19* and *Plandemic: Indoctornation* to demonstrate which strategies of resemanticization they employ to cast doubt on the official narrative of the pandemic and how their arguments are tied to a populist agenda.

1.   Conspiracy Theories as Counter-Narratives

It seems as if conspiracy theories have never been more popular and influential than in the past two decades. However, as Uscinski and Parent conclude in their quantitative study on the role of conspiracy theories in American public life since the 1890s, "[t]he data suggest one telling fact: we do not live in an age of conspiracy theories and have not for some time" (Uscinski and Parent 2014, 110–111). Their conclusion is confirmed by a plethora of qualitative studies on the role of conspiracy theorizing in Europe and North America since the early modern period, which all stress that it was perfectly normal to believe in conspiracy theories in previous ages (Bailyn 1967; Cubitt 1993; Butter 2014). Far into the twentieth century, the western world regarded conspiracy theories as a legitimate form of knowledge, rooted within the mainstream of society, believed by ordinary people as well as elites, corroborated by scholars and spread by the media. Had there been polls trying to capture a conspiracy mentality as they are conducted now, probably more than 90 percent of people in North America and Europe would have affirmed their belief in conspiracy theories one or two hundred years ago (Butter 2020, 93–99).

Accordingly, conspiracy theories often had significant impact on events and developments. For reasons of brevity, I restrict myself to examples from the United States, but many episodes from European history could be mentioned as well. During the seventeenth century, the Puritan settler-colonists in New England saw themselves as the victims of a conspiracy led by the devil and comprising Native Americans, witches, and Catholics (Butter 2014, 66–112). A century later, colonial leaders like George Washington, Thomas Jefferson and John Adams became convinced that the British colonies in America were the victims of a sinister plot orchestrated by King George III and his ministers. As Bernard Bailyn (1967) has demonstrated, this belief was one of the major driving forces behind the American Revolution. During the 1850s, then, the so-called "Slave Power conspiracy theory" became "the founding ideology of the Republican Party" and the most important cause of the Civil War (Butter 2014, 171). In his 1858 "House Divided" speech, for example, Abraham Lincoln accused the current president James Buchanan, his predecessor, the chief justice of the Supreme Court, and an influential Democratic congressman of having orchestrated all events of the past decade to further the goal of introducing slavery everywhere in the United States (Butter 2020, 40–42). A century later, during the Red Scare of the 1940s and 1950s, the fear of a Communist conspiracy masterminded in Moscow pervaded American society. It was regularly discussed in Congress, loyalty programs were initiated in response, and the Communist Party was virtually outlawed (Butter 2014, 236). A few years later, however, conspiracy theorizing stopped being normal both in the United States and in most of Europe.

The stigmatization of conspiracy theories, which resulted in their transformation from orthodox into heterodox knowledge and thus from official to counter-narratives, has been traced in detail for the United States by Katharina Thalmann (2019). There is no similar study for Western Europe yet, but the evidence suggests that conspiracy theories underwent the same shift in status there (McKenzie-McHarg and Fredheim 2017; Girard 2020). As Thalmann (2019, 25–69) demonstrates, in the United States, conspiracist beliefs were first problematized by social scientists, and this skepticism then gradually seeped into Americans' everyday consciousness. To cut a long story short, social scientists began to problematize conspiracy theories in two different ways during the 1940s and 1950s. Some scholars, most notably Karl Popper, argued that conspiracy theories were bad explanations of social and political processes because they overemphasized intentions and neglected unintended consequences and structural effects. Another group of scholars, among them Theodor W. Adorno and other members of the Frankfurt School, looked from their U.S. exile to Germany where the conspiracy theory of a Jewish-Bolshevist plot for world domination led to the Holocaust.

These scholars argued that conspiracy theories were not only wrong but also extremely dangerous.

These arguments were initially restricted to the ivory tower of academia and had no wider repercussions. During the 1950s, however, they were taken up by a new generation of researchers. Scholars such as the sociologist Edward Shils or the political scientist Seymour Martin Lipset switched their attention from totalitarianism in Europe to the situation in the USA, where many liberal intellectuals were suspected to be part of the communist conspiracy. To rebut these accusations, academics either tackled the conspiracy theorists in the manner of the Frankfurt School, branding them as "pseudo-conservative" or "populist", or they took the Popperist line, attacking their pattern of reasoning and labelling them "pseudoscientific". Unlike the work of Adorno or Popper, these studies attracted notice beyond the bounds of academia. This was due partly to the efforts of Shils, Lipset and others who adopted an accessible style that would reach a wider public, and partly to the help of multipliers outside universities. Many journalists also regarded the Red Scare conspiracy theories as a danger to American democracy and seized on the research findings, thereby helping to popularize them.

This development was reinforced by another factor that Thalmann also discusses. Not only were the ideas of Lasswell, Lipset and later Richard Hofstadter catching on outside universities; after World War II, more and more Americans were also going to university. Under the G.I. Bill of 1944, former mobbed soldiers were able to go to college. For soldiers from low income and ethnic groups who had previously been denied the chance to study, this represented a great opportunity, and many took advantage of it. Large numbers of students thus came into contact with studies explicitly critiquing conspiracist thinking and learned about more nuanced social science models emphasizing structural constraints over human agency.

The effect of these developments became quickly apparent. While the idea of large-scale communist subversion orchestrated from Moscow was firmly anchored in mainstream U.S. society in the mid-1950s, ten years later only members of the far-right John Birch Society and similar groups continued to believe in a communist plot to undermine American institutions. In this and other cases, conspiracy theories were no longer the official version of events. As they moved from the mainstream to the margins of society, they became counter-narratives that challenge generally accepted explanations.

Broadly speaking, the stigmatization of conspiracy theories has left their proponents with two options: they can pretend to be just asking questions about the official version to hide the fact that they are conspiracy theorists and to maintain their mainstream appeal, or they can consciously accept their marginal status and make a virtue of it by openly employing the language of plots and schemes (Thalmann 2019, 130). At a deeper level, however, the rhetorical maneuvers conspiracy theorists perform are always remarkably similar, no matter which of the two paths they choose. In fact, it is only at this historical moment that the strategies of semantic subversion and rhetorical inversion that this volume is interested in became relevant for conspiracy theories.

However, to say that conspiracy theories became a stigmatized form of knowledge does not mean that they became entirely unpopular. As many studies have shown, conspiracy theories have retained considerable popularity throughout the western world (Uscinski and Parent 2014), albeit at a much lower level than before they were challenged by the social sciences. What is more, at least in the United States, conspiracy theories appear to have undergone a process of destigmatization over the past decade. When Barack Obama was running for reelection in 2012, most Republican politicians were extremely unwilling to openly embrace the birther conspiracy theory, which claims that Obama was an illegitimate president because he was allegedly not born in the U.S. – at least when they were on the record (Butter 2014, 300). By now, however, the claim that the presidential election of 2020 was stolen and that Joe Biden is an illegitimate president and has become the major tenet of the Republican Party, and members who openly disagree like Liz Cheney have been demoted. A detailed discussion of these factors – among them, growing polarization – and actors – among them, of course, Donald Trump – have fueled this process of de-stigmatization and to what degree and which effects conspiracy theories have gained legitimacy again is beyond the scope of this chapter. Suffice it to say that the destigmatization has by no means affected all areas of American public life and thus not restored conspiracy theories to their earlier status as perfectly acceptable knowledge. While they can be more openly articulated now with impunity, it is exactly the fact that they contradict knowledge produced by traditional experts and epistemic authorities that makes them so attractive for Donald Trump and other populists. Due to the democratization of media use, they can spread them even when the traditional media still shun them, and thus position themselves against political, intellectual, and scientific elites (Thalmann 2019, 198).

2.   Conspiracy Theories and (Science-Related) Populism

While there is widespread agreement when it comes to defining "conspiracy theory", "populism" is a far more contested concept. Over the past twenty years, populism has been conceptualized as the underlying logic of the political (Laclau 2005), a rhetorical strategy (Barr 2009), a mode of political practice (Jansen 2011), a discourse (Aslanidis 2016), a performative style (Moffitt 2016), and, arguably most influentially, an ideology (Mudde and and Rovira Kaltwasser 2017). The dividing lines in these discussions run both within and between disciplines; frequently, they are related to more fundamental disagreements about, for example, the nature of democracy, representation, or ideology.

It is not my intention to intervene in this debate because the different approaches to populism agree on key features that suffice for my purposes here. As Woods, drawing on Stanley (2008), convincingly argues, most definitions of populism converge in the identification of four core elements: (1) the existence of the two groups of the people and the elite; (2) their antagonism; (3) the celebration of popular sovereignty; and (4) the moral glorification of the people and the critique of the elites (Woods 2014, 11). Moreover, the debates about the nature of populism are to a certain degree moot because different definitions focus on different aspects of a more comprehensive phenomenon. Rhetoric and style, on the one hand, and ideology and discourse, on the other, are, as Woods also points out, "integral to each other" (Woods 2014, 15). In fact, it is one of the central tenets of my discipline – American literary and cultural studies – that form and content are inextricably connected. Ideas do not exist independently of their representations: Language, narrative, and discourse do not simply express preexisting ideas but shape them in the process of articulation (Hall 1997).

The close connection between populism and conspiracy theory has been repeatedly addressed in recent years (see, for example, Fenster 2008; Castanho Silva, Vegetti and Littvay 2017; Taggart 2019), but, as Hawkins and Rovira Kaltwasser put it, "[d]espite the fact that various scholars have pointed out the link between populism and conspiratorial thinking ... there is a dearth of empirical research on this argument" (Hawkins and Rovira Kaltwasser 2017, 530). So far, the relationship has been most thoroughly theorized by Bergmann and Butter (2020). They argue that populism and conspiracy theory share several characteristics: they purport a Manichean worldview, reduce complex political land-scapes to binary opposition, and are usually driven by nostalgia for a golden past that only ever existed in the minds of those who bemoan its passing (Bergmann and Butter 2020, 333). In the Americas and most of Europe, that is, in countries in which conspiracy theories underwent the process of stigmatization discussed in the previous section, politicians can use them to perform the typical populist gesture of performing "bad manners" (Moffitt 2016, 59) or "flaunting of the low" (Ostiguy 2017, 84) in order to fashion themselves as anti-elitist. Overall, Bergmann and Butter consider conspiracy theories a secondary feature of populism:

> Conspiracy theories, then, offer a specific explanation as to why the elites act against the interests of the people. This explanation tends to co-exist within a populist movement or party with other explanations such as negligence or personal enrichment. In other words, conspiracy theories are a non-necessary element of populist discourse and ideology, and they are not necessarily believed by everybody in the populist movement or party in which they are circulating. (Bergmann and Butter 2020, 334)

Bergmann and Butter do not say so explicitly in this passage, but their focus is on the contrast between political elites and the people, as almost all literature that discusses the link between conspiracy theories and populism concentrates on this dimension. However, populists do not only frequently position themselves against the *political* establishment but also in opposition to *scientific* elites, and it is this dimension that I explore in the remainder of this chapter.

Mede and Schäfer have recently conceptualized such critiques of scholars, academics, and experts as "science-related populism" (Mede and Schäfer 2020, 480). At the core of this specific kind of populism is not the conflict between the people and the political elite, but that between the people and the "academic elite": "a subset of a general elite – those who have supreme epistemic authority and can make science-related decisions, that is, organizations such as universities or research institutes as well as individual scholars and scientific experts" (Mede and Schäfer 2020, 480). Whereas the conflict between the people and the political elite revolves around "decision-making sovereignty" (Mede and Schäfer 2020, 481), the people compete with the academic elite for "claims for *epistemic* authority, that is, for sovereignty over how 'true knowledge' is produced" (Mede and Schäfer 2020, 482; italics in the original). According to Mede and Schäfer, populists regard the truth claims of the academic elite as "*illegitimate*, because scientific approaches to knowledge production do not prioritize the everyday experiences and opinions of ordinary people, but rely on seemingly alienated theories developed in the proverbial ivory tower" (Mede and Schäfer 2020, 483; italics in the original). Referring to Ylä-Anttila's concept of "experienced-based common sense" (Ylä-Anttila 2018, 363), they conclude that "*[l]egitimate* truth-speaking sovereigns are, according to science-related populism, only the ordinary people themselves" because they derive their knowledge from common sense and their own experience (Ylä-Anttila 2020, 483; italics in the original).

However, this eventual theorization of science-related populism is a bit too one-sided and falls back behind an important distinction that Mede and Schäfer make earlier. Reviewing the extant scholarship on alternative epistemologies they identify two ways in which the truth claims of the academic elite are challenged (Mede and Schäfer 2020, 478–480). On the one hand, there is the fundamental challenge of the scientific method that their conceptualization of science-related populism later draws on. The way the academic elite produces knowledge is rejected in favor of common sense and personal experience; "I-Pistemologies" are seen as superior to traditional scientific epistemology (van Zoonen 2012). On the other hand, though, there is also a less fundamental challenge which does not question the validity of the scientific paradigm as such but claims that institutionalized science and generally acknowledged experts do not produce accurate knowledge. Allegedly, they are not as disinterested as they should be but either ideologically misguided, which makes them involuntarily produce falsehoods, or actively promoting the agenda of the political elites, which makes them intentionally produce falsehoods. Populists and others who criticize the academic elite in this way claim that there are better scientists and truly disinterested experts whose superior truth claims, however, are ignored, stigmatized, or silenced by the elite. I argue that in science-related populism, both strategies are usually combined, often in the same text; for example, in the *Plandemic* movies, as I will demonstrate in the next section.

In fact, drawing on both one's own commonsensical experience and alternative experts is characteristic not only of science-related populism, but also of the conspiracist discourse in the western world in the past decades in general. During the long period in which they were an accepted form of knowledge, conspiracy theories were articulated and believed by academic as well as other elites. Since they became counternarratives, however, they consciously position themselves against the truth claims of epistemic authorities who dismiss their claims as figments of the imagination. Usually, conspiracy theorists hold that they – or the experts they rely on – provide much better analyses than the experts heralded by the establishment. They claim that they and their experts are truly independent, disinterested and only committed to finding out the truth. Thus, they do not challenge scientific or scholarly methods but claim that they are the ones who are accurately applying them. Conspiracist texts of all kinds are filled with footnotes and appendices, graphs and tables, and conspiracy theorists quote studies and interpret data. As Richard Hofstadter remarked many years ago about the "paranoid style," his term for conspiracy theorizing, "[i]t is nothing if not 'scholarly' in technique" (Hofstadter 1964, 37). In recent years, however, this focus on alternative experts has been supplemented by an increasing reliance on one's own experience, perceptions, and common sense. As Andrew McKenzie-McHarg (2019) has demonstrated, this shift entails a parallel shift from written evidence to a focus on images, from experts to eyewitnesses, in conspiracist accounts. In conspiracy theories, then, the same strategies are at work as in science-related populism more generally.

Importantly for the purpose of this volume, these rhetorical strategies rely heavily on resemanticization. Let me just mention two examples here before I move on to the analysis of the *Plandemic* movies. First, what academic elites cast as coincidence, chance, or correlation, is reconfigured – re-emplotted would be the best term – as causality and intentional actions by conspiracy theorists. Since they imagine a world where every important event has been planned, they claim that those who benefit – or more correctly, allegedly benefit – from an event must be responsible for it. "Cui bono?" is thus their favorite question and most important strategy for identifying the conspirators. Accordingly, conspiracy theorists always tell their stories backward. They know who the culprits are early on in their investigation and their entire argument is geared towards confirming their suspicions.

By the same token, conspiracy theorists always cast doubt on members of the academic elite, arguing that they are incompetent and thus no real experts or questioning their integrity by claiming that they knowingly deceive the public to serve the sinister ends of the political elite. This move is then complemented by either challenging the scientific method and epistemology entirely, or by presenting their own alternative experts, whose credentials are played up. For example, during the pandemic, many German conspiracy theorists falsely claimed that virologist Christian Drosten, Germany's leading expert on the coronavirus, never properly completed his PhD and thus did not know what he was talking about. Simultaneously, they stressed the qualifications of known conspiracy theorists like Wolfgang Wodarg, who has a background in medicine but is neither a virologist nor an epidemiologist. As we will see, the *Plandemic* films employ these and related strategies throughout to suggest that the people are being deceived by academic elites in league with the masterminds behind the conspiracy.

3.   Resemanticization in the *Plandemic* Movies

The *Plandemic* series by documentary filmmaker Mikki Willis comprises two parts: the 26-minute short film *Plandemic: The Hidden Agenda Behind Covid-19*, which was released online on 4 May 2020, and the feature-length *Plandemic: Indoctornation*, which was released on 18 August 2020. As the titles of the two existing films already imply, the series alleges that the pandemic is not a natural event but has been carefully orchestrated to achieve sinister goals. While this conspiracy theory is only hinted at in the first part, which mostly spreads disinformation about the coronavirus and viruses in general, it is developed in much detail in the second part.

Plandemic: The Hidden Agenda Behind Covid-19 went viral immediately. One week after its release, it had been watched several million times on Twitter, Instagram, Facebook, and YouTube and garnered 2.5 million comments, likes, and shares on Facebook alone (Frenkel, Decker and Alba 2020). From the very beginning, Willis and his collaborators anticipated that the film would be deplatformed quickly and therefore encouraged their audience to download the film and share it through as many channels as possible. Thus, although the film was removed from the major platforms within a couple of weeks after its release, it continued to find an audience in WhatsApp groups, on platforms like BitChute or via clips on TikTok (Nazar and Pieters 2021). Its catchy title, which condenses the conspiracist claim to a single word, had already been circulating as a hashtag on Twitter before the film came out (Kearney, Chiang, and Massey 2020), but it was the documentary's virality that made it a shorthand employed by conspiracy theorists throughout the western world over the next two years. Since the sequel had been publicly announced, the big social media platforms were prepared when it was released three months later. The film was immediately removed from YouTube and flagged with warnings on Facebook and Twitter. According to its distributor, London Real, it was nevertheless watched 1.2 million times within the first 24 hours, a claim disputed by a Buzzfeed review, which asserts that the film had hardly any impact (Lytvynenko 2020).

The first *Plandemic* movie consists mostly of an interview with Judy Mikovits, a former scientist who became a staunch anti-vaccination activist after some controversial scientific claims she had made concerning the chronic fatigue syndrome were widely criticized and *Science* retracted an article of hers it had published. Talking to Mikki Willis, she makes several wrong claims about the virus and the government reaction and articulates conspiracist allegations. Although the film is subtitled "The Hidden Agenda Behind Covid-19," it does not develop any of the conspiracy theories she alludes to in depth. By contrast, the sequel unfolds a large global conspiracy theory that involves Bill Gates, John D. Rockefeller, Google, fact-checkers, and the news media.

Most importantly, *Plandemic: The Hidden Agenda Behind Covid-19* recasts Mikovits, who was ousted from the scientific community because of her untenable claims, as a genuine expert as far as viruses in general and the coronavirus in particular are concerned, and as one of the few people who refuse to be intimidated by the conspirators. To prove her expertise to the audience, the documentary early on falsely claims that one of her papers revolutionized HIV treatment. The reason why she lost her job and her scientific credentials, the film claims, is that she revealed truths about the nature of viruses that powerful actors did not want to become publicly known. As she tells Willis, she was set up and arrested without charges (in truth, the charges were dropped after a few days) to destroy her reputation and her career and thus to silence her. However, she refuses to give in because, as she affirms in the alarmist fashion characteristic of conspiracy theories: "If we don't stop this now, we can not only forget our republic and our freedom, but we can forget humanity because it will be killed by this agenda" (00:03:45–00:03:51).

Just as Mikovits is heroized, Anthony Fauci, the director of the National Institute of Allergy and Infectious Diseases (NIAID) and head of the US administration's coronavirus task force, is disqualified by the film in a corresponding move. His credentials as a researcher and policy adviser are challenged and he is charged with scientific misconduct instead. Moreover, Mikovits accuses him of being the mastermind behind the destruction of her career. Prompted into this direction by Willis, she says outrightly: "He directed the cover-up" (00:04:00–00:04:02) and calls on the public not to heed his advice concerning the pandemic: "What he's saying is absolute propaganda" (00:04:33–00:04:36). In the fashion typical of science-related populism, then, Fauci is cast as the member of a corrupt scientific elite that is not interested in the truth or the wellbeing of the people but promotes a corrupt agenda instead.

What follows almost automatically from this reversal of the roles of leading expert and scientific pariah is a complete reevaluation of the dominant discourse on the pandemic. Mikovits not only accuses the government of manipulating the numbers of Covid victims by counting everybody who died *with* the virus and even many that had not been tested for the virus as victims *of* Covid-19. She also claims that the virus did not emerge naturally but must be the result of a conscious manipulation in a laboratory of the version of the coronavirus responsible for the 2002–2003 pandemic: "It's very clear this virus was manipulated. … That's accelerated viral evolution. If it was a natural occurrence, it would take it up to 800 years to occur. This occurred from SARS-1 within a decade. That's not naturally occurring" (00:10:45–00:11:01). A little later, however, Mikovits also claims that the high death rate in northern Italy in the spring of 2020 was caused not by the coronavirus but by an untested new flu vaccine, and then claims that political elites and scientists are collaborating to take away peoples' civil liberties. Not only will the vaccine that they will eventually distribute be highly dangerous; its manufacture is also intentionally being delayed in order to impose lockdowns, mask-wearing and other measures.

Importantly, the scientific paradigm as such is hardly ever challenged in the film. On the contrary, Mikovits is built up as an excellent and courageous scientist, as somebody so committed to finding out and spreading the truth that she had to leave the entirely corrupted institutions of science. Thus, it is only logical that she says at the end of the film that her goal is to "restore faith in the promise of medicine" (00:21:41–00:21:43) – a phrase that echoes the title of her co-written book *Plague of Corruption: Restoring Faith in the Promise of Science*, which was published a few weeks before the documentary was released and which she is of course promoting through her appearance in Willis's film. However, there are a few moments in the film where Mikovits articulates ideas that challenge the scientific paradigm and promote a radically different epistemology instead. At one point, for example, she criticizes the government for closing the beaches in order to contain the spread of the virus: "Why would you close the beach? You've got sequences in the soil, in the sand, healing microbes in the ocean, in the saltwater," Mikovits asks (00:17:45–00:17:58), esoterically positioning the powers of nature against scientifically sound measures for contact restrictions. This shows that the two ways in which science-related populism challenges official scientific claims are not at all mutually exclusive and can be articulated together not only in the same text but even by the same person, indicating that the worldviews of conspiracy theorists are just as contradictory as those of other people. Of course, for the film this has the added benefit that it allows catering to two audiences who are united in their conspiracist opposition to the Covid restrictions: those who think that science has been corrupted and needs to be purged, and those who think that it is nonsense and needs to be transcended.

The film's agenda of substituting its conspiracy theories for the dominant view of the current crisis, of recasting the pandemic as a "plandemic", hinges to a large degree on its form – an aspect that Mede and Schäfer do not touch upon at all in their discussion of science-related populism. *Plandemic: The Hidden Agenda Behind Covid-19* employs many of the tropes of documentary filmmaking to signify authenticity and to corroborate its truth claims. Unlike an earlier generation of online conspiracy documentaries such as the *Loose Change* series (see Butter and Retterath 2010), the film's editing is calm and professional, and the lighting of the interview scene is flawless. The way Mikovits is framed by the camera in a close shot signifies her expert status, with a sidelight accentuating the feature of her face without casting sharp shadows. Frequent reverse shots show Willis, who is similarly lit and framed. He is further visually aligned with Mikovits because both are dressed in black. Listening attentively, nodding repeatedly, and focusing his steel-blue eyes on Miscovits, he functions as a model for how the audience is supposed to listen to her. The form of the film thus supports the wholesale resemanticization the narrative undertakes.

The same formal tropes are employed in the sequel, *Plandemic: Indoctornation*. Except for the first few minutes, however, the film's focus is not on Mikovits but on a whole array of experts whose statements are intercut with reverse shots of Willis listening and nodding in agreement. Generally, though, the narrative is much faster because the film covers far more ground than the first part and paints a much more comprehensive picture of the alleged conspiracy. As in contemporary conspiracy theory films, it is characterized by a high degree of "speed" – "a multiplicity of events [depicted] in brief scenes," as Fenster describes it, and "velocity", which refers to "the geographic, geopolitical, and cognitive aspects of the conspiracy narrative's movement," which is "both global and increasingly rapid as the narrative progresses" (Fenster 2008, 133–134). Over the course of seventy-five minutes, the film moves back and forth between the U.S., Wuhan, and Europe, and from the present to the early twentieth century and back to present. All of this is held together by the calm voice-over narration of Willis, who interprets the sheer endless array of clips from news reports, graphics, and statistics in his attempt to interpellate the audience as conspiracy theorists. In a nutshell, the film takes up and develops the claim from the first part that the virus was artificially manufactured to, on the one hand, generate profit for the pharmaceutical industry through the selling of vaccines, and, on the other, to serve the elites as a tool of population management.

This argument is first articulated by David Martin, the second part's leading expert about ten minutes into the film. At the beginning of this scene, we see Martin putting on a dark suit and a bow tie for his interview, an act that is obviously meant to underline his expert status. This is then corroborated by the captions, which highlight not only his PhD but also introduce him – bending the truth considerably because he runs a small company that assesses the value of other companies based on the patents that they own – as an "intelligence analyst" and thus as somebody who possesses insights that most common people do not have. Martin states correctly that the Center for Disease Control filed a patent for the 2003 coronavirus, but he implies that this was done to turn "coronavirus from a pathogen to profit" (00:10:59–00:11:01) and not to make sure that researchers had unrestricted access to the virus. Moreover, the film's narrative picks up on his claims by cutting to a montage of stock market analysts who compare the race to produce the first vaccine against Covid-19 to a gold rush.

Whereas all other "experts" that Willis talks to are present only in one scene or short sequence, the narrative returns again and again to Martin. Next to Willis's voice-over, he is the film's second anchor, and his scenes work to hold the film's fast-paced narrative together, as it is often difficult to follow. After each major section, the film fades to black and then returns to Martin to have him introduce the topic of the next section. In fact, Martin is the one who is literally connecting the dots for the audience by painting the broader picture and showing how everything is linked. This is supported by the sequences in which he appears with intercut images of a table on which pictures representing the topics of the different sections of the film such as social media companies, fact-checkers or the WHO are connected by an array of lines. Unsurprisingly, the image at the center shows a model of the coronavirus. The film thus visualizes its claim that the pandemic is not an event that occurred naturally but as the result of a carefully planned conspiracy.

After an introductory sequence in which the film takes up the criticism directed at the first part and introduces Martin and its overall claim, the first half of the film works to immunize the conspiracy theory that will be developed in the second part against critique. Using mostly the allegedly unfair treatment of Mikovits as an example, the film argues that fact-checkers are not interested in the truth but are used by elites to spread their propaganda. Wikipedia and the Google search engine, the film implies, are employed in identical fashion by those in power. The same goes for the media, ranging from news on the major networks to cable comedy shows, which, *Plandemic* alleges, have been controlled by the CIA for decades. Recasting all of these entities as part of the plot that the first part of the series began to uncover and that the second part now exposes completely, the narrative tries to make it impossible for viewers to verify and dismiss its claims.

The second half of the documentary, then, develops the conspiracist claims in detail. Whereas the narrative has so far focused – with a short detour on China – on the U.S. and the past few years, it now assumes a distinctively global perspective by focusing on the World Health Organization and the activities of the Bill & Melinda Gates Foundation in Africa and India. The film suggests that the U.S. medical system has been a sham for the past 100 years, since John D. Rockefeller realized that he could manipulate it to generate vast amounts of money. This claim is the starting point for the film's argument that the pandemic has been manufactured to cash in on the vaccines that are being developed to contain it. Moreover, the film contends that vaccines in general are unsafe and usually not needed and that the Covid vaccines will be particularly dangerous because they have been produced far too quickly. The film includes a clip from a CBS interview with Bill Gates in which the interviewer asks him about the high number of people participating in the trials who experienced "systemic side effects" (01:06:12–01:06:15). Gates's answer is, unfortunately, not very precise. Instead of saying that these side effects were mostly some fever or headaches, he remains vague, which creates the impression that he has been cornered and that the vaccines are very dangerous.

As the screen begins to fade to black, David Martin's voice-over declares: "This isn't a vaccine story. It's a population management story" (01:07:00–01:07:03). This is the film's second major conspiracist allegation: that the pandemic has been carefully orchestrated to reduce the number of people on the globe both through the virus and the vaccines. The goal of the plot is, as Martin puts it, "an exclusive playground for the entitled few" (01:07:09–01:07:11). The film locates the origins of this agenda in the 1974 Kissinger Report, which defined the purpose of U.S. foreign policy in Africa as "reduc[ing] the population" there (00:58:23–00:58:24). Completely taken out of context and severely misrepresented – the document talks about slowing the population *growth*, as is actually discernible in a quote highlighted in yellow – the report becomes another piece in the jigsaw that the film claims to be putting together. Kissinger of course has been one of the usual suspects of American conspiracy theories for decades and thus lends himself to be included in the film's accusation. *Plandemic: Indoctornation*'s archvillain, however, is Bill Gates.

The film spends considerable time to recast the public image of Bill Gates, professing to deconstruct the legend he has created for himself. The narrative – in parts, correctly – suggests that Gates is not quite the creative genius as which he is often perceived. Instead, he is cast as an awful human being who used his father's funds and contacts to build his empire and betray his business partner Paul Allen when he was fighting cancer. The film also claims that the Bill & Melinda Gates Foundation was only founded in 1998 to polish Gates's public image because Microsoft was being sued for antitrust violations. This allegation is articulated against a montage of scenes that show Gates in unfavorable moments during the trial. However, this is not true, as the foundation was set up in 1994 already. After playing up the negative consequences of the foundation's work in India and Africa – in a move that goes far beyond the legitimate criticism that has been voiced in non-conspiracist fashion by many parties – the attempt to cast Gates as an incarnation of evil culminates in making him a close friend of Jeffrey Epstein. Thus, when Willis's voice-over declares at the end of this section, "[p]ersonally, I would love to believe that one of the richest men in the world is giving away his fortune for the betterment of humanity... I wanna believe that his heart is as soft and warm as his sweaters. At the very least, I wanna believe that he is unaware of the damage he has done" (01:03:43–01:04:06), it is clear that Willis does not believe this, and neither should the audience.

After all, the film has gone to great lengths to "show" that the pandemic has been carefully planned by Gates's foundation. In fact, *Plandemic: Indoctornation* begins with and later returns for a whole section to Event 201 – a pandemic exercise organized by the Gates Foundation, The Johns Hopkins Center for Health Security, and the World Economic Forum in October 2019. During the exercise, the global spread of a coronavirus that first emerges in China and the reactions by politics, science and civil society were simulated to prepare governments and relevant institutions for such an outbreak, which, many experts agreed, would occur sooner rather than later. For conspiracy theorists, however, the event signifies something entirely different: it is the blueprint for the pandemic that began only a few months later, a clear instance of the "foreknowledge" of the conspirators. Since conspiracy theories imagine a world where nothing happens by accident, an occurrence such as Event 201 must be part of a plan and thus proves the guilt and complicity of the parties involved beyond a doubt (Butter 2020, 50). And this is exactly how *Plandemic* integrates the event into its argument.

Tellingly, just as the first part, *Plandemic: Indoctornation* hardly ever challenges the scientific paradigm as such and rather suggests that the scientific community is mostly corrupt. Hence, the film highlights the academic credentials of the many people it presents as experts on the pandemic and the plot behind it. In fact, in the introductory segment of the film Willis stresses that his argument is based on interviews with "scholars from all over the world, among them top doctors, distinguished scientists and Nobel laureates" (00:04:05–00:04:12). Like Mikovits in the first part, these experts are presented as heroic figures who speak the truth despite occasionally severe personal consequences. However, also as in the first part, there are short moments where the film's argument transforms into a more general denunciation of science. The most pronounced of these moments occurs in the section in which Rockefeller is accused of having corrupted the U.S. medical system. Since he wanted to sell his oil-based drugs, Willis declares, "medicines used for thousands of years were suddenly classified as 'alternative,' while the new petroleum-based, highly addictive, and patentable drugs were declared the gold standard... Rockefeller leveraged his political influence by pressing Congress to declare natural healing modalities 'unscientific quackery'" (00:43:50–00:44:19). For a moment, the narrative here presents science as the opposite of medicine and healing and as inherently problematic. As it accuses Rockefeller and his allies of a major resemanticization, it engages in such an act itself. Overall, though, just as most populist conspiracist discourse, the second *Plandemic* movie contends to present the better, untainted and thus true science.

4.   Conclusion

Conspiracy theories are always narratives, but, as I have argued, not always populist counter-narratives. However, throughout the western world where conspiracy theories underwent a process of stigmatization after World War II they have been functioning exactly as populist counter-narratives in the past decades. As they almost invariably position themselves against common wisdom and the official version of events, they challenge – just as populist discourse more generally – not only political but also scientific elites and accuse them of deceiving and acting against the interests of the people. As I demonstrated in my analysis of the two *Plandemic* movies, they employ various strategies of resemanticization. They recast events that just happened and are not controlled by anybody as part of a devious plan by translating coincidence and contingency into collusion; they dismiss the expertise and the motives of leading scientific voices in the then ongoing discussions because they consider them complicit in the conspiracy; in their stead, they work up the credentials of voices that provide radically different interpretations of the events they are concerned with to prove their conspiracist allegations. In the *Plandemic* movies, these scientific resemanticizations usually do not challenge the scientific paradigm as such but "merely" contend that those scholars and scientists that claim that the virus emerged naturally and is very dangerous are corrupt and therefore lying to the people. The conspiracy theorists therefore contend that they are listening to the better and – since they are working outside the system – more honest experts. By contrast, more radical challenges that replace the scientific method with other epistemologies occur only rarely. I would claim that this goes for most conspiracy theories, as they almost always tend to mimic academic discourse. However, this would need to be demonstrated on the basis of a far larger corpus.

Works Cited

Aslanidis, Paris (2016) Is populism an ideology? A refutation and a new perspective. *Political studies* 64(1), 88–104.

Bailyn, Bernard (1967) *The ideological origins of the American Revolution.* Cambridge: Belknap Press of Harvard University Press.

Barkun, Michael (2003) *A culture of conspiracy: apocalyptic visions in contemporary America.* Berkeley: University of California Press.

Barr, Robert R. (2009) Populists, outsiders and anti-establishment politics. *Party Politics.* 15(1), 29–48.

Bergmann, Eirikur and Michael Butter (2020) Conspiracy theory and populism. In: Michael Butter and Peter Knight (eds.) *Routledge handbook of conspiracy theories.* London: Routledge, 330–343.

Boukari, Oumarou and Joschka Philipps (2022) "Complòóót?" Theorizing about Covid-19 conspiracies in Côte d'Ivoire. In: Butter, Michael and Knight, Peter (eds.) *Covid conspiracy theories in global perspective.* London: Routledge. forthcoming.

Bratich, Jack Z. (2008) *Conspiracy panics: political rationality and popular culture.* Albany: State University of New York Press.

Butter, Michael (2014) *Plots, designs, and schemes: American conspiracy theories from the puritans to the present.* Berlin/Boston: De Gruyter, Linguae & Litterae.

Butter, Michael (2020) *The nature of conspiracy theories.* London: Polity Press.

Butter, Michael (2021) Conspiracy theories – conspiracy narratives. In: *DIEGESIS. Interdisciplinary E-Journal for Narrative Research/ Interdisziplinäres E-Journal für Erzählforschung* 10(1), 97–100.

Butter, Michael and Lisa Retterath (2010) From alerting the world to stabilizing its own community: The shifting cultural work of the *Loose Change* films. *Canadian Review of American Studies* 40(1), 25–44.

Butter, Michael and Peter Knight (eds.) (2020) *Routledge handbook of conspiracy theories.* London: Routledge.

Castanho Silva, Bruno, Federico Vegetti, and Levente Littvay (2017) The elite is up to something: exploring the relation between populism and belief in conspiracy theories. *Schweizerische Zeitschrift für Politik-wissenschaft.* 23(4), 423–443.

Cubitt, Geoffrey (1993) *The Jesuit myth: conspiracy theory and politics in nine-teenth-century France.* Oxford: Clarendon Press.

Deutschmann, Peter, Jens Herlth and Alois Woldan (eds.) (2020) *"Truth" and fiction. Conspiracy theories in Eastern European culture and literature.* Bielefeld: transcript.

Fenster, Mark (2008) *Conspiracy theories: secrecy and power in American culture.* Minneapolis: University of Minnesota Press.

Fiske, John (ed.) (1994) *Media matters: everyday culture and political change.* Minneapolis: University of Minnesota Press.

Frenkel, Sheera, Ben Decker and Davey Alba (2020) *How the 'Plandemic' movie and its falsehoods spread widely online.* Web: https://www.nytimes.com/2020/05/20/technology/plandemic-movie-youtube-facebook-coronavirus.html.

Girard, Pascal (2020) Conspiracy theories in Europe during the twentieth century. In: Butter, Michael and Peter Knight (eds.) *Routledge handbook of conspiracy theories.* London: Routledge, 569–581.

Gray, Matthew (2010) *Conspiracy theories in the Arab world: sources and politics.* London: Routledge.

Hall, Stuart (1997) *Representation: cultural representations and signifying practices.* Thousand Oaks: SAGE Publishing.

Hawkins, Kirk A. and Cristóbal Rovira Kaltwasser (2017) The ideational approach to populism. *Latin American Research Review* 52(4), 513–528.

Hofstadter, Richard (1964) *The paranoid style in American politics, and other essays.* Cambridge: Harvard University Press.

Jansen, Robert S. (2011) Populist mobilization: A new theoretical approach to populism. *Sociological Theory* 29(2), 75–96.

Kearney, Matthew D., Shawn C. Chiang and Philip M. Massey (2020) The Twitter origins and evolution of the COVID-19 "plandemic" conspiracy theory. *Harvard Kennedy School Misinformation Review* 1, 1–18. Web: https://misinforeview.hks.harvard.edu/article/the-twitter-origins-and-evolution-of-the-covid-19-plandemic-conspiracy-theory/.

Laclau, Ernesto (2005) *On populist reason.* New York: Verso.

Lytvynenko, Jane (2020) *The "Plandemic" sequel is here. We give it zero stars*. Web: https://www.buzzfeednews.com/article/janelytvynenko/plandemic-sequel-review.

McKenzie-McHarg, Andrew (2019) Conspiracy theory: the nineteenth-century prehistory of a twentieth-century concept. In: Uscinski, Joseph (ed.) *Conspiracy theories and the people who believe them*. New York: Oxford University Press, 62–81.

McKenzie-McHarg, Andrew and Rolf Fredheim (2017) Cock-ups and slapdowns: A quantitative analysis of conspiracy rhetoric in the British Parliament 1916–2015. *Historical methods: A journal of quantitative and interdisciplinary history* 50(3), 156–169.

Mede, Niels G. and Mike S. Schäfer (2020) Science-related populism: Conceptualizing populist demands toward science. *Public understanding of science* 29(5), 473–491.

Moffitt, Benjamin (2016) *The global rise of populism: performance, political style, and representation*. Palo Alto: Stanford University Press.

Mudde, Cas and Cristóbal Rovira Kaltwasser (2017) *Populism: a very short introduction*. New York: Oxford University Press.

Nazar, Shahin and Toine Pieters (2021) Plandemic revisited: A product of planned disinformation amplifying the COVID-19 "infodemic". *Frontiers in public health*. 9 (649930), 1–15.

Ostiguy, Pierre (2017) Populism: A socio-cultural approach. In: Rovira Kaltwasser, Cristóbal. et al. (eds.) *The Oxford handbook of populism*. Oxford: Oxford University Press, 73–97.

Plandemic: Indoctornation (2020). Directed by Mikki Willis [Documentary]. London,: London Real.

Plandemic: The Hidden Agenda Behind Covid-19 (2020). Directed by Mikki Willis [Documentary]. Ojai, CA: Elevate Films.

Rabo, Annika (2020) Conspiracy theory as occult cosmology in anthropology. In: Butter, Michael and Peter Knight (eds.) *Routledge handbook of conspiracy theories*. London: Routledge, 81–93.

Radnitz, Scott (2021) *Revealing schemes: The politics of conspiracy in Russia and the post-Soviet region*. Oxford: Oxford University Press.

Stanley, Ben (2008) The thin ideology of populism. *Journal of political ideologies* 13(1), 95–110.

Taggart, Paul (2019) Populism and "unpolitics." In: Fitzi, Gregor, Jürgen Mackert and Bryan S. Turner (eds.) *Populism and the crisis of democracy*, vol. 1. Abingdon: Routledge, 79–88.

Thalmann, Katharina (2019) *The stigmatization of conspiracy theory since the 1950s: 'A Plot to Make us Look Foolish'*. London: Routledge.

Uscinski, Joseph E. and Joseph M. Parent (2014) *American conspiracy theories*. New York: Oxford University Press.

Van Zoonen, Liesbet (2012) I-Pistemology: Changing truth claims in popular and political culture. *European journal of communication* 27(1), 56–67.

Woods, Dwayne (2014) *The many faces of populism: diverse but not disparate*. In: Wood, Dwayne and Barbara Wejnert (eds.) *The many faces of populism: current perspectives*. Bingley, Emerald, Research in Political Sociology 22, 1–26.

Ylä-Anttila, Tuomas (2018) Populist knowledge: "post-truth" repertoires of contesting epistemic authorities. *European journal of cultural and political sociology* 5(4), 356–388.

Populism, Populist Democracy, and the Shifting of Meanings
Subverting – Disfiguring – Transforming

Hans-Jürgen Puhle

In a number of papers I have written during the last years I have tried to find some answers to the question of what populist aspirations and politics, on the one hand, and the newly emerging structures of "populist democracy", on the other hand, and their interactions do to democracy in general, and to political communication and intermediation more in particular (e.g. Puhle 2020, 2018, 2017, 2015a). With regard to the topic of this volume one might have to go a bit further and look more into the mechanisms of agitation and propaganda, into the factors and vectors that constitute "Deutungsmacht" (within the new constellations of the public sphere), and the various processes of resemanticization and shifting of meanings that could be noticed in the orbit of populist mobilization and politics. For a start, the basic question might be put like this: Are contemporary populisms particularly prone (and how and why) to subverting, disfiguring and transforming the terms and topoi of political discourse and propaganda? And do populists (have to) rely more on "fake news" and "alternative facts" than others?

Here, we first would have to explain what we mean by "contemporary populisms". Who are the actors (and authors)? This obviously is a complex agenda and the analysis requires two short summaries: one of the findings on the varieties of populisms through the twentieth century, and another of the relevant dimensions and repercussions of what I have called the rise of "populist democracy", as one of the consequences of a new structural change of the public sphere ("Strukturwandel der Öffentlichkeit", Habermas 1962) during the last decades around the turn of the century (Puhle 2017). Then, in a third point, some populist strategies of semantic reallocation will be identified.

1.   Varieties of Populisms

There is no such thing as populism as such. What we are dealing with are varieties of populisms (the plural is important). First we find two basic types, one for more developed, and one for less developed countries. The "classic" U.S. Populists of the end of the nineteenth century have become the archetype of protest populisms in, for example, the more exclusionary peasant and protest movements in Europe since the 1920s. More or less at the same time, the Russian narodniki became (or were written into) the archetype of project populisms in less developed countries, such as the more inclusionary and mostly anti-imperialist populist (and national liberation) movements in the decolonizing world and in Latin America. In an effort to use the term in a parsimonious way, I am referring here to "populisms" (as "-isms"), i.e. particular movements with distinctive and meaningful aspirations that cannot be better characterized otherwise, e.g., by the term for their "political family" (from anarchists and communists to liberals, conservatives, or Christians), in contrast to "populist" elements, styles, mechanisms, or rhetoric which can be combined with any kind of political intentions on the Left or on the Right ("populist" as an adjective; for more details, and the following, see Puhle 2020).

There are, however, significant commonalities. As a first approximation, we might define populisms as social mobilizations and movements of protest and resistance against the status quo in the name of the "people", "the people's will", or the "common men", and not of specific classes or groups, with a corresponding ideology featuring a number or characteristic elements: Populists fight against the elites, the institutions, and the mechanisms of organized interests and politics; they see themselves as a grassroots movement voicing the sentiments of "just" indignation (an old topos) against what they consider to be the conspiracies of a corrupt "establishment" or "oligarchy" and its foreign allies, and an illegitimate usurpation of power that should belong to the people. One of their most important ideological features is the fiction of an immediate relationship between the people and its leaders with direct communication in two ways that does not need any intermediaries. Hence populists antagonize and try (if they can) to circumvent and weaken all kinds of "corps intermédiaires" with functions of control or accountability: parliaments, courts of justice, political parties, interest groups, and independent media. They are anti-liberal, and mostly anti-urban, anti-intellectual, and at least rhetorically against "Big Capital", corporations, trusts, and the more (and often "better") organized capitalist actors, but they are not outright anti-capitalist.

Populist movements basically are movements of an underdog culture: They see politics in moralistic, agonistic and dichotomousc terms and they cultivate all kinds of conspiracy narratives and myths. They polarize, and their most favored political strategy is the politics of fear and hatred. They have an explicit "Feindbild" (image of the enemy): it is the honest many against the corrupt few, the small good guys against the big bad guys. The bad guys are the great national and international corporations and organizations and their agents. The good guys are "the people", i.e., the moral majority (no matter their numbers), of those who were once called the "common men" or the "forgotten men". "The people" at the same time is an entity that is considered to be homogeneous, and excludes many "others", like "corrupt" elites, interests, foreigners, migrants, people of different culture, etc. Populists often are xenophobic, and care about their "identities" (which are often considered "endangered"). And when they speak of the "rule of the people" they usually mean the rule of the populists. They can be on the Right or on the Left. Given their close affinity to nationalism (by their invocation of "the people") they mostly are on the Right, but there are exceptions, e.g., the critics of globalization and the G8 summits, anti-capitalist protesters, leftist critics of the European Union (Puhle 2015a; Priester 2012; Canovan 1999).

Populists' relationships with the state and with democracy can be characterized as highly ambivalent: They usually favor a weak state as long as they fight it, and a strong state once they have conquered it. Furthermore, populist movements or regimes can be either democratic or undemocratic, or, in the case of regimes, tend to what we have called "defective democracies" (Merkel and Puhle et al. 2003), or what others might call "disfigured" (Urbinati 2014) or "illiberal democracies". Populist impacts on democracies oscillate between "threat" and "corrective". In many cases the mechanisms of direct acclamation and the reduction of the controlling potential of the "corps intermédiaires" inherent to populist politics have damaged the countervailing institutions and the balance of an "embedded democracy", and opened the path toward more manipulation from above, "guided" democracy, Bonapartism, or worse forms of autocracy (Merkel 2004). But there have also been other cases in which populist energies have strengthened and reinvigorated existing democratic systems. The most notable cases here have been the "classic" American Populists whose history in the longue durée has turned out to be a success story, given their lasting influence on the politics and policies of the "Progressives" in both parties that have informed American mainstream politics down to the 1990s (Puhle 1975, 142–154; Hofstadter 1955). The usual ambivalence, however, has become visible in a second line of populist legacies: in the protest movements of the right, from Father Coughlin and Huey Long via George Wallace and others all the way to Donald Trump who may not be a populist in substance, but certainly is in style and campaigning (Lipset and Raab 1970; Judis 2016).

Other "classical" cases of the twentieth century have shown more varieties. Among the protesters in the more developed world we can also find some North and Central European peasant movements, tax resisters and xenophobic protest organizations of the lower middle classes from the interwar period to the 1960s, also in Western Europe. One of the most prominent among them has been the short-lived Poujadist movement of small artisans and shopkeepers (UDCA) in France which, in 1956, got 56 Members of Parliament elected – one was Jean Marie Le Pen who later founded the Front National (Souillac 2007). Similar continuities between older movements and the more recent ones of a later wave can also be found in Scandinavia, Austria, Belgium and the Netherlands. The "classics" of the second type, the anti-imperialist and national-liberation populisms of what has been called the "Third World", enjoyed their peak time between the 1930s and the 1970s. They usually organized broad multi-class movements, mobilized against the "oligarchy" and foreign colonialist or imperialist powers, and had an interventionist and developmental agenda. In many cases they established regimes of some duration, some more democratic, some more authoritarian (Hermet 2001; Hermet et al. 2001; Mény and Surel 2002, and the pioneers in: Ionescu/Gellner 1969). Here we can distinguish various groups:

- Kemalists in Turkey, Kuomintang (KMT) in China, Congress Party in India, Sukarno's movement in Indonesia,
- the secular and often socialist Arab nationalists (Nasser, National Liberation Front (FLN) in Algeria, Baath parties, etc.),
- the classical African movements of decolonization in the 1950s, led by Nkrumah, Kenyatta, Nyerere; the African National Congress (ANC) in South Africa, etc.

For many years, the best studied area had been Latin America. Here the "classical" populists have marked a longer phase of transition, usually after revolutions or previous substantial reform politics (e.g. Di Tella 1965, 1997; Laclau 1981, 2005; Knight 1998; Weyland 2001; Coniff 1999; for the context: Collier and Collier 1991; Puhle 2007).

We can distinguish between three to four types:

a) postrevolutionary stabilizers (Partido Revolucionario Institucional/ PRI in Mexico, Movimiento Nacionalista Revolucionario/MNR in Bolivia; Cuba 1, Nicaragua 1, both before becoming outright Marxist-Leninist),
b) authoritarian regimes (Vargas in Brazil, Perón in Argentina), and
c) democratic populist movements in two waves:
    a. a first wave from late 1920s and 1930s (APRA in Peru, Acción Democrática in Venezuela, Partido Liberación Nacional in Costa Rica, Partido Revolucionario Dominicano, and in a way also the coalition of the Unidad Popular in Chile), and

b. a second wave, since the 1960s (basically the Christian Democrats in Chile, Venezuela [COPEI], El Salvador, Guatemala, or Acción Popular in Peru).

The two types mentioned – xenophobic protest populisms in the U.S. and in Europe, and populisms with developmental projects in most of the rest of the world – have established clear lines of continuities throughout the twentieth century. At the same time, they have increasingly mixed with new elements, producing also discontinuities and varieties of "hybrid" phenomena which seem to dominate present day populisms. In *Latin America*, e.g., various layers of populisms, from different periods, coexist. We could find movements with a longer tradition in Argentina's Peronists, in the parties of Concertación in Chile, Alianza Popular Revolucionaria Americana (APRA) in Peru or the Mexican PRI, and new movements, not without links to the past, in the Partido dos Trabalhadores (PT) in Brazil, the Movimiento al Socialismo (MAS) in Bolivia, Correa in Ecuador, or the erratic Chavismo in Venezuela. Often mixed approaches have prevailed (Roberts 2015, 2019; Weyland 2001, 2013; Mudde and Rovira Kaltwasser 2012; De la Torre 2015; Abromeit et al. 2016). One interesting fusion of old and new elements has been the Movimiento Regeneración Nacional (MORENA) and the presidency of López Obrador (often referred to by his initials AMLO) in Mexico. A different and rather new type that does not follow the traditional patterns of Latin American populism has been established in the movement and regime of Bolsonaro in Brazil, their ideological set-up much resembling those of Donald Trump and some European right-wing protest movements.

Among the protest populisms of the more developed world, the movements in the *United States* have also shown many continuities, those of the progressive mainstream as well as those of the Right. Here, too, new elements have been blended into them, so far ending, in the twenty-first century, in the reiterative hollowing and the destruction of the Republican Party, first by the Neocons and later by the Tea Party, so that Donald Trump could hijack it in 2016 and has not let it go since then (Hochschild 2016; Skocpol and Williamson 2012). Trump is a ruthless populist in communication and campaigning, but not that much in substance. His politics of the rich, by the rich and for the rich has never been a populist agenda.

Varieties of populist mixes and hybrids also prevail in *Europe* where, during the last decades, from Scandinavia to the Balkans and the Mediterranean, the most numerous movements have been those whom the Germans call "Rechtspopulisten": xenophobic right-wing extremists who often have also represented some continuities of the traditional ultra-nationalisms of the respective countries (e.g. Akkerman et al. 2015; Decker et al. 2015; Kriesi/Pappas 2015; Mudde 2007). The usual suspects here are the following:

- the "Progress" or "popular" parties in Scandinavia, from Mogens Glistrup in Denmark in the 1970s to the Danish People's Party (DDP), the Sweden Democrats, or the True Finns;
- the Front/Rassemblement National, and what became of it, in France, the Vlaams Blok/Belang in Belgium, the Democratic Center, Partij voor de Vrijheid (Party for Freedom, PVV) and the movements of Pim Fortuyn and Geert Wilders in the Netherlands, Blocher's Schweizerische Volkspartei (Swiss People's Party, SVP) in Switzerland, the FPÖ and its secessions in Austria, and in Great Britain the English Defence League, UK Independence Party (UKIP), many of the Tory Brexiteers, and the Brexit Party;
- in Italy the Lega; Berlusconi's Forza Italia seems to be a random case, and the Cinque Stelle (M5S) may be populists but not necessarily populists of the Right.
- In Spain, the rise of VOX began rather late in 2018;
- In Hungary FIDESZ (Hungarian Civic Alliance), and in Poland Prawo i Sprawiedliwość (Law and justice, PiS), if we do not count them, like some groups in Ireland, as traditional catholic ultra-nationalists, all of them modernized by new modes of communication;
- in Germany the "Republicans", the Deutsche Volksunion (*German People's Union*, DVU), the Schill Party, and finally the Alternative für Deutschland (Alternative for Germany, AfD) which was first elected into the German Bundestag in 2017.

However, not all right-wing extremists are populists, and not all populists are necessarily on the Right. We can also find them on the Left, among the critics of globalization and of the G7 (or G8) summits (attac, occupy, blockupy, the Federal Coordination of Internationalism/BUKO, Global Trade Watch), the anti-capitalist protesters and "indignados" triggered by the financial and institutional crisis of 2008/09, and the increasing number of critics of the European Union and its politics. Some of them have become influential players and parties which have significantly contributed to restructure the respective party systems. The most important among them have been SYRIZA in Greece and PODEMOS in Spain which both made it into government (Pappas 2014; Rivero 2014; Monedero 2014). They all have articulated populist aspirations, denouncing the sempiternal "conspiracies" of the banks, of capitalists and the elites, of the established parties and the "system", the European Union, the International Financial Institutions (IFI) and other agents of globalization, and asking for more justice, more direct, unmediated participation, and more respect, particularly for the "common people" (e.g. Rodrik 2017; Moffitt 2016; Knöbl 2016; Jörke and Selk 2017). Anti-EU rhetoric does, however, also come from the Right, and in some cases anti-globalist and anti-capitalist criticism overlaps or combines with traditional ultranationalist arguments.

2.   The Rise of "Populist Democracy"

The second phenomenon that ought to be summarized briefly in order to better understand the context is what could be called the rise of "populist democracy" – as one of the consequences of the structural change of the public sphere and of the conditions and constellations of political communication and mobilization that has occurred in the last decades around the turn of the century. This "Strukturwandel der Öffentlichkeit 2.0" has been triggered by a number of factors that have to do with: economic and institutional crises (since the late 1970s), advanced globalization, and the availability of new electronic media (particularly social media), and the various mixes of elements of "collective" and "connective action" (with the network logic) in political communication (Bennett and Segerberg 2013). Among its outcomes have been a comprehensive mediatization of politics and another decisive push, on a broad scale, toward strengthening the elements of "populist democracy" as a real-type structure, opposed to those of "liberal" or "embedded democracy" (for more details, see Puhle 2017). Its basic characteristic is the emphasis on the direct and immediate relationship, and the fiction (or the simulacrum) of a permanent two-ways communication between the voters and the leader(s), circumventing and marginalizing the "corps intermédiaires" designed to provide channels of control and accountability. These changes also tend to favor populist actors and politics and give them significant comparative advantages. And they have affected the mode and composition of political agency and intermediation as well as the institutions, and influenced the outcomes of many interactions (Puhle 2020).

We can observe some general trends: The mechanisms of populist democracy can help to enhance direct participation of the citizens, but they can also (and often do) favor fragmentation, disorder and manipulation, particularly when democracy is reduced to mere "audience democracy" (Manin 1997). Political mobilization has become much easier than before: faster, more comprehensive, better to coordinate, but also more fragmented, less sustainable, more ad hoc and short-termish. Shit- and shamestorms may eventually be devastating, but they are reliably short. Cooperation and coalitions have become more fluid. Political campaigning, and the skills required, have substantially changed; techniques of networking, symbolic action, theatrical events, simulation (see Ingolfur Blühdorn's "simulative democracy", 2013), and good entertainment are more in demand. And the increase in recruiting political personnel from actors (beginning with Ronald Reagan), communicators, TV hosts, comedians and other "political amateurs" has been significant.

What also stands out as a correlate of the politics of permanent mobilization and unmitigated partiality (e.g., "fake news", "alternative facts"), is the high degree of emotionalization and scandalization of political communication. It has been facilitated by the ease and directness of electronic communication which, on average, seems to favor a less formal and more brutal language, by the fragmentation conditioned by the network logic, and by the fact that traditional filters (like quality journalism or intra-organizational checks) are no longer in place. It also fits well with the populist preferences for "politics of fear", and the Freund/Feind (friend/foe) scheme which have favored polarization and radicalization from the start. The idea is that people shall even vote out of fear and guided by hate. Hence elections tend to be transformed into acclamations and plebiscites, and campaigning has become more and more "negative" (see the debates on "affective polarization", "negative partisanship", etc.; Iyengar et al. 2018; Abramowitz and Webster 2018).

These trends are further enhanced by a number of mechanisms that are related to the structure and functioning of the social media and also contribute to disfigure the perceptions of the political landscape and, e.g., of the strengths of the political competitors. In the new social media popularity, intensity and "strength" are basically measured by algorithms, and these (eventually together with a small bunch of hyperactive users) tend to favor emotions, and particularly negative emotions, such as hatred and rage. Negative emotions get more comments, more "likes", and the candidates and parties emitting them hence have unfair advantages in the net. To give just one example: At the beginning of 2022, the exchanges in Facebook conveyed the impression that the extreme right-wing AfD was the most popular party in Germany. At the same time, however, there was sufficient evidence for estimating that about one third of the top commentators for the AfD were fake profiles (*Der Spiegel* 4, 22.01.2022, 36–7). It is obvious that such constellations, like many other problems that have been raised by the techniques and practices of the social networks, are in need of more systematic monitoring, policing and regulation.

Here the logics of populist democracy and the mechanisms of the new media, on the one hand, and populist politics, pressures and messages, on the other, reinforce one another triggering a process of "Veralltäglichung" (cotidianization, quotidianization) of the aggressive and dividing mechanisms populist interactions can contain. These processes and aspirations have been backed up by a general loss of trust and solidarity and a growing disenchantment of the people with their governments and institutions (for more see Gunther/Montero/Puhle 2007, 29–74). They often appear as if they could no longer "deliver" as expected vis-à-vis the major problems at hand, such as transcultural migrations, the structural transformation from Fordist economies to knowledge economies, the impacts of advanced globalization for the labor markets, and rising inequalities, not to speak of other crises and catastrophes, like COVID-19 (Atkinson 2015; Piketty 2014; Merkel and Kneip 2018).

The structural change of the public sphere and the rise of "populist democracy" have enhanced certain trends that could already be observed earlier in the twentieth century: the tendencies toward more fragmentation, and toward more hybrids of old and new movements, as well as an increase in the mutual transcontinental and transoceanic learning processes. However, whereas in earlier times the movements became more similar and converged, up to a point, within the limits of their respective type (protest populism in the developed world, project populism in the less developed world), they now have started to go beyond: the dividing lines between the types have become blurred, and more fragmented and loose elements and molds ('Versatzstücke') are traveling around (which also contributes to the characteristic constellations of our time that have been labeled as "postmodern"). We can now find more project populisms in Europe and the U.S., and more protest populisms also in Latin America. The Bolsonaro movement in Brazil has been the first populist movement that has no longer followed the typical lines of Brazilian and Latin American populist traditions (which have been anti-imperialist, "desarrollista", and in a way "progressive"), but has taken the Trump movement for a model. The U.S. populists as well have taken in foreign influences and suggestions (often undemocratic ones).

3. Some Populist Strategies of Semantic Reallocation

Coming back to my initial question of whether and why contemporary populisms may have a greater affinity to (or a greater need of) rearranging, disfiguring and redefining the terms and topoi of political discourse and agitation, and whether and how they might succeed in this practice, we are facing a broad variety of phenomena differing in degree. First, we find an extended field of varieties of populisms, eventually even with blurred borderlines to non-populist, or not-so-much populist movements and politicians: more or less democratic and undemocratic, of the right and of the left, extremist and moderate, in opposition and in government. Second, we are facing different degrees of intensities with which the populists are mobilizing, prioritizing, occupying, subverting, disfiguring, and transforming the basic agendas of political discourse and agitation. How far they could go, and whether and how they might reach the lines of "fake news", "alternative knowledge" ("facts", "truth"), or of a complete "alternative reality" of their own, depends on how much interpretive power / Deutungsmacht they can muster. The amount of interpretive power, in its turn, usually will be conditioned by (1) the societal, political and cultural constellations and contexts of the situation, (2) the influence and power of the populist actors, and (3) the constellations of receptivity in the field. It basically is a question of influence and power (and of power differentials and power relations) in a given situation.

The easiest and least sophisticated way of political propaganda has always been what Hitler recommended in *Mein Kampf*: repeat simplistic propaganda formulae and outright lies again and again, so that some of it will stick in the end (Hitler 1925, ch. 6). Donald Trump appears to be a fan of this basic version one of whose advantages lies in its being operable at a reduced level of literacy. It has been done before, e.g., by Karl Rove in the last days of the Bush campaign of 2004 in rural areas, with reference to the Democrats' alleged plans for gay marriage. Such campaigns have also demonstrated that strategies like this will usually work easier and more smoothly and get more momentum in case they are backed up by a specific "creed" or ideology, at least by some of its patterns, or loose bits and pieces which can be referred to (there is no need to be too demanding here). These elements would not only invoke the standard mechanisms of prejudice (as it was understood by the early Frankfurt School) and outright partiality; they would also mobilize the logic of fundamentalist convictions and quasi-religious believing. Even if many details of fundamentalist beliefs may be exchangeable, the logic implied remains the same: What you believe is, in principle, no longer open to critical assessment or rational argument, not to speak of scientific evidence, so that the scope of what might be considered as being "true" or "real" widens enormously and becomes more arbitrary. "Facts" and "alternative facts" then play in the same league, and you may have your choice, without any scruples. Hence proceeding, e.g., from the classic labeling of the New Dealers as "socialists", or of welfare as a collectivist straitjacket, to the statements that Obama is a Muslim, or Joe Biden a Commie at the service of foreign interests and conspiracies, will become just a matter of degree, opening up innumerable possibilities for representing the world not as it is, but as you need it to appear in order to promote your campaign.

Populist belief systems, creeds and ideologies usually also display a peculiar subversiveness: It is, however, not the "good" and productive subversiveness of critique and reason that serves as a permanent "mole" triggering, between our "space of experience" and the "horizon of expectations", dialectical processes of change and potential "progress" (Koselleck 1979). In contrast, the subversiveness of populism is negative, and impregnated by one of its most salient characteristics which Nadia Urbinati (2019) has called its intransigent "antiestablishmentarianism". Populists hate and fight the "establishment" and what they might call the "system". Many of them, in the name of "the people", and of the people's democratic participation and empowerment, have subverted the guarantees and the institutional firmness and stability of democracies. It is, however, interesting that, in Western democracies, only a few of them have presented themselves as being outright and completely disloyal to democratic values and procedures, whereas the majority has preferred strategies of semi-loyalty, with much "doublespeak", purged or "re-invented" and re-defined terminology, and techniques of semantic reallocation (cf. the rhetoric of Jörg Haider, Marine Le Pen or Giorgia Meloni). Most of populist "Umdeutung" ("resemanticization") and the shifting of meanings has followed the lines of semi-loyalty with regard to democracy, taking advantage of strategies of piecemeal (and somewhat furtive) change and salami slicing tactics. (For the concept of semiloyalty, first Linz 1978.)

In these processes key terms of political communication, programmatic articulation and campaigning are disfigured and transformed, often gradually, but increasingly and continuously. They are semantically rearranged, adapted to and integrated into the populist vocabulary and belief system, so that in the end they reflect and correspond to the essentials of contemporary populism, in the average mostly on the right and not or not completely democratic. Coming back to what has been outlined in the beginning of this essay, these "essentials" (of a tendentially maximalist ideal type) could be summarized as follows (Puhle 2020):

- protest against the status quo, in the name of the "people";
- "people" conceived as homogeneous (also underdogs);
- agonistic schemes, dichotomous view of society, conspiracy narratives, moralistic indignation, polarization and politics of fear and hatred;
- antipluralistic, antiliberal positions;
- against elites, institutions, and experts;
- against intermediaries (parliaments, parties, courts of law, independent media);
- fiction of direct, unmediated relationship and communication between leaders and followers;
- (mostly) exclusionary nationalism or nativism.

Besides the protest against the "establishment" and the "system" the first key element is the invocation of "the people". For populists this is not a statistical term, or the ensemble of the citizens, but rather a subjective and affective term: It is "We the people", the "good" or "common" people, often underdogs who are all alike and all "friends". In an agonistically structured world where friends fight foes, and "us" fight "them", the good guys (mostly the smaller ones) fight the bad guys (mostly the bigger ones). So, the term "people" has to be redefined, and the criteria for belonging are changing. Not all of those who may live next door and speak our language belong to the "people", and to the respective "nation": The elites usually do not, and eventually many others, too, particularly minorities and immigrants, the more so if they are culturally different. The populist concept of the "people" has an exclusionary, often xenophobic bias. The elites, in particular, are considered to be allies of foreign interests and (oligarchic or cosmopolitan) protagonists of the conspiracies against the common, hard-working and underprivileged people.

The same happens to other key terms of the political discourse referring to concepts like freedom, security, culture, citizenship, or "the system", to institutions such as parliaments, parties, pressure groups, courts of law, the media (e.g., the press becoming the "Lügenpresse"), or to the various vehicles of mobilization, not to speak of all the affective symbols of an inward-looking community. In a polarized world, characterized by politics of fear and hatred between friend and foe, there is only black and white, good and evil, and almost every term can become a voluntaristic "Kampfbegriff" (battle term) which is either occupied or "captured" (for the "good" cause), or disfigured and rearranged. This is particularly the case with the notion and the meaning of "democracy" which is completely redefined. Whatever else may be the specifics in a particular case, for populists in general an "embedded" or "liberal democracy", as it has been described, with all its checks and balances (Merkel and Puhle et al. 2003), is no longer a democracy. For them "democracy" is a simulacrum of participation with various simulations of "immediacy" (for those who belong), it is anti-pluralist, anti-liberal, anti-institutional, and at present in many cases also "anti-genderwahnsinn". "Feindbilder" have to be tangible.

One of the favored strategies of populist agitators besides resemanticization is outright reality denial, such as the denial of climate change, in the interest of the chemical agroindustry, extractivist entrepreneurs and many others, or Covid-19 denial, directed against the politics and policies of the established mainstream, or denial of electoral defeat, as in the case of Donald Trump who invented "illegal voting ballots" after the November 2020 elections. Such strategies combine repeated basic lies (as Hitler and others had recommended) with more systematic "alternative facts" and the respective conspiracy narratives, often also with an evocation of fundamentalist belief systems, in order to produce simulacra of hermetic "alternative" realities that are similar to those cultivated in Mafia circles, by Mexican drug cartels, or under totalitarian rule. These inventions and fancies then would guide and channel the mobilization of the populists' followers and could be further exploited in the course of future campaigns.

On the whole, it appears that populists would have to rely more than non-populists on building their politics and communication on such mechanisms of subverting, disfiguring and transforming the terms and topoi of political discourse and agitation. Not only because they usually have less substance to offer and, due to their strategies of polarization, have a greater need for mobilization, and hence for additional vehicles of identification and legitimation. They also value affective politics of indignation and resentment over rational aspirations and arguments, and have a rather peculiar black-and-white view of the world that in most cases does not correspond to the constellations of real-existing societies and to the concepts and institutions of liberal democracy. Hence, they have to take refuge in the mechanisms of prejudice, in myths and legends of conspiracies and in fundamentalist beliefs which then have to be made plausible to potential followers and voters. Here the techniques of resemanticization, shifting of meanings and transforming existing narratives come in. They seem to be in higher demand among populist campaigners than they would be among traditional non-populist Conservatives, Liberals or Social Democrats.

If they could, and if the others let them, populist agitators would try to subvert, disfigure, transform, and re-invent the world according to their peculiar narratives and aspirations, beginning with semantics. The friends of a free society and of an embedded democracy should not let them succeed. They should criticize their language, unmask their intentions, contain their efforts and resist their aspirations, by critical discourse, critique of ideology, and not least by well communicated politics and policies that address the problems of the people adequately. No pasarán!

Works Cited

Abramowitz, Alan I. and Steve W. Webster (2018) Negative Partisanship: Why Americans Dislike Parties But Behave Like Rabid Partisans. *Political Psychology* 39(S1), 119–135, Web: https://doi.org/10.1111/pops.12 479.

Abromeit, John et al. (eds.) (2016) *Transformations of Populism in Europe and the Americas. History and Recent Tendencies*. New York: Bloomsbury Academic.

Akkerman, Tjitske et al. (eds.) (2015) *Radical Right-Wing Populist Parties in Western Europe: Into the Mainstream?* London: Routledge.

Atkinson, Anthony B. (2015) *Inequality. What Can Be Done?* Cambridge: Harvard University Press.

Bennett, W. Lance and Alexandra Segerberg (2013) *The Logic of Connective Action. Digital Media and the Personalization of Contentious Politics*. Cambridge: Cambridge University Press.

Berlin, Isaiah (1968) (Summary) To Define Populism. Precis of the conference held in London 1967. *Government and Opposition* 3(2), 137–179.

Bertelsmann Stiftung (ed.) (2020) Transformation Index BTI 2020. Governance in International Comparison. Gütersloh: Bertelsmann Stiftung. https://www.bti-project.org.

Blühdorn, Ingolfur (2013) *Simulative Demokratie. Neue Politik nach der postdemokratischen Wende*. Frankfurt: Suhrkamp.

Canovan, Margaret (1981) *Populism*. London: Junction Books.

Canovan, Margaret (1999) Trust the People! Populism and the two faces of democracy. *Political Studies* 47(1), 2–16.

Castells, Manuel (1996–1998) *The Information Age*. 3 vols. Oxford: Blackwell.

Collier, Ruth Berins and David Collier (1991) *Shaping the Political Arena. Critical Junctures, the Labor Movement, and Regime Dynamics in Latin America*. Princeton: Princeton University Press.

Conniff, Michael L. (ed.) (1999) *Populism in Latin America*. Tuscaloosa: University of Alabama Press.

De la Torre, Carlos (2018) Populism Revived: Donald Trump and the Latin American Leftist Populists. *The Americas* 47(4), 734–38.

De la Torre, Carlos (ed.) (2015) *The Promise and Perils of Populism. Global Perspectives*. Lexington: University Press of Kentucky.

De la Torre, Carlos (ed.) (2019) *Routledge International Handbook of Global Populism*. Abingdon: Routledge.

Decker, Frank, Bernd Henningsen and Kjetil Jakobsen (eds.) (2015) *Rechtspopulismus und Rechtsextremismus in Europa*. Baden-Baden: Nomos.

Di Tella, Torcuato S. (1965) Populism and Reform in Latin America. In: Veliz, Claudio (ed.) *Obstacles to Change in Latin America*. London: Oxford University Press, 47–74.

Di Tella, Torcuato S. (1997) Populism into the Twenty-first Century. *Government and Opposition* 32, 187–200.

Dubiel, Helmut (ed.) (1986) *Populismus und Aufklärung*. Frankfurt: Suhrkamp.

Freeden, Michael (1998) Is Nationalism a Distinct Ideology? *Political Studies* 46, 748–765.

Gidron, Noam and Bart Bonikowski (2013) Varieties of Populism: Literature Review and Research Agenda. *Weatherhead Working Paper Series* 13–0004, Cambridge: Harvard University.

Gunther, Richard, José Ramón Montero and Juan J. Linz (eds.) (2002) *Political Parties: Old Concepts and New Challenges*. Oxford: Oxford University Press.

Gunther, Richard, José Ramón Montero and Hans-Jürgen Puhle (eds.) (2007) *Democracy, Intermediation, and Voting on Four Continents*. Oxford: Oxford University Press.

Gunther, Richard, Paul A. Beck, Petro C. Magalhães and Alejandro Moreno (eds.) (2016) *Voting in Old and New Democracies*. New York: Routledge.

Habermas, Jürgen (1990) *Strukturwandel der Öffentlichkeit*. 1962. Repr. Frankfurt am Main: Suhrkamp.

Heinisch, Reinhard C., Christina Holtz-Bacha and Oscar Mazzoleni (eds.) (2017) *Political Populism. A Handbook*. Baden-Baden : Nomos.

Hermet, Guy (1989) *Le peuple contre la démocratie* Paris : Fayard.

Hermet, Guy (2001) *Les populismes dans le monde*. Paris : Fayard.

Hermet, Guy, Soledad Loaeza and Jean François Prud'homme (eds.) (2001) *Del populismo de los antiguos al populismo de los modernos*. México: El Colegio de México.

Hitler, Adolf (1925) *Mein Kampf*. Vol. 1, München: Franz Eher Nf.

Hochschild, Arlie Russell (2016) *Strangers in Their Own Land. Anger and Mourning on the American Right. A Journey to the Heart of Our Political Divide*. New York: New Press.

Hofstadter, Richard (1955) *The Age of Reform*. New York: Vintage Books.

Ionescu, Ghita and Ernest Gellner (eds.) (1969) *Populism. Its Meanings and National Characteristics*. London: Weidenfeld and Nicolson.

Iyengar, Shanto et al. (2018) The Origins and Consequences of Affective Polarization in the United States. *Annual Review of Political Science* 22(1), 1–18, DOI 10.1146/annurev-polisci-051117-073034.

Jörke, Dirk and Veith Selk (2017) *Theorien des Populismus. Zur Einführung*. Hamburg: Junius.

Judis, John P. (2016) *The Populist Explosion. How the Great Recession Transformed American and European Politics*. New York: Columbia Global Reports.

Katz, Richard S. and Peter Mair (2002) The Ascendancy of the Party in Public Office: Party Organizational Change in Twentieth-Century Democracies. In: Gunther, Richard, José Ramon Montero and Juan J. Linz (eds.) *Political Parties. Old Concepts and New Challenges*. Oxford: Oxford University Press, 113–135.

Kirchheimer, Otto (1966) The Transformation of the Western European Party System. In: La Palombara, Joseph and Myron Weiner (eds.): *Political Parties and Political Development*. Princeton: Princeton University Press, 177–200. Knight, Alan (1998) Populism and Neo-populism in Latin America, especially Mexico. *Journal of Latin American Studies* 30(2), 223–248.

Knöbl, Wolfgang (2016) Über alte und neue Gespenster. Historisch-systematische Anmerkungen zum "Populismus". *Mittelweg 36* 25(6), 8–35.

Koselleck, Reinhart (1979) "Erfahrungsraum" und "Erwartungshorizont" – zwei historische Kategorien. In: Koselleck, Reinhart, *Vergangene*

Zukunft. Zur Semantik geschichtlicher Zeiten. Frankfurt am Main: Suhrkamp, 349–375.

Kriesi, Hanspeter and Takis S. Pappas (eds.) (2015) *European Populism in the Shadow of the Great Recession*. Colchester: ECPR Press.

Laclau, Ernesto (1981) *Politik und Ideologie im Marxismus. Kapitalismus – Faschismus – Populismus*. Berlin: Argument-Verlag, 123–185.

Laclau, Ernesto (2005) *On Populist Reason*. London: Verso.

Levitsky, Steven and Daniel Ziblatt (2018) *How Democracies Die: What History Reveals About our Future*. New York: Viking.

Linz, Juan J. (1978) *The Breakdown of Democratic Regimes: Crisis, Breakdown and Reequilibration*. Baltimore: Johns Hopkins University Press.

Lipset, Seymour Martin and Earl Raab (1970) *The Politics of Unreason. Right-Wing Extremism in America, 1790–1970*. New York: Harper & Row.

Maihold, Günther (ed.) (2020) *Cultura, comunicación y crimen organizado en México*. Berlin: ed. tranvía.

Manin, Bernard (1997) *Principles of Representative Government*. Cambridge: Cambridge University Press.

Manow, Philip (2018) *Die Politische Ökonomie des Populismus*. Berlin: Suhrkamp.

Marx, Karl (1960) Der achtzehnte Brumaire des Louis Bonaparte. 1852. In: *Marx-Engels-Werke* (MEW), vol. 8, Berlin: Dietz Verlag, 111–207.

Mény, Yves and Yves Surel (eds.) (2002) *Democracies and the Populist Challenge*. Basingstoke: Palgrave Macmillan.

Merkel, Wolfgang (2004) Embedded and Defective Democracies. *Democratization* 11(5), 33–58.

Merkel, Wolfgang and Sascha Kneip (eds.) (2018) *Democracy and Crisis. Challenges in Turbulent Times*. Wiesbaden: Springer VS.

Merkel, Wolfgang, Hans-Jürgen Puhle et al. (2003) *Defekte Demokratie*. Vol. 1: Theorie. Opladen: Leske + Budrich.

Moffitt, Benjamin (2016) *The Global Rise of Populism. Performance, Political Style, and Representation*. Stanford: Stanford University Press.

Monedero, Juan Carlos (2014) *Curso urgente de política para gente decente*. Barcelona: Seix Barral.

Mouffe, Chantal (2018) *Für einen linken Populismus*. Berlin: Suhrkamp.

Mounk, Yascha (2018) *The People vs. Democracy. Why Our Freedom Is in Danger and How to Save It*. Cambridge: Harvard University Press.

Mudde, Cas (2007) *Populist Radical Right Parties in Europe*. Cambridge: Cambridge University Press.

Mudde, Cas and Cristóbal Rovira Kaltwasser (2017) *Populism. A Very Short Introduction*. Oxford: Oxford University Press.

Mudde, Cas and Cristóbal Rovira Kaltwasser (eds.) (2012) *Populism in Europe and the Americas. Threat or Corrective for Democracy?* Cambridge: Cambridge University Press.

Müller, Jan-Werner (2016) *What Is Populism?* Philadelphia: University of Pennsylvania Press.

Norris, Pippa and Ronald Inglehart (2019) *Cultural Backlash. Trump, Brexit, and Authoritarian Populism*. Cambridge: Cambridge University Press.

Panizza, Francisco (ed.) (2005) *Populism and the Mirror of Democracy*. London: Verso.

Pappas, Takis S. (2014) Populist democracies: post-authoritarian Greece and post-communist Hungary. *Government and Opposition* 49(1), 1–23.

Piketty, Thomas (2014) *Capital in the Twenty-First Century*. Cambridge: Harvard University Press.

Priester, Karin (2012) *Rechter und linker Populismus. Annäherung an ein Chamäleon*. Frankfurt: Campus.

Puhle, Hans-Jürgen (1975) *Politische Agrarbewegungen in kapitalistischen Industriegesellschaften. Deutschland, USA und Frankreich im 20. Jahrhundert* Göttingen: Vandenhoeck & Ruprecht.

Puhle, Hans-Jürgen (1986) Was ist Populismus? In: Dubiel, Helmut (ed.): *Populismus und Aufklärung*. Frankfurt am Main: Suhrkamp, 12–32 (first publ. in: *Politik und Kultur* 10, 1983, 22–43).

Puhle, Hans-Jürgen (2002) Still the Age of Catch-allism? "Volksparteien" and "Parteienstaat" in Crisis and Re-equilibration. In: Gunther, Richard, José Ramón Montero and Juan J. Linz (eds.): *Political Parties: Old Concepts and New Challenges*. Oxford: Oxford University Press, 58–83.

Puhle, Hans-Jürgen (2007) Zwischen Diktatur und Demokratie. Stufen der politischen Entwicklung in Lateinamerika im 20. Jahrhundert.

In: Bernecker, Walther L. et al. (eds.): *Lateinamerika 1870–2000. Geschichte und Gesellschaft*. Wien: Promedia, 15–33.

Puhle, Hans-Jürgen (2015a) Populismus: Form oder Inhalt? Protest oder Projekt? In: Puhle, Hans-Jürgen *Protest, Parteien, Interventionsstaat. Organisierte Politik und Demokratieprobleme im Wandel*. Göttingen: Vandenhoeck & Ruprecht, 91–117.

Puhle, Hans-Jürgen (2015b) "Embedded Democracy" und "Defekte Demokratien": Probleme demokratischer Konsolidierung und ihrer Teilregime. In: Puhle, Hans-Jürgen: *Protest, Parteien, Interventionsstaat. Organisierte Politik und Demokratieprobleme im Wandel*. Göttingen: Vandenhoeck & Ruprecht, 161–183.

Puhle, Hans-Jürgen (2017) Auf dem Weg zur populistischen Demokratie. Ein neuer Strukturwandel der Öffentlichkeit und seine Folgen. In: Croissant, Aurel et al. (eds.): *Demokratie, Diktatur und Gerechtigkeit. Festschrift für Wolfgang Merkel*. Wiesbaden: Springer VS, 467–484.

Puhle, Hans-Jürgen (2018) Populismos y democracia en el siglo XXI. *La Maleta de Portbou. Revista de Humanidades y Economía* 32, nov.-dic. 2018, 12–19.

Puhle, Hans-Jürgen (2020) Populism and Democracy in the 21st Century. *SCRIPTS Working Paper Series* No. 2, Cluster of Excellence "Contestations of the Liberal Script", Berlin: Freie Universität Berlin. Web: https://www.scripts-berlin.eu/publications/Publications-PDF /SCRIPTS_Working_Paper_02_Web.pdf.

Rivero, Jacobo (2014) *Conversación con Pablo Iglesias*. Madrid: Turpial.

Roberts, Kenneth M. (2014) Populism, Social Movements, and Popular Subjectivity. In: Della Porta, Donatella and Mario Diani (eds.): *The Oxford Handbook of Social Movements*. Oxford: Oxford University Press: DOI: 10.1093/oxfordhb/9780199678402.013.27.

Roberts, Kenneth M. (2015) Populism, Political Mobilization and Crisis of Political Representation. In: De la Torre, Carlos (ed.): *The Promise and Perils of Populism. Global Perspectives*. Lexington: University Press of Kentucky, 140–158.

Roberts, Kenneth M. (2019) Bipolar Disorders: Varieties of Capitalism and Populist Out-Flanking on the Left and Right. *Polity* 51(4), 641–653. Web: http://dx.doi.org/10.1086/705377.

Rodrik, Dani (2017) Populism and the Economics of Globalization. *Working Paper* 23559. Cambridge: National Bureau of Economic Research. Web: http://j.mp/2sowhXj.

Rovira Kaltwasser, Cristóbal, Paul Taggart, Paulina Ochoa Espejo and Pierre Ostiguy (eds.) (2017) *The Oxford Handbook of Populism*. New York: Oxford University Press.

Schmitter, Philippe C. (2018) "Real-existing" democracy and its discontents: Sources, conditions, causes, symptoms and prospects. Paper presented at the conference "The Crisis of Western Liberal Democracy?" Shanghai: Fudan University, 27–28 October.

Skocpol, Theda and Vanessa Williamson (2012) *The Tea Party and the Remaking of Republican Conservatism*. Oxford : Oxford University Press.

Souillac, Romain (2007) *Le mouvement Poujade : de la défense professionnelle au populisme nationaliste, 1953–1962*. Paris: Presses de Sciences Po.

Taggart, Paul (2000) *Populism*. Buckingham: Open University Press.

Taggart, Paul and Cristóbal Rovira Kaltwasser (2016) Dealing with populists in government. A framework for analysis. *Democratization* 23(2), 201–220.

Urbinati, Nadia (2014) *Democracy Disfigured. Opinion, Truth and the People*. Cambridge: Harvard University Press.

Urbinati, Nadia (2019) *Me the People. How Populism Transforms Democracy*. Cambridge: Harvard University Press.

Weyland, Kurt (2001) Clarifying a Contested Concept: Populism in the Study of Latin American Politics. *Comparative Politics* 34(1), 1–22.

Weyland, Kurt (2013) Latin America's Authoritarian Drift. The Threat from the Populist Left. *Journal of Democracy* 24, 18–32.

Legitimizing Colonial Rule in the Twenty-First Century
Discursive Strategies of the AfD's Politics of Remembrance

Aram Ziai

This chapter[1] sets out to analyze how the German right-wing party AfD (Alternative für Deutschland) attempts to legitimize colonial rule and resemanticize colonialism as an endeavor which cannot be seen as entirely criminal and negative. The first section will deal with the social and historical context of this attempt, which is characterized by the rise of postcolonial (and more recently decolonial) studies, an increasing political awareness of colonialism and racism through political campaigns reaching a wider public, and a revisionist backlash against this process from the political right. The second section will outline the method employed, which can briefly be characterized as a poststructuralist discourse analysis. The third section will then focus on the motion to the German Bundestag entitled "A nuanced cultural-political engagement with the German colonial period" ("Die deutsche Kolonialzeit kulturpolitisch differenziert aufarbeiten")[2] submitted by the AfD, which will be taken as a case in point to be analyzed. Covering

---

1   Many thanks to the editors for numerous helpful comments. A short and very early draft of the argument was presented in German in the Frankfurter Rundschau. https://www.fr.de/kultur/gesellschaft/unter-kolonialen-haerten-versteht-13548449.html.
2   All translations are by the author.

issues from the genocide in Southwest Africa to the debate on museums and restitution, it claims to strive for a scientific and non-ideological view of German colonialism in the politics of remembrance and a more nuanced view on its merits and flaws, in contrast to an allegedly hegemonic and biased perspective dominated by cultural Marxism and postcolonial studies which has managed to portray colonial rule as simply criminal.

The article will reconstruct the argument and analyze it from the perspective of discourse analysis, taking into account the wider academic and public debate which can be shown to be either ignored or distorted in the AfD paper. It will trace its attempts to resignify and instrumentalize existing academic and political concepts, establish conceptual links and construct a new narrative which has the effect of legitimizing racist colonial rule in the twenty-first century and aims at commemorating German colonialism for its achievements.

1.   Context

The AfD's attempt to resemanticize colonialism has to be seen as part of a broader wave of revisionist policies of knowledge which are a reaction to the increasing recognition of postcolonial and decolonial studies in academia and, connected to this, political campaigns targeting colonialism and racism. These three aspects of the context will be discussed in this section.

Postcolonial approaches investigate the aftermath of colonial rule after formal decolonization, the "legacies of colonialism" (Loomba 1998, 12) and the "continuing cultural and political ramifications of colonialism in both colonizing and colonized societies" (Young 2016, 6). They focus on the "production of knowledge about the Other" (Williams and Chrisman 1994, 8). Yet postcolonial theory usually perceives itself as critical theory which aims at progressive social change, such as when Loomba describes the "contestation of colonial domination and the legacies of colonialism" as the program of postcolonial studies (Loomba 1998, 12). It can thus be argued that postcolonial theory clearly takes an anticolonial and anti-imperial political position, which means it is not confined to the critique of discourse but is also concerned with economic exploitation (Young 2016, 58; see also Conrad and Randeria 2002, 24; Castro Varela and Dhawan 2005, 8; Kerner 2012, 11; Ziai 2012, 293). At the same time most theorists of postcolonial studies would agree to Stuart Hall when he differentiates postcolonial studies from a "clear-cut politics of binary oppositions" between good and bad which renders the complex situations of colonialism intelligible (Hall 1996, 244).

Since the early iconic works of postcolonial theory (Said 1978; Spivak 1988; Hall 1992; Bhabha 1994; McClintock 1995; Chakrabarty 2000), it has become increasingly recognized – first in literary and cultural studies, but increasingly also in the social sciences – exemplified in the work of Bhambra (2007, 2013) and Shilliam (2011). In development studies, the postcolonial critique of the Post-Development school has had a marked influence on the discipline (Ziai 2017).

Yet the rising influence of the critique of colonialism and colonial racism was not confined to academia: it had repercussions in the public sphere. The presence of a history of slavery and racism was highlighted by the Black Lives Matter (BLM) movement which began after the shooting of Trayvon Martin and the acquittal of the perpetrator in 2012, but has since been regularly rekindled by ongoing lethal police violence against Blacks in the U.S., such as the killing of George Floyd in 2020. The movement has inspired mass protests not only in the U.S., but in a number of other countries as well (in Europe, Australia, New Zealand, Brazil and Japan). In addition, BLM protests also seem to have an effect on media attention: in the two months after the killing of George Floyd, our postcolonial activist group in Kassel received many more requests for interviews than in the whole previous year (and usually the reference to these current political events was made by the journalists themselves).

Since 2015, the Rhodes Must Fall movement has similarly contributed to a public debate on racism, and specifically on colonialism and the question whether and how colonizers should be remembered in the twenty-first century. The removal of the statue of Cecil Rhodes from the campus of the University of Cape Town had repercussions in other universities in and beyond South Africa, be it in removing colonial monuments in Great Britain and Belgium, such as the statue of slave trader Edward Colston which was thrown into the harbor of Bristol, or in decolonizing the curriculum. The ensuing Fees Must Fall movement claimed that colonialism and Apartheid lived on in present-day South Africa through racialized social inequality.

So a critical perspective on colonialism has gained prominence in the twenty-first century, not only in academic postcolonial and decolonial studies, but also in the wider public debate. Against this backdrop, there has been a backlash against this critical view on colonialism in the past years. On the international stage, probably the most prominent vindication of colonialism came from political scientist Bruce Gilley (2017) and was published in *Third World Quarterly* (of all journals), which had hitherto been seen as critical and anticolonial. Although the majority of members of the editorial board stepped down because of this publication (Richey et al. 2019), and although numerous determined rebuttals of the Gilley article have been written (e.g., Hira 2017; Klein 2018; Rodriguez 2018), *TWQ* had given a platform to the "original" hypothesis that colonialism was beneficial for people under European rule.

In the German context, the argument about the benefits of colonialism for the colonized had been made in 2015 by journalists in renowned liberal and conservative newspapers. They argued that decolonization had proven to worsen the situation in formerly colonized countries, suggesting (just like Gilley) a contemporary form of European colonialism as a solution (Martenstein 2015; Stein 2015). While this did not produce any public outcry, an interview with the commissioner for Africa of the German government, Günter Nooke, did so in 2018 when it was published by a Berlin newspaper. In the interview, the conservative politician claimed that the Cold War had been "more detrimental to Africa" than colonialism and that the latter had "contributed to separate the continent from archaic structures." He envisioned special economic zones in Africa in which African migrants heading for Europe could be resettled, governed by the World Bank or the EU or European states (Nooke 2018). In the following year, the AfD invited Gilley to give a talk in the German parliament entitled "The Case for German Colonialism" in which he reiterated his argument from the *TWQ* article with special reference to the German colonies (Gilley 2019).

2. Method

The research question how the AfD legitimizes colonialism will be investigated using as an object of analysis the motion submitted by the AfD party in the German parliament entitled "A nuanced cultural-political engagement with the German colonial period" ("Die deutsche Kolonialzeit kulturpolitisch differenziert aufarbeiten") from December 2019. The text has been chosen because it covers a wide range of aspects concerning a politics of remembrance regarding colonialism and can (with officially 31 AfD delegates being the authors) be seen as representative of the party's view of the topic (AfD 2019). It forms a centerpiece in the AfD's strategy in the battle over the meaning of colonialism in Germany, which is accompanied by events such as the publication of a paper on the renaming of streets (AfD 2020), the invitation of Gilley and a resolution on the alleged instrumentalization of the German colonial period by "leftist ideologues".[3] What sets it apart from these other attempts is that it directly tries to influence German cultural policy in the parliament. Recently, it has been followed up by another motion in the Bundestag which used the accusations of antisemitism against the art exhibition Documenta to demand a complete stop to any public funding for postcolonial studies (AfD 2022).

The text will be submitted to an analysis of its arguments which examines (following Foucault 1980) the interconnections between power and knowledge and the discursive construction of German colonialism,

---

3   AfD-Fraktion im Landtag Schleswig-Holstein: "Schluss mit Schuld und Sühne – für eine differenzierte Betrachtung der deutschen Kolonialgeschichte!" 10.06.2021. Web: https://www.openpr.de/news/1212091/Schluss-mit-Schuld-und-Suehne-fuer-eine-differenzierte-Betrachtung-der-deutschen-Kolonialges chichte.html.

bearing in mind the social and political context of the publication. Additionally, the statements in the text will be compared to the academic debate on the topic, pointing out certain misrepresentations and misconceptions. Based on the poststructuralist analytical method of Laclau and Mouffe (2001), the essay will look at these texts' strategies of resemanticization, the volatility between signifiers and signifieds, and the construction and disruption of chains of equivalence.

3.   Analysis

"Deutsche Kolonialzeit kulturpolitisch differenziert aufarbeiten" comprises twelve pages and covers different aspects related to the question how to deal with the colonial past in Germany: the renaming of streets; the restitution of cultural artifacts from museums; the handling of the colonial war in German South-West Africa (today's Namibia); present-day cultural politics and in general the political evaluation of the period of German colonialism. The text starts with a diagnosis of facts (AfD 2019, 1–2) followed by political demands (AfD 2019, 2–3) and a more detailed justification of them (AfD 2019, 4–12). The motion proposes that the parliament demands from the government, a) to ensure that in German curricula, culture and politics a "nuanced" view on German colonialism will be promoted which emphasizes the beneficial aspects of this period for those subjected; b) to reject any demands for reparation by descendants of the Herero and Nama; c) to reject any demands for restitution of cultural artifacts from colonial contexts (based on a categorization of these contexts as criminal); and d) to call on municipalities to keep and if need be contextualize colonial street names (AfD 2019, 2–3). The different aspects of the text will be examined in the following sub-sections.

3.1. The Colonial War Against the Herero and Nama: No Genocide

The longest part of the text is dedicated to disproving that the colonial war against the Herero and Nama in German South-West Africa was a genocide (AfD 2019, 4–9). This can be explained because the text links the predominant negative judgement on German colonialism to Germany's violent colonial wars. The text readily admits that there were "hardships and cruelties" (AfD 2019, 2) and "without a doubt a disproportionate use of violence" on the side of the Germans (AfD 2019, 4), but it then claims that it was "out of the question that this amounted to genocide or that there was a continuity between this war and the crimes of National Socialism" (AfD 2019, 1). German colonial policy, the text contends, had learned from these "serious mistakes" and initiated reforms which led to an improvement in living standards of the colonized people (AfD 2019, 4). The central claim that there was no genocide in German South-West Africa rests on several arguments, some of which are, according to the text, backed up by respected German historians. I will look at them in chronological order.

Argument 1: No Continuity Between Colonialism and National Socialism

Based on the research of an expert on German colonial wars, Susanne Kuß from the University of Bern, who is quoted at length, the text argues that the hypothesis of a direct continuity between German colonial wars and National Socialist policies of extermination was based on speculation and did not rest on solid evidence (AfD 2019, 5). However, the text suggests that the controversy about this continuity (which in fact exists among historians) indicates that there is a controversy about the question of genocide (which does not exist, at least not in the contemporary academic debate). Kuß, who is indeed skeptical about the continuity hypothesis, is very clear about the colonial war against the Herero and Nama: "The colonial war in German South-West Africa is special in so far as it culminated in genocide" (Kuß 2014, 333, see also her detailed reflection on the categorization of this colonial war as genocide in Kuß 2018).

To use her as a principal witness that there was no genocide is disingenuous. This move is made possible through the unacceptable conflation of the question of continuity and the question of genocide, as if there was an equation between genocide and the Holocaust. Allegedly disproving the continuity thesis, the authors pretend that this now also disproves the genocidal quality of the German wars in Africa. (The genocidal quality of the Holocaust is readily accepted, which can be interpreted as part of the AfD's discursive strategy as will be discussed in the conclusion.) This conflation – or rather intentional confusion – gives rise to the impression that the AfD position was indeed shared by a number of respectable historians, which is not the case.

Argument 2: The Policy of Extermination was Criticized by German Authorities

The text is quoting German critics of Generalleutnant von Trotha, the governor of German South-West Africa and chief commander of the German troops, who was responsible for the policy of extermination against the Herero and Nama. The governor of German East Africa criticized the "ruthless manner" in which von Trotha conducted the war and Chancellor von Bülow claimed that his intentions "contradicted the principles of Christianity and humanity" (AfD 2019, 5). Yet the German government today ignored this and criticizes the "terrible injustice committed by our ancestors" (AfD 2019, 5). The criticism indicates that the policy of extermination did not find unanimous support within the German government (see also AfD 2019, 8–9). But again, it is difficult to see in what way this could constitute an argument against the categorization of the violent deeds as genocide. The last quote suggests that the point might be an inappropriate generalization: some of "our ancestors" could have been critics of the colonial policies. This is certainly correct, but irrelevant for the question of whether there was a genocide. Von Trotha may not have acted in accordance with every member of the German government, but he was the representative of the German state in charge of the military operation. And it seems that the German army general staff shared his intent when it writes in the war report:

This bold undertaking shows the ruthless energy of the German leadership in the pursuit of the defeated enemy in brilliant light. No effort, no privation was spared to rob the enemy of the last vestige of his power of resistance; like a deer hunted half to death, he was chased from waterhole to waterhole until he finally became a victim of the nature of his own country. The waterless Omaheke was to complete what the German weapons had begun: The annihilation of the Herero people (cited in Kößler and Melber 2018, 226–27).

It is interesting to note how the responsibility for the genocide is transferred from the German perpetrators to the "nature" of Africa.

Argument 3: The Claim to Genocide was Promoted by GDR Historiography

The text again relies on a respected historian, Christiane Bürger, author of an award-winning PhD thesis on the topic, who is quoted extensively (twenty-seven times) to make the point that GDR historiography a) defined the colonial war in German South-West Africa as genocide; b) saw a causal connection between the colonial and the National Socialist genocide; and c) was influenced and instrumentalized by political anti-bourgeois guidelines of the authoritarian socialist state (AfD, 2019, 5–8). The text quotes Bürger's statement that "The genocide against the Herero and the continuity between colonialism and National Socialism became a normative interpretation of history which resonated especially with the political left in the Federal Republic who supported the Anti-Apartheid movement and the independence of Namibia" (quoted in AfD 2019, 8). While the text implies that c) is an argument which devalues a) and b), and while the quote is taken to mean that this "normative" (is there a non-normative one?) interpretation is patently wrong, this is not what Bürger is saying. Indeed, she unambiguously talks about the "first German genocide in the year 1904" (Bürger 2013, 3). So Bürger does say: GDR historiography called the violence against the Herero and Nama genocide and there was a political influence on GDR historiography, but she does not say: only because there was a political influence it was called a genocide. Additionally, the discursive strategy of a conflation of the continuity hypothesis and categorization of genocide is employed once more, while the two positions are in fact separate: one can readily deny a direct continuity between colonialism and Nationalist Socialism without denying that each of them was a genocide. Again, the text uses a respected historian as a witness for a claim she has never made. Further, the text seeks to discredit the genocide claim because it allegedly originated in GDR historiography.

Argument 4: The German Policy of Extermination was Ineffective

A journalist from the news magazine *Der Spiegel* and a third female historian, Brigitte Lau, are cited to argue that the German troops had been unable to effectively imprison the remaining Herero in the Omaheke desert. Further, many of the soldiers had been suffering from diseases and exhaustion (AfD 2019, 9). Again, this may or may not be the case, but these questions are irrelevant for the categorization of the military action as genocide. According to the UN Convention on the Prevention and Punishment of the Crime of Genocide, the crime is constituted by

> any of the following acts committed with intent to destroy, in whole or in part, a national, ethnical, racial or religious group, as such: (a) Killing members of the group; . . . (c) Deliberately inflicting on the group conditions of life calculated to bring about its physical destruction in whole or in part. (Chalk and Jonassohn 1988, 44)

There is no doubt that Generalleutnant von Trotha voiced his intention to destroy the Herero people: "I believe that the nation as such has to be destroyed," he wrote to the chief of staff (Gewald 2004, 116). After the military victory in the battle of Waterberg he issued orders to his soldiers to pursue the losers and to shoot at armed or unarmed Herero to drive them into the Omaheke desert where many thousands of them died (Zimmerer 2004, 50–52). The precise number of survivors (between 17,000 and 40,000 of a people of 70,000–100.000; Zimmerer 2004, 243n16) and thus the effectiveness of the extermination policy is irrelevant for the identification of the crime. That the "extermination order" was retracted six weeks later (AfD 2019, 9) (which could be read as an addendum to argument 2) is a fact which does neither alter the intent nor the deed.

The four arguments brought forward by the AfD document are partly valid (2 and 3), partly contested (1 and 4), but none of them does in any way constitute an argument against the categorization of the colonial warfare in German South-West Africa as a genocide, although the text suggests that this was the case. This effect is produced by the discursive strategies of equation, appropriating and discrediting. The first strategy (argument 1) works by constructing a chain of equivalence between categorizing German colonial policy as genocidal and claiming direct links between colonial genocide and National Socialist genocide. The second strategy (argument 1 and 3) works through deceptively appropriating some historians' skepticism about the historical continuity thesis as evidence that the colonial policy did not amount to genocide. The third strategy (argument 3) works through discrediting the argument on the grounds of its origin: if the ideologically driven historiography of the GDR proclaimed it was a genocide, then it probably was not. Arguments 2 and 4 seem to simply rely on readers' ignorance of the UN genocide convention.

All in all, the strategy of "Deutsche Kolonialzeit kulturpolitisch differenziert aufarbeiten" is to suggest that the categorization of the war crimes as genocide is contested among historians and a product of ideological GDR historiography. Both claims are spurious. In analogy to Herman and Chomsky (1988), these strategies could be described as "manufacturing dissent" where there is none, at least not among contemporary academic historians. The objective seems to be to delegitimize the characterization of German colonialism as criminal by casting doubt on the consensual genocide thesis. This interpretation is suggested by the AfD itself:

> The period of German colonial rule, which ended 100 years ago, is evaluated as negative today, or even as entirely criminal. This evaluation is based above all on the manner in which the German Empire waged war in some African colonies in the first phase of its colonial rule. (AfD 2019, 4).

3.2. The Benefits for the Colonized

That the objective of the text even goes beyond downplaying the crimes of German colonial rule becomes clearly visible in those sections where it attempts to legitimize it by pointing out its alleged benefits for the colonized. Interestingly, already in the first paragraph the text refers to the statement of the Commissioner for Africa, Günter Nooke, and his statement that colonialism had "contributed to disengage Africa from archaic structures" (AfD 2019, 1). Nooke, the text says, merely articulated the view of "prominent historians" like Prof. Egon Flaig (AfD 2019, 10). Flaig in turn claims that European colonialism had put an end to slavery in Africa and made possible new paths for the continent after "a thousand-year history of most bloody violence and genocides" (Flaig, quoted in AfD 2019, 11). In particular imperial Germany's reforms in colonial rule introduced by secretary of state Bernhard Dernburg between 1907 and1910, the text claims, had led to a "significant improvement of living conditions" (AfD 2019, 4) and an expansion of infrastructure, especially the railways (AfD 2019, 4, 11).

The reference to Nooke, a member of the respected conservative party (CDU), is again an appropriating move, but this time one which is justified. However, his statement knowingly or unknowingly reproduces the stereotype of a backward and barbarian Africa in need of "civilization" and "development" – which was (and is until today) the most significant myth legitimizing European colonial rule around the world. While the appropriation of the historian Flaig is also justified, it seems to add academic expertise to the position emphasizing the benefits of colonialism. Yet Flaig is actually no expert of European colonialism or modern history in general. His PhD thesis and second book dealt with ancient history, with Greek cultural history and Roman emperors.[4] His book on the global history of slavery, which the text quotes, is an apology of European colonial slavery which resemanticizes European slavery in Africa as liberation – and has received disastrous scholarly

---

4   Wikipedia: Egon Flaig. Web: https://de.wikipedia.org/wiki/Egon_Flaig.

reviews.[5] In her review, Felicitas Schmieder writes that Flaig's book was "not meeting elementary requirements of academic texts." She claims that it ignores historical facts, reproduces "the ideological justification of European wars of conquest by the European colonial powers," and indeed makes the reviewer wonder why an academic publisher had accepted the manuscript (Schmieder 2010).

What about the archaic structures that colonialism allegedly had pushed back in Africa? While it is correct that, after having profited from the slave trade for centuries, European powers (including Germany) outlawed slavery in many regions especially in the later nineteenth and early twentieth century, it was often replaced by other forms of forced labor. One example for German colonial rule is Cameroon, where the deputy governor Heinrich Leist ordered freed African slaves to work for him. When they dared to demand wages, he had their women whipped (Speitkamp 2005, 68, 138). While the AfD's claim concerning the eventual outlawing of the slave trade is not factually incorrect, its not mentioning other forms of forced labor by colonial and imperial powers skews the representation of colonialism to serve an apologetic desire.

The AfD text's claim about the improvement of living conditions under German colonial rule as a consequence of the colonial "reform policy" under secretary of state Dernburg is postulated, but nowhere supported by evidence. Historical research does not endorse the view. Dernburg did in fact abolish the tax on huts and limited corporal punishment, but during his office mixed-race marriages remained forbidden, forced labor and land theft went on as before, and German colonial policy was still geared to maximize the exploitation of indigenous labor power (Speitkamp 2005, 140–41; van Laak 2005, 8; Utermark 2011, 343–46). In his PhD thesis on the Dernburg reforms in German colonial policy, the historian Sören Utermark concludes: "There has definitely been no fundamental improvement of the living conditions of Africans in the German colonies in the Dernburg era. On the contrary, Dernburg's policy

---

of reform has accelerated the process of impoverishment of the indigenous population" (Utermark 2011, 344). Regarding the expansion of infrastructure and especially the railways, historical research points out a) that the actual work of building the infrastructure was performed by African forced laborers; b) that its objective was to allow for a more effective exploitation of natural resources exported from the colonies; and c) that it also served the transport of soldiers to the front and the transport of prisoners of war into concentration camps (Zimmerer 2004, 27; Zeller 2004, 72; Rodney 2018, 251–52; Grewe 2018, 501). All three points render it quite difficult to argue that the expansion of infrastructure benefitted the colonized or even entailed "significant improvements of living conditions." Again, the text exhibits an extremely partial reading of history which systematically leaves out significant facts that do not fit the premeditated conclusion: that the Europeans did the Africans a great service by conquering their countries and establishing an undemocratic system of racialized rule. This discursive strategy could be called a selective reading. As David Campbell (1998) has pointed out, this strategy is a standard technique wherever political struggles require the construction of narratives on the basis of some facts while ignoring other facts inconvenient to the cause. However, rarely has the contortion of historical facts been as blatant as here.

The alleged benefits of German colonial rule pointed out in "Deutsche Kolonialzeit kulturpolitisch differenziert aufarbeiten" serve to discredit what is described as the "undifferentiated and untenable categorization of the entire colonial period as 'criminal'" (AfD 2019, 3). As similar points are made on pages 1, 2, 4, and 10, this can be identified as the central thesis of the text. The AfD criticizes that the politics of remembrance of the German government mentions German colonialism next to the dictatorships of National Socialism and State Socialism in the GDR (AfD 2019, 4). In their view, this does not do justice to the benign foreign rule of the German Empire. So, their central discursive objective seems to be to disrupt the chain of equivalence between these three regimes and to achieve a status for German colonial rule as not entirely negative or criminal, based on their own "nuanced" view on the period. This has repercussions for present debates on restitution, reparations and further issues connected to North-South relations like migration and development co-operation.

3.3. Postcolonial Studies and Cultural Marxism

If German colonial rule is not guilty of genocide and partly led to improvements for the living conditions of the colonized, as "Deutsche Kolonialzeit kulturpolitisch differenziert aufarbeiten" claims, this begs the question why it is viewed so negatively in the German public and recently even by the German government. The AfD's answer is that since the 1990s there was an ideologically driven anti-Western "postcolonial turn" leading to a "discourse of guilt," although a closer look reveals that behind the "fancy labels" of postcolonial or decolonial studies we find "nothing more than a restaging of anti-imperialist theories inspired by cultural Marxism" (AfD 2019, 9). The recent focus on culture, identities and the deconstruction of knowledge had led to a shift from the history of the real to that of discourse. "Post- or decolonial studies do not care about the facts any longer" and in their "most extreme variants deny that there is a connection between the history located in the world of language and the world of real history" (AfD 2019, 10). The text quotes a statement accusing the approach to use "intellectual terror" in their discrediting of critics like Nooke or Gilley as racists and in attacking the Enlightenment principles of universality and freedom of speech while ignoring basic academic standards (AfD 2019, 10).

Part of this diagnosis is certainly correct. As mentioned in section 1, the postcolonial turn – first in literary and cultural studies, later in history and finally in the social sciences – did shift the perspective on colonialism. That this was driven by ideology is of course true if by ideology we understand a political world view. In this case it was driven by a political world view which decidedly rejects asymmetries based on colonial assumptions of some people being less rational and capable of self-government than others. If ideology is understood in opposition to science, then the text fails to provide evidence showing where the postcolonial approach is less scientific than other perceptions of North-South relations. The characterization as "anti-Western" is certainly wrong regarding postcolonial critics like Homi Bhabha (1994), who insists on deconstructing the dichotomies between powerful colonizers and helpless colonized, or Stuart Hall who points out that postcolonial studies depart from a "clear-cut politics of binary oppositions" (Hall 1996, 244). The attribution of all crimes of colonialism to the West is certainly avoided here. Yet there may be a grain of truth in the characterization of "anti-Western" of some of the more radical proponents of decolonial studies such as Hamid Dabashi (2015) or Walter Mignolo (2015). And the same might hold true for some accusations of racism launched by followers of this school, although the point of contention probably is how wide or narrow a definition of the term racism is appropriate. The relationship between postcolonialism and Marxism proclaimed in "Deutsche Kolonialzeit kulturpolitisch differenziert aufarbeiten" seems to have been assumed on political grounds while remaining ignorant of the criticism that the latter camp articulated towards the former (and partly vice versa). However, to deduce from a poststructuralist epistemology that some (!) of the postcolonial and decolonial authors share that they would not care about facts, is simply a gross misrepresentation which can only be explained by the intent to discredit this school of thought. As for the attacks on Enlightenment principles and universality, for most of the post- and decolonial scholars their criticism is primarily that these principles were applied only to the White (and male and propertied) part of the population – as shown by France's execution of women's rights proponent Olympe de Gouge and of the warfare conducted against rebellious slaves in Saint Domingue (today's Haiti). Both had merely demanded equal rights.

Finally, the AfD's claim about the impingement of the freedom of speech in today's academia is hardly representative of postcolonial studies scholars in general. The paranoid focus on occasional cases of anti-racist "cancel culture" obscures the view on the much more massive attack on academic freedoms conducted by right-wing regimes muzzling universities in Hungary, Turkey, Russia and Iran, but also reactionary attempts to link anti-racism to Islamist terrorism and Stalinist censorship in some European states.[6]

We can see that the discursive strategy of discrediting is applied again on the grounds of an association with Marxism, but also through labelling postcolonial studies as "anti-Western" – as if such characterizations would suffice to rob any argument of its plausibility. Obviously the AfD seeks to establish discursive limits in the public space which function as if this was the case, based on a binary logic. In the chains of equivalence constructed in the text, the critique of colonialism (in the name of equal rights) is associated with "ideological" Marxism, anti-Westernism, anti-Enlightenment thinking, authoritarianism and intellectual terrorism, while on the other side of the discursive fence we find those who defend freedom of speech, the Enlightenment, the West – and beneficial colonial rule over cultural inferiors outside of Europe. Even beyond the question in how far it makes sense to associate only the critique of colonialism with ideology, but not the defense of the West: The construction of these chains of equivalence suggests that sympathy for one element of the chain by implication leads to favoring the others as well; it serves the overarching aim of legitimizing colonial rule and resemanticizing it as liberating and benign.

3.4. Current Debates on Restitution, Reparations and Street Names

This positive resemanticization of colonialism has major consequences for current debates about restitution of cultural artifacts from German museums, the naming of streets after colonial officers and politicians, and the question of reparations for former colonies. These public initiatives are attributed to the influence of postcolonial studies and cultural Marxism.

---

6   Decolonising Development. Coast Action CA19129: Statement in the threat of academic authoritarianism. Web: https://decolonise.eu/statement-on-the-thr eat-of-academic-authoritarianism/

Regarding the debate about restitution of cultural artifacts in European museums, the AfD argues in "Deutsche Kolonialzeit kulturpolitisch differenziert aufarbeiten" that colonialism could not be reduced to the "original sin" of colonial violence but that the work of many decades for the "collective memory of humanity" had to be taken into account (AfD 2019, 11). Quoting media theory professor Erhard Schüttpelz, they claim that the European museums had contributed to preserve "history and soul of the African peoples" (AfD 2019, 11). This and the concept of inalienable property should be turned against the "inquisitorial logic" of the "propagandists of restitution" who would assume the owners of such artifacts to be guilty of robbery (AfD 2019, 12). Restitution, the text claims, would transform this inalienable property to "profane," "commercial property" which would lead to historical and anthropological amnesia (AfD 2019, 12). The "sale of indulgences" ("Ablasshandel") with which the promoters of restitution would assume to get rid of the "contaminations" and the "multi-dimensionality" of the colonial period should be countered determinedly (AfD 2019, 12).

Interestingly, this argument reverses the roles: those who insist on remembering the crimes of colonialism are made responsible for amnesia and commercializing the cultural artifacts of the colonized. Again, the motive of a more differentiated view on the complex situation of colonialism is invoked. And again, different arguments have to be disentangled. Obvious polemics about inquisition and propaganda aside, the AfD says the following: The first argument claims that the artifacts belonged to the collective memory of humanity and not simply to those who had originally crafted them: Europeans define that African artifacts do not belong to them, but to the whole of humanity – and the defenders of nationalism suddenly become the pioneers of cosmopolitanism. The second argument claims that by keeping them in their museums, the keepers had preserved not only the artifacts, but the history and soul of the African peoples: Europeans have done both humanity and Africans a great service in appropriating and preserving these artifacts, because, and this is a necessary implication, Africans themselves would not have been capable of preserving them (and thus, the text adds, their history and their soul). A (more implicit) third argument seems to be that the museums themselves, through their decade-long care for the artifacts, had become the rightful owners: if one manages to keep stolen goods long enough, they are magically transformed from stolen goods into rightful property. The fourth argument is that by returning the artifacts to their rightful owners, the artifacts would lose their non-profane (sacred?) quality and become commodities: A clear case of subversive semantics: Suddenly having second thoughts about their own rules of property, the robbers become the preservers, the profaners become the defenders of the sanctity of the artifacts in the name of a common heritage of humanity. The fifth and last argument assumes that those who demand restitutions would do so in an illusionary attempt to leave behind the complexities of colonialism for a morally pure, uncontaminated image of it, using the analogy of medieval Christians paying money for their sins so that they could still go to heaven. Serious attempts to alleviate colonial debt are cynically reinterpreted as attempts at historical amnesia and purification. This amounts to saying: colonialism was a complex and dirty business and you cannot change that by simply giving back stolen goods – and therefore we should keep the goods. Here, all sorts of ascriptions to and characterizations of artifacts of non-European origin, but also to (seemingly history-less) African people are being invoked to represent the matter as complicated and obscure the simple solution that stolen goods should be given back.[7] In the AfD view, robbery can still be legitimate if the robbed goods are defined as common human heritage, transforming them into a higher, "inalienable" (AfD 2019, 12) kind of property. If the rightful owners are defined as unable to preserve their own history and identity, returning their possessions would amount to their imminent destruction – apart from giving in to historically amnesiac propaganda. The notorious right-nationalist "Schlussstrichmentalität" – the desire to erase the unsavory parts of the national past and let it be forgotten – is here subversively projected on those who initiated the collective memory of German colonialism in the first place.

---

7   For a more detailed discussion of these questions see Sarr and Savoy 2018.

Regarding the question of reparations, "Deutsche Kolonialzeit kulturpolitisch differenziert aufarbeiten" demands that there should be no reparations for the victims of colonial warfare. Curiously, as a justification the authors do not emphasize the alleged benefits of colonial rule mentioned throughout the text (see section 3.2) but point to the financial transfers to Namibia in the context of development cooperation (870 million Euros, or 348 Euros per person; AfD 2019, 1). This, the authors propose, would prove that Germany has faced its historical responsibility. Therefore, demands for reparation should be emphatically rejected (AfD 2019, 3). While it may be controversial whether forced labor and genocide can be financially compensated in the first place, the sum seems massively inadequate in the light of the crimes committed under German colonial rule. Would the AfD parliamentarians see this as an adequate compensation if Germany had been occupied and plundered for decades and ravaged by war and a part of its people worked to death in concentration camps? The double standards are obvious.

Concerning the streets named after colonial "pioneers" or "travelers," "Deutsche Kolonialzeit kulturpolitisch differenziert aufarbeiten" rejects the "undifferentiated perspective" of renaming them (AfD 2019, 2). Personalities whose actions needed to be understood in the historical context of "claims for civilization" but partly could be seen as "honorable" even according to present-day standards (e.g., against slavery), so the argument goes, should not be indiscriminately named "colonial criminals" (AfD 2019, 2). Also, this renaming would "erase history" from public spaces (AfD 2019, 2). Therefore, controversial names should be kept and where appropriate put into historical context (AfD 2019, 3). However, if all names of streets name after colonial officers and politicians should be kept, it is difficult to see in what way this would be a more differentiated perspective than replacing them. Likewise, the threat of amnesia or erasing history is invoked, despite the obvious facts that the postcolonial and decolonial initiatives are precisely oriented toward remembering history, but from a different perspective. Neither would new street names (e.g., remembering people involved in anti-colonial struggles) erase history, but they would recenter official historical memory. German history certainly has not been erased by renaming the countless

Adolf-Hitler-streets after the end of the Third Reich. Just as in the context of restitution, a new and more critical way of dealing with history is rhetorically subverted into a threat of collective amnesia.

4.   Conclusion

"Deutsche Kolonialzeit" employs numerous discursive strategies to legitimize colonial rule. The most remarkable ones are, first, that the AfD claims to occupy a strictly scientific perspective based on facts, using seventy-four footnotes and quoting numerous professors to invoke academic authority, denouncing normative interpretations and ideologically driven arguments from the critics of colonialism, while at the same time either ignoring or distorting facts and academic research which does not fit into their argument about imperial Germany's benign colonialism. One of the most blatant moves is to suggest that prominent historians questioned the fact that the colonial war against the Herero and Nama was a genocide while in fact they say the opposite. Secondly, the text discursively constructs a chain of equivalences between on the one hand the Enlightenment, universal values, the West and an affirmative view of colonialism and, on the other, between postcolonial and decolonial studies, Marxism, the GDR, a world of discourse unrelated to facts, anti-Western sentiments, unfounded accusations of racism and intellectual terror. The objective of these discursive strategies is to legitimize German colonial rule.

The narrative about the benefits of German colonial rule has been shown to be misguided and based on an extremely selective reading of history. Replacing slavery with another kind of forced labor and forcing the indigenous population to build infrastructure under deadly conditions can hardly be regarded as beneficial for the colonized. Just as Walter Rodney had envisioned (Rodney 2018, 246): "It would be an act of the most brazen fraud to weigh the paltry social amenities provided during the colonial epoch against the exploitation, and to arrive at the conclusion that the good outweighed the bad." However, I would argue that even if the weighing is obviously unfavorable for the sympathizers of colonialism, the act of weighing itself should be interrogated. Because even if the colonizers had in fact established health systems which benefitted the colonized, would this legitimize the subjugation and destruction of pre-colonial societies? In the context of Germany, none but the most die-hard right-wing extremists would dare to publicly defend National Socialism because of its successes in reducing unemployment and building motorways. The respect towards the victims (acquired in long decades of fighting for a self-critical politics of remembrance) has led to certain discursive red lines in the public debate. As shown by "Pros and Cons debates" in textbooks in German secondary schools (Marmer and Ziai 2015), such boundaries do not yet exist in the treatment of colonialism in Germany. It seems that so far, some victims are more equal than others.

We can conclude that the legitimization of German colonial rule in "Deutsche Kolonialzeit kulturpolitisch differenziert aufarbeiten" has the objective of breaking the chain of equivalence between National Socialism, Socialist dictatorship and Empire in German history. While the former two are almost unequivocally denounced as "unjust regimes," the AfD desperately attempts to rehabilitate the third. It seriously argues that a political system based on racist superiority of White Europeans should not be seen as criminal in principle and deserves a more nuanced evaluation. This can be understood in the context of the German public debate and the discursive boundaries mentioned above: after the battle for a positive image of National Socialism has been lost in the past decades (the Historikerstreit and the controversy about the Wehrmachtsausstellung probably have been the last nails in the coffin), for the new right in Germany the Empire has become the sole object for retaining a positive image of German nationalism, militarism, masculinism and superiority. And here they feel that they are losing the battle for hegemony to postcolonial studies and "cultural Marxism". In this context, they are conceding the criminal character of National Socialism and the hegemonic view on the Holocaust only to claim that colonialism has to be seen in a more positive light and that postcolonial critics engage in Stalinist and antisemitic practices (see also AfD 2022). The analyzed text should thus be read as an attempt to turn the tide in this losing battle. This article can be seen academically as an analysis of the discursive strategies and factual flaws in this attempt – and politically as an opposing contribution in this battle.

Works Cited

AfD (2019) Die deutsche Kolonialzeit kulturpolitisch differenziert aufarbeiten. Deutscher Bundestag Drucksache 19/15784.

AfD (2020) Straßenumbenennungen. Positionspapier der AfD-Bundestagsfraktion Arbeitskreis Kultur und Medien. Web: https://afdbund estag.de/wp-content/uploads/2020/06/afd_btf_stra%C3%9Fenumb enennungen_digitale_version.pdf.

AfD (2022) Jetzt Konsequenzen aus dem Antisemitismus-Skandal auf der documenta ziehen – Förderung des Postkolonialismus umgehend einstellen. Deutscher Bundestag Drucksache 20/2598.

Bhabha, Homi (1994) *The Location of Culture*. London: Routledge.

Bhambra, Gurminder (2007) Sociology and Postcolonialism: Another "Missing" Revolution? *Sociology* 41(5), 871–884.

Bhambra, Gurminder (2013) The Possibilities of, and for, Global Sociology: A Postcolonial Perspective. In: *Political Power and Social Theory* 24, 295–314.

Bürger, Christiane (2013) Ein "Richtiges Afrikabild." Das Koloniale Namibia und die frühe Historiografie der DDR. *Focus on German Studies* 20, 3–18.

Campbell, David (1998) *National Deconstruction. Violence, Identity, and Justice in Bosnia*. Minneapolis: University of Minnesota Press.

Castro Varela, Maria do Mar and Nikita Dawahn (2005) *Postkoloniale Theorie. Eine kritische Einführung*. Bielefeld: transcript.

Chakrabarty, Dipesh (2000) *Provincializing Europe. Postcolonial Thought and Historical Difference*. Princeton: Princeton University Press.

Chalk, Frank and Kurt Jonassohn (1990) *The History and Sociology of Genocide. Analyses and Case Studies*. New Haven: Yale University Press.

Conrad, Sebastian and Shalini Randeria (eds.) (2002) *Jenseits des Eurozentrismus. Postkoloniale Perspektiven in den Geschichts- und Kulturwissenschaften*. Frankfurt a. M.: Campus.

Dabashi, Hamid (2015) *Can Non-Europeans Think?* London: Zed Books.

Foucault, Michel (1980) Truth and Power. In: *Power/Knowledge. Selected Interviews & Other Writings 1972–1977*. New York: Pantheon Books, 109–133.

Gewald, Jan-Bart (2004) Kolonisierung, Völkermord und Wiederkehr. Die Herero von Namibia 1890–1923. In: Zimmerer, Jürgen and Joachim Zeller (eds.) 2004: *Völkermord in Deutsch-Südwestafrika. Der Kolonialkrieg (1904–1908) in Namibia und seine Folgen*. Berlin: Ch. Links Verlag, 105–120.

Gilley, Bruce (2017) The Case for Colonialism. *Third World Quarterly*. Web: http://dx.doi.org/10.1080/01436597.2017.1369037.

Gilley, Bruce (2019) The Case for German Colonialism. Web: https://www.researchgate.net/publication/338555799_The_Case_for_German_Colonialism.

Grewe, Bernd-Stefan (2018) Das schwierige Erbe des Kolonialismus. Probleme und Potenziale für den Geschichtsunterricht. In: Bechhaus-Gerst, Marianne and Joachim Zeller (eds.) *Deutschland postkolonial? Die Gegenwart der imperialen Vergangenheit*. Berlin: Metropol-Verlag, 473–502.

Hall, Stuart (1996) When was "the Postcolonial"? Thinking at the Limit. In: Iain Chambers and Lidia Curti (eds.) (1996) *The Post-Colonial Question. Common Skies, Divided Horizons*. London: Routledge, 242–260.

Herman, Edward and Noam Chomsky (1988) *Manufacturing Consent. The Political Economy of the Mass Media*. New York: Pantheon Books.

Hira, Sandew (2017) A Decolonial Critique of the Racist Case for Colonialism. In: *Decolonial International Network*. Web: https://din.today/sandewhira/a-decolonial-critique-of-the-racist-case-for-colonialism/.

Kerner, Ina (2012) *Postkoloniale Theorien zur Einführung*. Stuttgart: Junius.

Klein, Martin A. (2018) A Critique of Colonial Rule: A Response to Bruce Gilley. *Australasian Review of African Studies* 39(1), 39–52.

Kößler, Reinhart and Henning Melber (2018) Völkermord – Anerkennung ohne Entschuldigung und Entschädigung? Verwicklungen in verwobene Geschichte. In: Bechhaus-Gerst, Marianne and Joachim Zeller (eds.) (2018) *Deutschland postkolonial? Die Gegenwart der imperialen Vergangenheit*. Berlin: Metropol-Verlag, 223–242.

Kuß, Susanne (2014) Kolonialkriege und Raum. In: *Militärgeschichtliche Zeitschrift* 73, 333–348.

Kuß, Susanne (2018) Postkolonialismus und Genozid. In: Bechhaus-Gerst, Marianne and Joachim Zeller (eds.) *Deutschland postkolonial? Die Gegenwart der imperialen Vergangenheit*. Berlin: Metropol-Verlag, 204–222.

Laclau, Ernesto and Chantal Mouffe (2001/1985) *Hegemony and Socialist Strategy. Towards a Radical Democratic Politics*. London: Verso.

Loomba, Ania (1998) *Colonialism/Postcolonialism*. London: Routledge.

Marmer, Elina and Aram Ziai (2015) Racism in the Teaching of 'Development' in German Secondary School Textbooks. *Critical Literacy* 9(2), 64–84.

Martenstein, Harald (2015) Über Mittel gegen die Ursachen des Flüchtlingsstroms. In: *ZEITmagazin* Nr. 41/2015. Web: https://www.zeit.de/zeit-magazin/2015/41/harald-martenstein-fluechtlinge-kolonialismus?utm_referrer=https%3A%2F%2Fwww.startpage.com%2F.

McClintock, Anne (1995) *Imperial Leather: Race, Gender and Sexuality in the Colonial Contest*. London: Routledge.

Mignolo, Walter (2015) Foreword: Yes, we can. Hamid Dabashi (2015) *Can Non-Europeans Think?* London: Zed Books. viii-xlii.

Nooke, Günter (2018) Wir haben lange Zeit zu viel im Hilfsmodus gedacht. In: *B.Z.* (7 October) Web: https://www.bz-berlin.de/deutschland/afrikabeauftragter-guenter-nooke-der-kalte-krieg-hat-afrika-mehr-geschadet-als-die-kolonialzeit.

Richey, Lisa Ann, David Simon, Ilan Kapoor and Stefano Ponte (2019) Academic Neocolonialism: Clickbait and the Perils of Commercial Publishing. Web: https://aidnography.blogspot.com/2019/03/academic-neocolonialism-clickbait-perils-publishing-third-world-quarterly-richey-simon-kapoor-ponte.html.

Rodney, Walter (2018/1972) *How Europe underdeveloped Africa*. London: Verso.

Rodriguez, Amardo (2018) A case against colonialism. *Postcolonial Studies* 21(2), 254–259.

Said, Edward (1978) *Orientalism*. New York : Vintage.

Sarr, Felwine and Bénédicte Savoy (2018) *Restituer le patrimoine africain*. Paris: P. Rey-Seuil.

Schmieder, Ulrike (2010) Rezension von E. Flaig, *Weltgeschichte der Sklaverei*. Web: https://www.connections.clio-online.net/publicationrev iew/id/reb-13299.

Shilliam, Robbie (ed.) (2011) *International Relations and Non-Western Thought. Imperialism, colonialism and investigations of global modernity*. London: Routledge.

Speitkamp, Winfried (2005) *Deutsche Kolonialgeschichte*. Stuttgart: Reclam.

Spivak, Gayatri Chakravorty (1988) Can the Subaltern Speak? In: Williams, Patrick and Laura Chrisman (eds.) *Colonial Discourse and Post-Colonial Theory. A Reader*. New York: Columbia University Press, 66–111.

Stein, Hannes (2015) Die Entkolonialisierung war eine Katastrophe. In: *Die Welt* (6 December). Web: http://www.welt.de/149662414.

Utermark, Sören (2011) "Schwarzer Untertan versus schwarzer Bruder." Bernhard Dernburgs Reformen in den Kolonien Deutsch-Ostafrika, Deutsch-Südwestafrika, Togo und Kamerun. Diss., Univ. Kassel, Fachbereich Gesellschaftswissenschaften. Web: https://kobra.uni-k assel.de/bitstream/handle/123456789/2012082441677/DissertationS oerenUtermark.pdf?sequence=5&isAllowed=y.

Van Laak, Dirk (2005) Deutschland in Afrika. Der Kolonialismus und seine Nachwirkungen. *Aus Politik und Zeitgeschichte* 4/2005, 3–11.

Williams, Patrick and Laura Chrisman (eds.) (1994) *Colonial Discourse and Post-Colonial Theory. A Reader*. New York: Columbia University Press.

Young, Robert C. (2016) *Postcolonialism. A Historical Introduction*. 2nd ed. Oxford: Blackwell.

Zeller, Joachim (2004) "Ombepera i koza – Die Kälte tötet mich." Zur Geschichte des Konzentrationslagers in Swakopmund (1904–1908).

In: Zimmerer, Jürgen and Joachim Zeller (eds.) *Völkermord in Deutsch-Südwestafrika. Der Kolonialkrieg (1904–1908) in Namibia und seine Folgen.* Berlin: Ch. Links Verlag, 64–79.

Ziai, Aram (2012) Postkoloniale Studien und Politikwissenschaft: Komplementäre Defizite, Stand der Forschung und Perspektiven. *Politische Vierteljahresschrift* 53(2), 292–323.

Ziai, Aram (2017) "I am not a Post-Developmentalist, but…" The Influence of Post-Development on Development Studies. *Third World Quarterly* 38(12), 2719–2734.

Zimmerer, Jürgen (2004) Krieg, KZ und Völkermord in Südwestafrika. Der erste deutsche Genozid. In: Zimmerer, Jürgen and Joachim Zeller (eds.) *Völkermord in Deutsch-Südwestafrika. Der Kolonialkrieg (1904–1908) in Namibia und seine Folgen.* Berlin: Ch. Links Verlag, 45–63.

The Origins of Replacement Narratives and the Resemanticization of Feminism in Two Novels of the Far Right

Enrico Schlickeisen

When Brenton Tarrant, a right-wing terrorist, attacked two mosques and killed fifty-one people in Christchurch, New Zealand in 2019, he live-streamed his deed on the internet for the world to witness. He also left behind an 87-page manifesto.[1] This electronic document was circulated on online message boards such as the now-defunct 8chan. It was supposed to explain the attacker's motivations and worldview and was meant to inspire copycats, very much in the same way Anders Behring Breivik had intended to do with a similar manifesto named *2038 – A Dec-*

---

[1] After the attack, New Zealand officials and media refrained from communicating the attacker's name in order to prevent a further circulation of his ideas. Further motivation behind this strategy was not to concede the perpetrator special importance over the memorial of the victims. In this article however, I will disclose the attacker's full name and use his manifesto as a quotable source. The document was distributed all over the internet after the Christchurch shooting but to this day it is difficult to find a host that adheres to the standards of academic research. The version of the document that I refer to has been downloaded from the website of the Italian newspaper Il Foglio and is similar to the version of the document that circulated on the website formerly known as 8chan. It is my deeply held belief that it is necessary to explicitly define the agents and strategies of all different forms of neo-Nazism in order to effectively combat them.

laration of European Independence in 2011.[2] The opening lines of the main text of the Christchurch attacker's manifesto, *The Great Replacement*, are a threefold repetition of the sentence "It's the birthrates" (Tarrant 2019, 4). The replacement narrative that is outlined over the following pages of the manifesto and that allegedly motivated the attack is one of the most potent and prominent of the current Far Right. Its basic assessment is that the white "race" is dying out – either through supposedly natural demographic change or through a deliberate attack perpetuated by nebulous forces that advocate unchecked mass migration.

In its demographic and sociological simplicity, the narrative is eerily reminiscent of Jean Raspail's 1973 novel *The Camp of the Saints*. At the very center of the book's plot lies the question to what ends a society would go to protect its own racial and cultural identity in the face of demographic and cultural change. The narrative that was named "Great Replacement" and that motivated the Christchurch shooter and many others to commit acts of political violence takes a prominent position in Raspail's novel. This is one of the reasons why I selected this book for closer analysis. *Sea Changes*, written by Derek Turner almost forty years later, is another novel with a prominent migration theme, although it is more subtle in tone. Rather than the imminent and dystopian threat of irrefutable and sudden destruction of a country's identity through abrupt demographic change, it instead emphasizes the strong emotional reaction of Western society towards the death of migrants during their attempt to enter the country illegally. In spite of a violation of the proper process of providing asylum, a strong sentiment of migration-friendly sympathy and moralistic righteousness is purported by the barely fictionalized media apparatus while simultaneously discarding any reasonable objections to open borders and multiculturalism. This hospitality towards strangers is described as a "psychosis" (Raspail 2018, ix) in Tito Perdue's preface

---

2   For a detailed explanation regarding the use of Breivik's manifesto as an academic source see above. After the attack in Utøya, the 1500-page manifesto was
distributed through several websites such as scribd.com and archive.org. The
version I am using for this text is linked in my bibliography.

of Raspail's book; as a "project [...] to turn a highly heterogeneous (*diverse!*) into an undifferentiated [...] something or another" (Raspail 2018, ix). Both books share the motif of a modern liberal society that fails to defend itself against the threat of the migrant other and of transformation through replacement and that instead celebrates its own decadence, ultimately leading to its demise. Both books feature characters that exhibit an almost obscene obliviousness to the violence that even a liberal democracy has to employ in order to defend itself against anything that reduces the proper process to apply for asylum or immigration to absurdity.

Another prominent aspect of both novels is their depiction of women, women's plot functions and the related assumptions about gender stereotypes and gender politics, which is representative of much right-wing literature. In both novels, feminism and gender equality are reframed as harmful in the struggle to preserve a constructed Western identity. The analysis of contemporary right-wing ideology and media reveals a paradoxical position regarding gender politics. Strong opposition to feminism and gender equality appears to be a common feature as they are often depicted as "clientelistic and largely misguided" and opposed to what is constructed as the traditional gendered reality of most women and men (Sprengholz 2021, 498). Furthermore, scholars such as Angela Nagle have written about the influence of the so-called "manosphere" and other antifeminist online communities on contemporary right-wing movements that hold feminism responsible for their own lack of romantic and physical intimacy (Nagle 2017; Dietze and Strick 2008). Most members of these online communities consider themselves to be "betas", subordinate to the more attractive and successful alpha males and therefore not entitled to love (Nagle 2017, 89). The pessimism created through this self- imposed binary serves as common ground in order to legitimize the misogyny expressed by those communities. Any progressive movements that enable women to freely choose their partners or to have sex outside of a relationship are therefore perceived as hostile because a traditional patriarchal family is idealized as a retrotopian (Baumann 2017) ideal that ensures sexual contact for beta males.

However, particularly in right-wing party politics, but also in groups such as Generation Identity or the European Génération Identitaire, there is the notable tendency to reframe arguments of women's rights and equality in order to justify anti-migration policies. The phenomenon of a "feminist right-wing populism" (Hadj-Abdou 2010, 117) is even more surprising considering the emphasis on traditional family models and gender roles exhibited by most of the far right. The consideration of multiculturalism as a threat to gender equality originated in the late 1990s, when prominent feminist voices such as Harvard professor Susan Moller Okin (1997) began to ask, "Is multiculturalism bad for women?" Okin argued that concessions to diversity and the demands of religious minorities threatened liberal notions of gender equality. Okin's critics argued that her argumentation was paternalist (especially of immigrant women) and tended to locate patriarchal oppression as mostly imported from foreign cultures (Fekete 2006, 13). The policies of radical right populist parties and actors such as the German AfD attempt to construct two women's rights narratives. On the one hand, there is a unified heartland, an "us" that has to resist and reject gender ideology as superimposed, and on the other hand, that the heartland has to resist Muslim immigration and multiculturalism in order not to endanger gender equality (Sprengholz 2021, 11). Depending on the communicative situation, the heartland can therefore be constructed as traditional or progressive. This article seeks to analyze from a literary perspective the intratextual function of progressive female characters and feminist narratives for both books, but also within the broader context of contemporary right-wing discursive strategies.

Both books have in common their fictionalization of the alt-right discourse surrounding the notion of cultural Marxism. Far from the intellectual concept developed by Gramsci and the Frankfurt school, cultural Marxism in right-wing discourse is mostly a continuation of the Nazis' idea of "cultural bolshevism" (Mirlees 2018, 53). According to Tanner Mirlees, the phrase "cultural Marxism" was used as "an anti-Semitic epithet and as cudgel for attacking any group of people or modernist cultural trend that they perceived to be corrupting or leading to the degeneracy of traditional German society" (Mirlees 2018, 53). In the same tradition, "the alt-right's story about cultural Marxism in America represents cultural Marxists as a malicious elite that is consolidating its power over America and controlling the Federal government, the media and cultural industries, the higher education system, public discourse and opinion at the expense of white conservatives" (Mirlees 2018, 56).

Although I chose both books as exemplary for right-wing literature, the latter is not in any way an established genre that can be classified entirely through its topoi or stylistic choices. As I argue, it is rather a context-dependent grouping that relies additionally on extratextual aspects such as the political activities and opinions of authors and their readership. Furthermore, the media that enable the discussion, evaluation and circulation of literature strongly influence literature's political perception. In contrast to the vast body of work that has been done on the influence of the digital sphere on, and the use of media by, right-wing parties, movements and individuals, fictional literature as a phenomenon on the political right has been largely under-researched in that context. Notable exceptions are Crawford Gribben's (2009) and Daniel Silliman's (2021) works on Evangelical fiction. Regarding nonfiction, much secondary literature has been published on the ideological origins and development of the modern far-right (Sedgwick 2019; Beiner 2018; MacLean 2017; Mudde 2019).

My interest in modern right-wing fiction was sparked first when I came across a "Guide to Right-wing literature" on 4chan's /lit/ board. Besides Raspail's *The Camp of the Saints*, this primer contained fiction written by Ernst Jünger, Joseph Conrad, Kurt Vonnegut and other authors and was very obviously meant to give non-initiated prospects an introduction to far-right thought.[3]

In the same way this guide contained all sorts of different texts, books that circulate within the right-wing public sphere or that particularly appeal to audiences beyond the mainstream conservative spectrum

---

3   4chan and other anonymous messaging boards are notoriously ephemeral. Contents rarely exist longer than a few days unless they are downloaded or archived otherwise. A copy of the image is archived at https://4chanlit.fando m.com/wiki/Conservative_literature.

are generally diverse in their contents, language and genre. Ranging from evangelical science fiction such as the popular *Left Behind* series by Tim LaHaye and Jerry B. Jenkins, to re-appropriated and re-read classics such as George Orwell's *1984*, a large variety of books are being read among the Right. I selected the abovementioned books as representative works of migration-critical fiction because both have been widely circulated among an anglophone readership and well received among readers of the far-right. According to the U.S. media organization National Public Radio, *The Camp of the Saints* was explicitly mentioned by Donald Trump's Senior Political adviser Stephen Miller in a leaked email to the far-Right news outlet *Breitbart*, together with a plea to use its contents in order to promote White supremacist ideas (Garcia-Navarro 2019). Steve Bannon, co-founder of *Breitbart*, had referred Raspail's novel as early as 2015 in the context of the influx of refugees in Europe. "It's been almost a *Camp of the Saints*-type invasion into Central and then Western and Northern Europe" (Blumenthal and Rieger 2017),[4] he said in an interview to Alabama state senator Jeff Sessions and repeatedly referenced the book in following statements. To some degree, this serves as an indicator that the ideas, positions and discursive strategies formulated in the book have been recognized as beneficial or at least discursively stimulating to those on the Right.

While *The Camp of the Saints* by now has had almost five decades to establish its reputation, Derek Turner's *Sea Changes* was published in 2012, when the advent of Trumpism and Brexit were yet to come and the 2015/16 migration movements that fueled right-wing mobilization all over Europe had not yet occurred. Indicators for the novel's circulation can be found in its author's connections to the British and international right-wing media. In a 2012 interview with the right-wing online blog *Affirmative Right*, Turner himself compares his work to Raspail's *The Camp*

---

4   Excerpts from this interview can be found in an article from Huffington Post (https://www.huffpost.com/entry/steve-bannon-camp-of-the-saints-i mmigration_n_58b75206e4b0284854b3dc03) and a recording of the interview is still available on SoundCloud: https://soundcloud.com/siriusxm-news-issue s/the-american-people-are-angry.

of the Saints (Nowicki 2012). Turner, who was born in Dublin, worked as a political essayist for the British quarterlies *Right Now!* and its predecessor *Quarterly Review* (Turner 2012, 425). He is a frequent guest in other media, such as the German alt-right blog *Sezession*. The 2018 German translation of the book was published by the *Jungeuropa Verlag*, which is adjacent to the German branch of Generation Identity (Boehnke and Thran and Wunderwald 2019, 138). Richard Spencer, one of the coiners of the term "alt-right", wrote an editorial for this translation, which may serve as another indicator for the transnational character of the right-wing literature industry or possibly the contemporary Right in general.

Controversially discussed since its publication, *The Camp of the Saints* has been praised as a courageous foreboding of the future by some and simultaneously dismissed as racist and insulting by others (Tanton 1994). Its plot is summarized rather quickly: an armada of approximately one million migrants from the Ganges region board numerous dilapidated ships and set out for Europe. Initially, attempts at humanitarian aid are undertaken by the Western world and most of the French mass media cultivate an actively anti-racist spirit of welcoming the fleet that resonates with the fundamental values of the French Republic. Some of the characters uphold the charade of *Willkommenskultur* out of mere opportunism and others simply do not expect the armada to land in Europe. As the plot progresses, the arrival of the armada becomes at first a possibility and later a certainty. Put under pressure by public opinion and its own humanist ideals, the French government desperately attempts to find a humanitarian solution and a possibility to prevent the refugees from landing. When the armada apathetically rejects all aid and continues on its course, public order increasingly disintegrates and a mass exodus of people from South to North is set in motion because of the general population's fear of the newcomers. The French army is deployed to the coast in order to repel the arrivants through the use of force, but most of its soldiers' defect because they cannot stand the idea of shooting the poor and defenseless immigrants. When the ships ultimately arrive at the Côte d'Azur, the masses of immigrants quite literally overrun everything and everyone in their way, ironically those first that were most eager to welcome them. The final chapters describe the aftermath of the settlement of the one million Indians that radically changes France and destroys its European and Christian culture. The book ends with several more fleets setting sail from different parts of the Global South.

Derek Turner's *Sea Changes* strikes a chord that is equally critical of migration. Compared to *The Camp of the Saints* with its dystopian pessimism, the theme in *Sea Changes* emphasizes the reaction of British society to illegal immigration rather than Raspail's fatalistic outlook on the end of western civilization. Turner himself referred to current liberal anti-racist discourse as "modern racial neuroses" (Nowicki 2012). After several bodies of immigrants with gunshot wounds wash up on the shores of a rural British village in the first chapter, journalists, politicians and starlets put into motion schemes for their own political gain under the banner of anti-racism and pro-migration positions. The story is told with frequent changes in the focal characters with a recurrent focus on Ibraham Nassouf, a young Iraqi migrant who used to be a petty criminal before he embarked on his odyssey to Europe. After about half of the book it is revealed that Ibraham was on the same boat as the other migrants but was the only survivor. The timeline after the shipwreck occurred is mainly shaped by contrasting the opportunistic journalist John Leyden and other actors of "pc culture" with the farmer Dan Gowt, who is interviewed shortly after the discovery and who is presented as the embodiment of British rural racism. Leyden, a celebrated journalist who prides himself for his ability to bring to light all kinds of injustices, is a closeted racist and sexist himself. After Ibraham awakes and untruthfully presents himself as part of the opposition against Saddam Hussein, he is idolized as a "Miracle Migrant" (Turner 2012, 391) and most of the media advocate a strict policy that imposes sanctions on racist behavior and encourages diversity. Only very few voices, among them the populist columnist Albert Norman, oppose that general sentiment. Towards the end of the book, another journalist is attacked by antifascists who mistook him for Norman. Ibraham's claims to be a political dissident are ultimately proven false, but he is granted asylum nevertheless. He still ends up unhappy and disillusioned in a cheap housing estate without employment. Ultimately, the novel is inconclusive. There is no solution to the conflict, the ending is anticlimactic and Ibraham has been merely a pawn of other actors for their own personal, political or moral benefit who never appeared to have cares about him as a person in the first place.

As mentioned above, the narrative of the "Great Replacement" is one of the most prominent among the current Far Right but far from new. More so, it is a direct continuation of an ongoing right-wing demographic and cultural discourse that has been narratively reframed. The Austrian Branch of the Identitarians (*Identitäre Bewegung*) has protested the "Great Replacement" under this name prominently since 2014 (Goetz 2021, 67). The narrative itself, however, has existed for decades within the broader Right under different names and in different iterations. The term "Great Replacement" can be traced back to French right-wing intellectual Renaud Camus, who published a book that was titled accordingly in 2001. The right-wing desire to preserve the existence of a culturally and racially predominantly white population is mostly negotiated in cultural terms, especially in the discourses of those parts of the Far Right that attempt to uphold an impression of civility and democratic legitimacy. More radical proponents, however, argue biologically and consider "the autochthonous 'people' as a unique species that needs to be preserved, or as an organism that needs to be kept clean and that cannot take too many foreign influences, and that is put in mortal danger by amalgamation" (Goetz 2021, 63).

Due to the heritage of the National Socialist state, German speakers are more hesitant to refer to categories of "race" in their argumentation. The use of "White Genocide" as a phrase for ongoing demographic change is therefore more prominent outside of Germany. Instead, terms such as *Umvolkung* and *Volkstod* are used in order to obscure the specific reference to the White population, although they also clearly contain a racial component. According to Judith Goetz, differences in terminology between Europe and the US can mainly be traced back to regional taboos (Goetz 2021, 63). However, regardless of the terminology that is used, right-wing discourses and narratives surrounding demographic change generally consist of three elements: "firstly, the decline in birth rate of the autochthonous population; secondly the 'exchange of populations' due to immigration, multiculturalism and Islamization; and thirdly, the 'senescence' or ageing of society" (Goetz 2021, 62). "Society" and "population" are in this case equated with "the people", an imagined homogenous biological community with common ancestors (Kopke 2017, 57).

The perceived problem of a demographic shift is generally explained as a result of the emancipation movements of the past decades. According to right-wing discourses, feminism and various postcolonial emancipation movements have effected/brought about a decline of the traditional family. Women were enabled to pursue professional careers instead of traditional caretaker roles in families, which in turn led to a general lowering of birth rates. However, proponents of right-wing demographic ideas do not promote a general increase in population number but rather advocate for strict control about which parts of the population increase their birthrate. While they do wish for an increase of birthrates of white, autochthonous segments, they lament the dangers or try to restrict an increase of non-white, immigrant segments within the national population. This perceived opposition of racial in-group and out-group is often contrasted with the rapid population growth in the Global South (Goetz 2021, 63).

These concepts of demographic changes and the diffusion of allegedly separate homogenous populations have been more thoroughly discussed since the early 1900s under the term *Umvolkung* (ethnic replacement) (Kellerslohn 2016). In 1936, Max Boehm, an author on German folkdom, differentiated between three semantic levels of *Umvolkung: assimilation, dissimilation* and *ethnomorphosis* (Kellerslohn 2016, 358). While the former two refer to the integration and reversal of integration of ethnic groups, ethnomorphosis refers to the infiltration of foreign populations into the autochthonous population that is negotiated in either biological or cultural terms (Kellerslohn 2016, 358). It is therefore the semantic component that is most prominent in current conspiracy narratives. In contrast to the concept of *Volkstod* (death of the people), that more strongly emphasizes the perceived negative, fatal and irrevocable outcome of demographic changes, the conspiracy narrative of the "Great Replacement" includes the notion of explicit or implicit participation of political elites in that process (Kopke 2017, 57). The dissemination and discursive reproduction of this narrative is not limited to far-right fringe groups, but has found its way into the broader political discourse. In a 2015 speech, Björn Höcke, leader of the Thuringian branch and a prominent member of the German right-wing populist party AfD (*Alternative für Deutschland*, Alternative for Germany), contended that chancellor Angela Merkel was either deranged for allowing refugees to enter the country in 2015, or complicit in a larger, geopolitical plan to destabilize Europe (Kemper 2016). Conspiracy narratives such as the "Great Replacement" narrative obscure the historical origins and global dimensions of the Syrian refugee crisis.

Analytically, the replacement narratives in Raspail's and Turner's novels consist of three broader categories of people: those being replaced, those responsible for or perpetuating the replacement, and those who come to replace. These three human groups have different amounts of agency and motivation. It is particularly the second category, the perpetrators, who are imagined to be in control of the situation. These malicious elites are contrasted with two separate concepts of "the people" that are both imagined as homogenous: the supposedly "native" European population and the foreigners who immigrate, or rather invade their realm. Particularly the first two categories are largely adjacent to the discourse through which populism constructs the aforementioned cultural and political "us" vs. "them" – a construct that largely follows the two-dimensional model proposed by Pierre-André Taguieff (1995). The "us" and "them" are defined both in horizontal and vertical dimensions. Vertically, the dichotomy is constructed between "the people" and "the elite". Rhetorically, an adherence to "the people" is promoted, regardless of the populists' material or social conditions. "The elite", however, represents a class of opportunistic, self-serving and individuals laying claim to political correctness while lacking common decency and sense. The horizontal dimension expresses the opposition of perceived insiders and outsiders, "between 'people like us', those who share our way of life, and those on the outside who threaten our way of life" (Brubaker 2017, 2). Recent populist characterizations therefore place political, economic and cultural elites both "on top" and "outside", as Brubaker argues. This distinction is particularly observable in the characters in both books, as I will outline later.

Regarding the narrative of the "Great Replacement", the sixth edition of Norman Shapiro's English translation of *The Camp of the Saints* contains an extensive foreword by Jean Raspail himself, both for the original publication in 1973 but also for the 2011 reprint. The latter is an essay named "Big Other". In it, Raspail reflects on the mixed reception of the novel during the almost fifty years since its publication but more importantly provides a prime example and brief summary for the primary element of the "Great Reset", the demographic change:

> [...] in reality, it's about an ingoing submersion, over the years, whose catastrophic fullness won't register on us until the watershed of 2045–2050, when the passing of the final demographic tipping point will be under way: In France and the countries around us, in the urbanized zones where two-thirds of the population live, 50 percent of the inhabitants below the age of 55 will be of non-European extraction. After which, this percentage will only keep climbing as a corollary of the weight of the two or three billion individuals, mainly from Africa and Asia, who will have been added to the six billion human beings the earth has today, and against whom our original Europe will be able to put up only its rump birth rate and its glorious senescence. (Raspail 2018, xxvii)

In this essay, Raspail anticipates the arguments that the Christchurch shooter would use years later (Tarrant 2019). Raspail allegorically equates the well-known biological factors of European descent, birthrates and demographic development with the cultural dangers he associates with migration. To Raspail, it is out of the question that "all persons and nations have the sacred right to preserve their differences and identities, in the name of their own future and their own past" (Raspail 2018, xiii). Potential accusations of racism are refuted through reference to Dartmouth professor Jeffrey Hart who is quoted writing that "Raspail is not writing about race, he is writing about civilization" (qt. in Raspail 2018, xiv).

The Camp of the Saints fictionally reinforces Raspail's stated opinions, offering more insight regarding the "Great Replacement" narrative through its plot and characters. More so, the novel provides a fictionalized version of all the necessary components of that narrative. It comprises the necessary threat of the "Other", the benefactors and accomplices in the process of replacement and it includes those who either tragically suffer the results of the replacement or desperately fight it.

Right in the first chapter, which temporally takes place on the evening before the landing of the refugees, the character of Calguès is introduced. A former professor of Literature, Calguès is one of the few people who remained in their homes on the southern coast of France as the armada approached. The character serves as a personification of traditionalist values. He is an educated, well-read man who is used to the luxuries, comforts and privileges of Western European culture. As a character, he functions as an observer of the events that are unfolding. Calguès, the stoic remnant of the France that is ceasing to exist, is contrasted with a leftist hippie who has traveled to the South in order to observe the arrival of the armada. Representing the tragedy of the demise of French culture, Calguès is confronted with someone who applauds and welcomes that change. The nameless leftist has a radically Christian-humanist perspective, he claims that "there's a million Christs on those boats" (Raspail 2018, 10). Following the composition of the "Great Replacement" narrative, the hippie is probably closest to an accomplice of the replacement process, although he holds no political influence whatsoever. Following the revelation of his views, Calguès shoots him without further ado.

This naïve idea of the "million Christs" is contrasted with chapters that describe life on the boats of the armada. Only few characters are described in more detail, among them the leader of the armada, a misshapen child that is only named the "turd-eater" (Raspail 2018, 40) who serves as a proto-religious figure and spiritual guide to those aboard the ship, a travesty of the Christ figure showing that the text also turns against the Christian doctrine of human love. The thousands of other people are mostly described as an amorphous mass of indistinct, dark-skinned bodies that barely have any individual qualities beyond occasional mentions of age or gender. Most of the unnamed people aboard the armada act only as a collective. The revocation of individual qualities and personalities enables both other characters and the reader to ignore any personal moral judgement about the situation in the face of an existential threat. This dehumanization is particularly exemplified in chapter 20 of *The Camp of the Saints* in which the process of using human excrements in order to fuel the fires needed to cook rice is described. The explicit description is immediately contrasted with a depiction of orgiastic group sex involving children: "And everywhere, a mass of hands and mouths, of phalluses and rumps. Young boys passed from hand to hand. Young girls, barely ripe, lying together cheek to thigh, asleep in a languid maze of arms, and legs, and flowing hair, waking to the silent play of eager lips" (Raspail 2018, 108). Particularly in this passage, the refugees are reduced to a faceless mass of filth and debauched, uncontrollable sexuality: a monstrous, amorphous and threatening body.

Throughout the entire novel, the notable dichotomy of political stances that is expressed in Calguès' encounter with the hippie, is a recurring theme. On the one hand, there are those that bear political responsibility for the arrival of the armada. Public figures who influence the country's opinion into welcoming the immigrants are contrasted with characters that exhibit migration-friendly positions for political or moral reasons are among them. The journalist Ben Suad, also known as Clément Dio, is a prime example in this regard. He is the editor of a newspaper with a large readership and from the moment he is introduced as a character, it is clear that he is somewhat of an antithesis to Calgués. Although this character was invented almost fifty years ago, he reads like an anticipation of the strawman the current Far Right brings up as an antagonist to their own hostile position towards migration. In *The Camp of the Saints*, Raspail leaves no doubt that Dio's actions are malicious and self-serving. In the chapter in which he is introduced, he is described as "a spider deep in the midst of French public opinion" (Raspail 2018, 68). Raspail writes further that "one thing never changed: his contempt for tradition, his scorn for Western man per se, and above all the patriotic Frenchman" (Raspail 2018, 69). A similar character is the radio host Albert Dufort, who similarly enjoys presenting himself as a fighter for a righteous cause. Both Dufort and Dio do not primarily adhere to these ideals due to a deeper belief in universal humanism but rather for their own vanity and profit. A similar character in *Sea Changes* is John Leyden, who is a celebrated journalist and who has mastered the art of stirring public opinion towards social justice and generating outrage towards any sort of injustice. In the same way as Dio, John upholds a façade of political correctness and moral superiority but is in reality focused on his personal benefit. Furthermore, he has strong narcissistic tendencies, objectifies women in his immediate surrounding and is himself not free of racist thought and practice (Turner 2012, 373). Regarding the abovementioned two dimensions of populism, these members of the media industry are both economically "on top" (as they are part of a financially well-endowed and well-educated elite) and "outside" (as they act against the supposed immediate interests and wellbeing of the general population). In practice, this framing is used to justify and legitimize opposition to the perceived outsiders. Both Tarrant's and Breivik's manifestos fashion their authors as rightful fighters against an oppressive and elitist political caste (Breivik 2011; Tarrant 2019).

In *Sea Changes*, the farmer Dan Gowt, who is described as a simple and hard-working manual laborer from a rural village, is presented as an antithesis and victim to the ambitions of a morally corrupt media class. Gowt is the personification of the good-hearted "small man" who is out of touch with an increasingly academic and self-referential culture of political correctness personified by people like John Leyden. Despite attempts to clear his name, Dan Gowt is relentlessly smeared and labelled as a racist after initially making insensitive remarks right at the scene of the shipwreck. Besides Ibraham, Gowt is the character that is easiest to sympathize with, since he embodies traits and values that are associated with honesty and authenticity. In both populist dimensions, he is part of the in-group. Vertically, he is part of "the people" as he is living a frugal life with little to no societal or economic influence. Horizontally, he is "inside" due to his historical connection and admiration for the farm he inherited from his father. Gowt is, in right-wing terms, autochthonous, part of a supposedly native population. With this portrayal, he serves as the ideal projection screen for conservative self-identification.

An identification of those that are "outside" in *Sea Changes* is made particularly obvious in the chapter "Vox Metrop", which features a panel discussion in which John Leyden and representatives of several political parties and NGOs partake. Their populist framing as "outsiders" is narratively constructed through their depiction as incredibly self-righteous and arrogant but morally flawed individuals. Although most of them have enough political agency to be invited to a televised panel discussion, all of them are presented as unlikeable and estranged from the concerns of honest and hard-working people such as Dan Gowt. An example is Richard Simpson, a Member of Parliament for the leftist Worker's Party. Nicknamed "Spitson" (Turner 2012, 89) due to his pronunciation and accent, he is represented as a relic from a past political era of labor disputes that is quite unfamiliar with the cosmopolitan and PC notion of an inclusive society. Evan Dafydd is a representative of another political party named Fair Play Alliance. A bureaucrat and a bore, he is on the show as the "Coalition spokesperson for Transgendered Ethnic Minorities, and as rotating chair of the Fair Play for Islam Forum" (Turner 2012, 90). Particularly Carole Hassan, a devout Muslim convert and spokesperson for the Muslim Alliance, evokes in the reader an uneasiness that is mirrored in the audience of the panel discussion. While there is no objection from the other participants of the discussion, it is mentioned that "her concentration on Islam made some in the audience uneasy" (Turner 2012, 99). Apart from a general description of the aforementioned characters, this feeling of unease is mostly evoked indirectly. When a man from the audience makes the cautious remark that immigration control is still needed despite the incident, he is mocked and treated "as out of place as a Neanderthal lumbering down Oxford Street" (Turner 2012, 101). The self-righteousness of the panel and the rest of the audience's reaction feels cruel and uncalled for, which in return makes it easier to sympathize with those who are silenced and mocked and therefore locate the political protagonists and NGO and media representatives as out of touch with the concerns of reasonable and ordinary people. They are therefore "outside" and "on top" in populist terms.

While in *The Camp of the Saints*, the classification of "elites" and "outsiders" is relatively easy, it lacks a clearly identifiable "inside" counterpart. Calgués, while having a historical connection and a strong affection towards the region where he lives, is not the ideal example for "the people" due to his job in academia. Furthermore, there are those like Dio and Dufort who have grasped the severity of the situation early on, but who are silenced by public opinion control and "professional do-gooders". In most cases, they unsuccessfully attempt to act as a voice of reason in the discourse. One such character is the reactionary journalist Machefer who works for a small and unsuccessful newspaper with very limited success. Politically, "Machefer's paper was neither right nor left, nor even lukewarm middle of the road. It would lash out, often where least expected, tilting at the windmills of hackneyed opinion" (Raspail 2018, 75). This ability for a transgressive populism makes Machefer the ideal counterpart to a media apparatus that is seemingly forced into line.

Under the impression of books like Samuel Huntington's *Clash of Civilizations* (1992) and changes in Western party politics, the past two decades have witnessed a growing skepticism regarding the compatibility of a supposed "Western" culture and "non-Western" immigrant communities, particularly of Muslim faith. In contrast to the above-mentioned replacement narratives that have prominent racial undertones, arguments about the incompatibility of the gains of feminism with the acceptance of Muslim lifestyles mostly rely on cultural arguments.

Much in the same way that replacement narratives are fueling radicalization and inspiring violent action, an emerging anti-feminist and anti-LGBTQ* sentiment is providing a gateway and a framework for right-wing radicalization. Considering feminists and feminism as adversaries to the national and racial well-being appears to be the smallest common denominator between conservatives and far-right extremists. The "manosphere", an online subculture that seeks the preservation of male privilege and an end to an alleged discrimination of men, has been a fertile ground for anti-feminist and right-wing discourses over the last years (Nagle 2017). The relationship to feminism both within online and offline communities on the political right, however, is remarkably two-fold. On the one hand, feminist or egalitarian views challenge traditional gender roles and notions of a hierarchy based on biological difference. Any ideology that enables women to choose their lifestyle and partnership model autonomously supposedly lowers a nation's birthrate, which consequently affects population size. Particularly in this regard, narratives of "White Genocide" and anti-feminist discourses intersect. On the other hand, there is a visible tendency to "outsource" the sexism innate in those arguments and to appropriate supposedly feminist stances in order to underline cultural or racial differences to the "other". According to Ruth Wodak,

> [s]trangers within and outside are perceived as threatening (Christian) civilization, accompanied by a gendered discourse which, on the one hand, appeals to a liberation of women according to Human Rights conventions and is directed against Muslim women and, on the other hand, restricts women's rights via traditional Christian religious values directed against the freedom to choose abortion and to live independent lives (Wodak 2015, 181).

This dichotomy is perpetuated in both of the novels. In both books, there are notable instances of women who embody this duality, particularly through sexually tantalizing behavior or as persons onto whom sexual anxieties are projected. In *Sea Changes*, the lawyer Joanna Karatakis is such a figure. When the protagonist, Ibraham, is accommodated in a decrepit refugee camp in Greece, he develops an almost obsessive behavior and fantasizes about her. In the chapters, it remains ambiguous whether the provocative behavior that Ibraham notices is actually just the product of his imagination. In the descriptions of their interactions, it is made obvious that the male gaze and Ibraham's attraction towards Ms. Karatakis influence the narrative reliability of Ibraham as a focalizer for the narrative. When he attempts to kiss Ms. Karatakis, he is dragged out of the room by a translator and his rejection is made abundantly clear. The professional relationship between them is destroyed and Ibraham feels like he is "banished forever from paradise" when the mental image he has built up around her is met with a sudden physical rejection

(Turner 2012, 178). This immediate physical reaction is an expression of a sudden change in the power dynamics between the characters. Ibraham changes from a person Ms. Karatakis empathizes with and cares for to a sexually abusive offender, the predatory "Other". In a riot that takes place in the camp a few weeks later, a female guard is raped which again reflects a change in power dynamics and solidifies the representation of the migrant other as uncontrollable sexual predator.

In *The Camp of the Saints*, a comparable character is Iris Nan-Chan, girlfriend of Clèment Dio and a member of the liberal elite that exhibits the same reversal of power dynamics. When Dio and Nan-Chan head to the south of France to witness the arrival of the armada, they do so from an emphatic, humanist perspective that exhibits both scorn for their country and a paternalism and naiveté towards the migrant other. When she and Dio attempt to spend the night at a hotel that has been overtaken by a band of leftists and migrants, Nan-Chan is raped and commits suicide as a consequence.

Sexualized violence as a consequence or punishment for characters who exhibit pro-immigration stances occur several times throughout the book. Another case is Lydia, a member of the group of leftist militants under a leader named Panama Ranger. Lydia, too, expresses through her membership in Panama Ranger's group a decidedly pro-immigrant stance. As a minor character, Lydia remains very flat. The only information about her that can be gathered is that she is sexually promiscuous (Raspail 2018, 252). In the chapters that function as an epilogue it is revealed that after the arrival of the armada, she spent time in a brothel that offered mandatory services to the newly arrived Hindus (Raspail 2018, 269). Ultimately, she dies full of regret and self-loathing. Again, rape, sexualized violence and death are in the book's logic the consequence for behavior that harms the nation's identity and biological survival.

Unsurprisingly, neither novel contains complex female characters. They appear to exist only in two iterations: as weak characters or members of an assumed "elite". The weaker female characters need male protection because they are in danger, particularly from the migrant masculine other. An exception to the general lack of agency regarding females are those characters that are part of the populist conception of "the elite". Both books generally follow or anticipate the right-wing assertion that migration of people with non-western culture and values is a threat to women's emancipation and safety. Simultaneously, in both novels there are instances in which particularly emancipated women suffer sexualized violence. Not surprisingly, the texts do not adhere to the feminist conception of patriarchy as a set of social relations that transcends borders and cultures, but rather locate the origin of oppression on the side of foreign male invaders. The rhetorical and narrative strategies of reframing, or resemanticizing, feminist themes serves to justify anti-immigration policies. Both novels subvert feminist ideas, transforming them into instruments of xenophobic anti-immigration narratives.

In conclusion, both books employ elements of the "Great Replacement" narrative, albeit with different emphases. While *The Camp of the Saints* emphasizes both the irreversible national catastrophe of the replacement and the events leading up to it, *Sea Changes* lacks such a cataclysmic incident. What the novels have in common is their focus on the conditions of and the individual contributions to such a replacement. While characters from both novels act maliciously or selfishly, they share a dismissal of societal relations and fundamental humanitarian values which they represent as hindrances to the preservation of national culture and ethnic survival. In both Raspail's and Turner's fictions it is not individual wrongdoing that leads to catastrophe, but rather a collectively grown political culture that has learned to embrace Christian-humanitarian values of diversity and multiculturalism over the tendency to protect one's own racial and cultural identity.

Works Cited

Beiner, Ronald (2018) *Dangerous Minds: Nietzsche, Heidegger, and the Return of the Far Right*. Philadelphia: University of Pennsylvania Press.

Blumenthal, Paul and J.M. Rieger (2017) *This Stunningly Racist French Novel Is How Steve Bannon Explains the World*. Huffington Post (1 January). Web: https://www.huffpost.com/entry/steve-bannon-camp-of-the-saints-immigration_n_58b75206e4b0284854b3dc03.

Boehnke, Lukas, Malte Thran and Jacob Wunderwald, Jacob (eds.) (2019) *Rechtspopulismus Im Fokus: Theoretische und praktische Herausforderungen für die politische Bildung* [Online], Wiesbaden: Springer VS. Web: https://ebookcentral.proquest.com/lib/kxp/detail.action?docI D=5588740.

Brubaker, Rogers (2017) Between Nationalism and Civilizationism: the European Populist Moment in Comparative Perspective. *Ethnic and Racial Studies* 40(8), 1191–1226.

Dietze, Gabriele and Simon Strick (2017) *Der Aufstand der Betamännchen.* Gender-Blog der Zeitschrift für Medienwissenschaft. Web: https://z fmedienwissenschaft.de/node/1096.

Fekete, Liz (2006) Enlightened Fundamentalism? Immigration, Feminism and the Right. *Race & Class* 48(2), 1–22.

Garcia-Navarro, Lulu (2019) Stephen Miller and *The Camp Of The Saints.* A White Nationalist Reference. NPR. Web: https://ww w.npr.org/2019/11/19/780552636/stephen-miller-and-the-camp-of-t he-saints-a-white-nationalist-reference?t=1624609820835.

Goetz, Judith (2021) "The Great Replacement": Reproduction and Population Policies of the Far Right, Taking the Identitarians as an Example. *DiGeSt – Journal of Diversity and Gender Studies* 8(1), 59–74.

Gribben, Crawford (2009) *Writing the Rapture: Prophecy Fiction in Evangelical America.* New York: Oxford University Press.

Hadj-Abdou, Leila (2010) Anti-Migrationspolitik im Namen der Geschlechtergerechtigkeit. Das Paradox des "Feministischen Rechtspopulismus". *Femina Politica* 2, 117–119.

Kellerslohn, Helmut (2019) Umvolkung. In: Gießelmann, Bente, Benjamin Kerst, Robin Richterich, Lenard Suermann and Fabian Virchow (eds.) *Handwörterbuch Rechtsextremer Kampfbegriffe*, 2nd ed. Frankfurt/ M.: Wochenschau Verlag, 356–371.

Kemper, Andreas (2016) "… die neurotische Phase überwinden, in der wir uns seit siebzig Jahren befinden." Zur Differenz von Konservativismus und Faschismus am Beispiel der "historischen Mission" Björn Höckes (AfD). Rosa-Luxemburg-Stiftung Thüringen.

Web: https://th.rosalux.de/publikation/id/3961/die-neurotische-ph
ase-ueberwinden-in-der-wir-uns-seit-siebzig-jahren-befinden.

Kopke, Christoph (2017) Verschwörungsmythen und Feindbilder in der AfD und in der neuen Protestbewegung von rechts. *Neue Kriminalpolitik*, 29(1), 49–61.

MacLean, Nancy (2017) *Democracy in Chains: The Deep History of the Radical Right's Stealth Plan for America*. New York: Viking.

Mirlees, Tanner (2018) The Alt-right's Discourse on "Cultural Marxism": A Political Instrument of Intersectional Hate. *Atlantis* 39(19, 49–69. Web: https://journals.msvu.ca/index.php/atlantis/article/vi ew/5403/pdf_55.

Mudde, Cas (2019) *The Far Right Today*. Cambridge: Polity Press.

Nagle, Angela (2017) *Kill All Normies: The Online Culture Wars from Tumblr and 4chan to the Alt-Right and Trump*. Winchester, Washington: Zero Books.

Nowicki, Andy (2012) *Sea Changes: An Interview with Derek Turner*. Affirmative Right. Web: https://affirmativeright.blogspot.com/2014/03/sea -changes-interview-with-derek-turner.html.

Okin, Susan M. (1999) *Is Multiculturalism Bad for Women?* Princeton: Princeton University Press.

Raspail, Jean (2018) *The Camp of the Saints*. Sixth American edition. Petoskey: Social Contract Press.

Sedgwick, Mark (ed.) (2019) *Key Thinkers of the Radical Right: Behind the New Threat to Liberal Democracy*. Oxford: Oxford University Press, 2019.

Silliman, Daniel (2021) *Reading Evangelicals: How Christian Fiction shaped a Culture and a Faith*, Grand Rapids: William B. Eerdmans Publishing Company

Sprengholz, Maximilian (2021) Post-feminist German heartland: On the Women's Rights Narrative of the Radical-Right Populist Party Alternative für Deutschland in the Bundestag. *European Journal of Women's Studies* 28(4), 1–16.

Taguieff, Pierre-André (1995) Political Science Confronts Populism: From a Conceptual Mirage to a Real Problem. *Telos* 103, 9–43.

Tanton, John (1994–1995) The Camp of the Saints Revisited. *The Social Contract*, 5(2), 83.

Turner, Derek (2012) *Sea Changes*. Alexandria: Washington Summit Publishers.

Wodak, Ruth (2015) *The Politics of Fear: What Right-Wing Populist Discourses Mean*, Los Angeles: SAGE.

Indignants of the World, Unite?
Mobilizations of Indignation in Alter- and Anti-Globalism

Christine Unrau

1. Introduction

In 2011, former Résistance fighter Stéphane Hessel (2011) published a manifesto in which he called on everyone, especially the youth of the world, to be indignant: *Indignez-vous!* In many respects, this can be read as a renewed call along the lines of the Communist Manifesto, which in its final phrase asks the workers of all countries to unite. This time, however, the exhortation is directed, first and foremost, at a feeling, instead of an action. Several movements took up this call, including the Spanish *Indignados*, who identified themselves as "the outraged". This boom of indignation is linked with globalization in multiple ways: Not only is it a global phenomenon which has various origins and circulated along certain lines of global communication. What is more, many of the objects and triggers of indignation are linked with what the respective activists identify as aspects of economic, social and cultural globalization.

The surge of indignation is not limited to those who carry the term in their name, like the *Indignados*. For example, long before Hessel's manifesto, the Mexican Zapatistas, inspirers of the Global Justice Movement, organized an international event called *Festival de la Digna Rabia* (Festival of Dignified Rage). Importantly, it is not limited to progressive movements whose actions are directed against forms of exclusion, neoliberalism or financialization. The expression of indignation is common among far right intellectuals and activists as well. The goals of the various groups of activists which recur to indignation are diametrically opposed. These observations immediately lead to the question: How can we interpret and react to the invocation and *re-semanticization* of indignation in the context of globalization?

By analyzing and reflecting on narratives of indignation in anti-globalism and alter-globalism, this chapter aims at contributing to a larger debate, in Political Theory, International Relations and beyond, on the significance of emotions for politics. While the post-war era was characterized by the priority to keep emotions out of politics, especially against the background of totalitarian manipulations of racial hatred and fanatic nationalism (Arendt 1963), there is now a rediscovery of the importance of emotions for politics. Among other aspects, political philosophers have explored the importance of emotions for overcoming the status quo in political movements (Walzer 2002), for the generation of belonging and support for values such as justice and democracy (Nussbaum 2013) and for ethical deliberation itself (Jeffery 2011). Especially in debates about justice, the exclusivity of universal rational criteria has been challenged and the experience of indignation has gained center stage as a sensorium for social suffering, in liberal (Shklar 1990), as well as feminist and decolonial political thought (Campello 2021). Some authors have also begun to discuss the relevance of political emotions in the context of globalization and the various alterglobalisms, as well as anti-globalist mobilizations (Pleyers 2010; Pulcini 2013; Bringel/Pleyers 2017; Unrau 2018; Freistein et al. 2022).

While studies on far-right anti-globalism have so far focused on emotions like fear (Wodak 2015), humiliation (Homolar/Löfflmann 2021), or resentment (Heins/Unrau 2020), the focus on indignation has the potential to highlight convergences, but also crucial differences between right-wing anti-globalism and left-wing alter-globalism. It also shows how the ideological assemblages of a global right is increasingly capitalizing on seemingly emancipatory claims that are either derived from or mimic those made by left wing movements (Abrahamsen et al. 2020; Drolet/Williams 2022). In the terminology of this volume, this phenomenon of appropriation could in fact be a form of *re-semanticiza-tion*.

The chapter will proceed in four steps: First, I will specify the material of analysis by distinguishing between alter- and anti-globalist movements that share a condemnation of current forms of "globalism" or "globalization". Second, I will briefly elaborate on the conceptual and methodological bases of the subsequent analysis, with a focus on the notion of *indignation* and the relationship between experience, narration and politics. Third, I will give a structured account of the recourse to indignation in both alter- and anti-global movements, identifying some of the multiple origins of the phenomenon and suggesting a distinction between the different invocations of indignation as *motivation, mode* and *goal* of political action. Fourth, based on this structured overview, the normative validity of recurring to the emotion of indignation in the context of globalization will be discussed.

The purpose of this exercise of taking stock, comparing and evaluating is not to subscribe to some emotional version of horseshoe theory, according to which far right and left anti- and alter-global mobilization narratives coincide in their recourse to indignation. On the contrary, what I aim at showing is that the recourse to indignation as a motivation, mode and goal of political action can neither undermine nor guarantee the normative legitimacy of the respective political concerns. What matters is the way in which indignation is experienced, narrated and mobilized. In the conclusion, I will sketch out some preliminary considerations concerning the initial question how to evaluate the role of indignation in alter- and anti-global activism.

2.   What's Wrong with the Global? Opposition to Globalization Between Alter- and Anti-Globalism

The body of analyzed material comprises different forms of texts – including philosophical works, song texts, journalistic pieces and various self-representations of movement organizations on homepages etc. Not only do they differ in style and mode of presentation, they also come from very different political orientations. What they have in common is that they represent some form of reaction to the processes commonly summarized under the label of globalization – most broadly understood as the "widening, deepening and speeding up of worldwide interconnectedness" (Held/McGrew 2007, 1), especially in their accelerated and intensified form which can be observed after the end of the Cold War and the post-bipolar constellation. These processes include, but are not limited to intensified international trade and financial transactions, increased importance and power of multinational corporations, the imposition of financial policies based on privatization and austerity, facilitated travelling, transplanetary communications, hybridization of ways of life and intensified migration (e.g., Giddens 1994, 4; Appadurai 1996, 17; Beck 1997, 28–29; Scholte 2005, 8). All of these processes lead to permanent crossings of national boundaries and some – especially those which have to do with the economic integration of the world and the imposition of neoliberal economic policies – are perceived to have caused an increase in individual insecurity and a permanent threat of unemployment and loss of status (Bauman 2000, 2001).

The texts analyzed in this chapter take issue with different aspects of these processes and envision alternative futures. They can be divided into two groups: The first group, which has been labeled as "globalization from below" (Brecher et al. 2000), "global justice movement" (della Porta 2007) or "alter-globalization" (Pleyers 2010) generally embraces and celebrates those aspects of globalization which have to do with facilitated travelling, migration and communication but sharply criticizes the boundaries erected against the free movement of persons, the unequal distribution of wealth, the transfer of binding decision-making power to international financial institutions like the IMF and the WTO, as well as the excessive power of multinational corporations. There are significant differences within this group of movements and authors as to the various visions of an alternative form of globalization – ranging from a reform of international institutions to radical transformation starting from below – and also with regard to the proposed repertoires of action. At the same time, however, there is a web of cross-references and common convictions which allow for the identification of one movement of movements. Temporarily, it found its common denominator in the motto "Another world is possible" and established its own cycle of protests and meetings, the most important one being the World Social Forum, which first took place in Porto Alegre, Brazil, in 2001. Examples from this group discussed below include texts by the Mexican *Zapatista* movement, which declared "war" on the Mexican government and neoliberal globalization in 1994, as well as movement intellectuals like Pierre Bourdieu, Michael Hardt and Antonio Negri. The intellectual roots of this movement are multiple, ranging from Keynesian economics to different strands of unorthodox Marxism, including dependency theory, Italian Autonomism and Latin American liberation theology (Unrau 2018, 35–37).

The *Indignados* movement in Spain, as well as *Occupy* and others, belong to a different protest cycle, which started after the financial crisis of 2008/09. During this protest circle, "neoliberal globalization" was no longer the most prominent point of reference when naming the relevant grievances. "Neoliberalism", however, survived as a key term and many of the earlier grievances addressed by the *Global Justice Movement* remained relevant. Along these lines, Hessel's *Indignez-vous* urged young people to resist the "oppression by an actual international dictatorship of the financial markets, which threatens peace and democracy" (Hessel 2011).

The group of far-right intellectuals and activists examined here cannot be attributed to an analogous web of social movements. While their basic values and orientations are diametrically opposed to those of the *Global Justice Movement* and its successors, they share a concern with "globalization", or "globalism". Their alternative visions of the future revolve around a re-erection of national and/or ethnic boundaries and a reestablishment of closed communities, even if those are sometimes imagined as part of wider "civilizational" empires. While there are considerable tensions and contradictions between various strands, a loose coalition of far-right self-ascribed anti-globalist thinkers and movements emerges, who converge on their goal of retrieving "innate culture", an emphasis on identity and a rejection of "liberal" international norms (De Orellana/Michelsen 2019; Drolet/Williams 2018; Griffin 2017).

Examples discussed in the following study include representatives of right-wing extremist movements from the1990s, such as the Italian rock group *Zetazeroalpha*, which is closely associated with the neo-fascist and explicitly anti-globalist squatters' movement *Casa Pound*. A more recent example of an anti-immigrant movement which emerged only around 2015 is the German *Pegida* – "Patriotic Europeans against the Islamization of the Occident." Although less outspokenly anti-systemic than groups like *Casa Pound*, *Pegida* clearly plays with radical modes of the rhetoric of indignation (Heins/Unrau 2020). Besides the protagonists of the intellectual movement referred to as the *New Right*, including Alain de Benoist, more recent far right ideologues have appeared in the context of the rise of populist radical right parties. One example is Marc Jongen, one of the most programmatic thinkers of the German "Alternative for Germany" (AfD) party. His intellectual teacher Peter Sloterdijk will also be taken into account since he constantly straddles the boundaries between the critical intellectual and the anti-immigrant rhetorician. The intellectual roots of this very loose network of thinkers and activists are broad and at times disconnected. For example, while some thinkers play with references to Germanic paganism, or share a Nietzschean anti-Christian attitude, others idealize Christianity as a cultural marker and anti-relativist tradition of thought (Schieder 2020, 221). A wide-spread heritage in far-right anti-globalism is that of the so-called *Conservative Revolution* with Carl Schmitt as its hero (Drolet/ Williams 2022, 26).

For reasons of feasibility and linguistic capacities, the origin of the discussed texts is restricted to Western and Southern Europe, Latin America and North America. The time span covered here is largely from the beginning of the 1990s, which marks the end of the bipolar world and thus the starting point of the last, most intensive and most self-reflexive era of globalization, to the present.

3. Fighting Against Indignity?
Indignation as Experience and Narration

In his famous considerations on Political Theory, Isaiah Berlin (1978 [1961], 148) explains its role using the question of obedience: "When we ask, what is perhaps the most fundamental of all political questions, 'Why should anyone obey anyone else?', we ask not 'Why do men obey?'". This latter question, according to him, might be answered by "empirical psychology, anthropology and sociology". By contrast, "[w]hen we ask why a man should obey, we are asking for the explanation of what is normative in such notions as authority, sovereignty, liberty, and the justification of their validity in political arguments" (Berlin 1978, 148). Similarly, this chapter shifts the focus from the question why people are indignant or which actions are prompted by indignation, which have been explored extensively by sociologists of social movements (Goodwin et al. 2001; Jasper 2014), to the normative implications of recourses to indignation in the context of the current world order. However, the aim is not to separate theoretical considerations from the crucial insights provided by sociology, psychology and interdisciplinary emotion research, but to bring them together.

When it comes to tentatively assessing the various recourses to indignation, the conceptual and political history of the emotion has to play a role. In fact, indignation has a long – and political – history, which is worth recapitulating in order to make sense of current uses. In the *Rhetoric*, Aristotle interprets indignation (for which he uses the verb "to nemesan" – "to be indignant") as the mirror image of compassion: While compassion is pain felt for others' undeserved misfortune, indignation refers to undeserved wellbeing (Aristotle 2020, 1386 b 10 ff.). As opposed to envy, which is also triggered by others' well-being (Aristotle 2020, 1386 b 18), indignation is a specific reaction to phenomena such as undeserved wealth or undeserved positions of power (Aristotle 2020, 1387 a9 ff.).

The Italian and Latin words used by Machiavelli ("sdegno": Machiavelli 1996 [1531], 370) and Spinoza ("indignatio": Spinoza 1994 [1677], 61) convey the characteristic of being an offence against somebody's "dignity". This understanding of indignation as a "proof of existence"

(Bromell 2013) of intrinsic dignity and as a sensorium for its violation was reflected on in the context of experiences of slavery and, later, discrimination of Black Americans. Similarly, theories of citizenship and recognition have drawn on the experience of indignation as an indicator of injustice and exclusion in the political realm (Shklar 1990; Honneth 1992; Brighi 2016). Especially decolonial and feminist approaches have questioned the role of rationality as the exclusive criterion for the assessment of justice claims and foregrounded the implications of personal emotional experience (Lorde 1981; Hoggett and Thompson 2002; Campello 2021).

Before assessing the various recourses to indignation in alter- and anti-global movements, it is necessary to have a closer look at them. Against this background, the special emphasis in the analysis of the material is on its experiential content and how it is narrated. In the large and growing interdisciplinary literature on emotions, there is a certain convergence in understanding emotions as "hybrid" forms of experience which comprise both a physical, bodily, and a cognitive mode of getting in touch with reality (Roth 2003, 296; Jeffery 2011, 147). Importantly, we can never have access to these experiences directly, but only to their symbolic articulation. Also, the experience of reality is always already shaped by the symbols, narratives and discourses which are available at a certain moment in time (also Taylor 1985, 37).

Experiences of indignation and exhortations to be indignant can be expressed directly, as exemplified by Hessel's call *Indignez-Vous*. However, they can also be articulated indirectly via storytelling, e.g. through certain plots and the attribution of roles. Therefore, when taking stock of recourses to indignation in alter- and anti-global movements, the focus lies on the narrative articulations of indignation. Thus, the methodology of narrative analysis, with its emphasis on roles, plots and metaphors, becomes relevant in the context of this analysis. How are the roles of villains, victims and heroes ascribed to the protagonists of the respective stories? Which metaphors are deployed? Is there a special plot structure, such as decline, rise or decline-and-rise which can be discerned? And, importantly, which myths, legends and other elements of a given repertoire of stories are recurred to (Czarniawska 2004; Mayer 2014; Shenhav 2015; Freistein and Gadinger 2019)?

4.   Taking Stock: Indignation in Alter-Global and Anti-Global Movements

Since the interest lies on the mobilization of indignation with a view to action against the current form of world order, the analysis will focus on the respective relationship between experience and action: Firstly, recourse to indignation as a *motivation* of political action will be taken into account, i.e., arguments that take the form of "We need to act because we experience indignation". Secondly, the focus will shift to indignation as a *mode* of political action. This regards arguments like "We take action by expressing, articulating and living based on indignation". Thirdly, I will turn to arguments about indignation as a *goal* of political action, i.e. calls to act in order to arouse indignation in others.

Motivation

The first common way of invoking indignation is as a motive for action. Among many others, Pierre Bourdieu articulates this relationship between rage/indignation and political action in the introduction of his collection of political texts entitled *Contre-feux*: "I would not have engaged in taking a public stance if I had not had, each time, the feeling – which might have been illusionary – to be constrained to do so by a kind of legitimate outrage, which was sometimes close to something like a feeling of duty" (Bourdieu 1998, 7).[1] He expresses the meaning of indignation as a motivation for action by recurring to his own personal story, which led him from academia to the position of being a public intellectual. By using the word "constrained", he presents the experience of rage as a force, something that acted against his first impulse, which might have been to stay in the comfort of the "ivory tower". The temporal specification "each

---

1   All translations from sources that are not originally in English are my own.

time" makes it clear that it was a repeated experience and not a singular event.

Indignation as a motivation for action can also be found in *Commonwealth*, the third part of Michael Hardt's and Antonio Negri's trilogy on globalization: "In indignation, as Spinoza reminds us, we discover our power to act against oppression and challenge the causes of our collective suffering. In the expression of indignation our very existence rebels" (Hardt and Negri 2009, 236). With their recourse to Spinoza, Hardt and Negri inscribe their own interpretation in a long history of indignation as a topic of political philosophy. The generic "we" they use can refer to the authors themselves, and to all of those who, from their perspective, form the "Multitude" in its struggle against "Empire".

In *Indignez-Vous* by Stéphane Hessel we find a similar celebration of indignation, here in the mode of a direct appeal to the reader: "I wish for you all, each of you, to have your own motive for indignation. It is precious. When something outrages you as I was outraged by Nazism, then people become militant, strong, and engaged" (Hessel 2011). Thus, he presents himself as the hero that he was, fighting the Nazi invasion, but not in order to emphasize the singularity of his act. Instead, he presents himself as an example that is worthy of emulation when the reasons for outrage persist even after the demise of Nazism.

The *Democracia real ya* campaign in Spain, which was in part inspired by Hessel's manifesto and in turn inspired the mobilizations of the *Indignados* movement (Antentas 2015), also identified indignation as that which motivated its members across all ideological divisions:

> Some of us think of themselves as more progressive, others as more conservative. Some are believers, others aren't. Some of us have clearly defined ideologies, others think of themselves as apolitical... But we are all concerned and indignant in view of the political, economic and social panorama that surrounds us. Of the corruption of the politicians, businessmen and bankers...Of the defenselessness of the ordinary citizen (*Democracia real ya* 2011).

Here, the individual experience of indignation is collectivized and turned into both the motivation of action, and the moment of identification which separates heroes ("ordinary citizens") from villains ("politicians, businessmen and bankers").

While both Hardt/Negri and Hessel interpret indignation as a way of connecting with the inner self and finding motivation and strength for action, theologians close to the Global Justice Movement associate indignation with a spiritual experience of the divine: "[T]he experience of ethical indignation, which leads to social commitment, has been and must be interpreted as a true spiritual experience" (Míguez et al 2009, 5).

Social commitment against the grievances which cause indignation is thereby presented as a commitment born out of divine revelation. Here, we see an interesting parallel with the views expressed by German philosopher Peter Sloterdijk. He presents rage (and indignation, which he does not differentiate clearly) as concomitant with the birth of European culture and a fundamental human capacity: Given that it appears in the first sentence of the *Iliad*, the oldest European work of literature, he calls it "the first word of Europe" (Sloterdijk 2010, 2)[2] and emphasizes that this rage, in Homer's world, is seen as "belonging to the realm of the higher powers" (Sloterdijk 2010, 4) and "granted from above" (Sloterdijk 2010, 5). In Sloterdijk's reconstruction of ancient rage, it is transmitted through participation between the gods and humans. By anchoring his considerations on rage and indignation in ancient Greek literature, Sloterdijk not only nobilitates the emotion in question but also emphasizes his concern with tradition: In fact, early on in his book he speaks about "our cultural tradition" and inserts the question "is this 'our' still valid?", thereby already insinuating that "our tradition" may be threatened and should be retrieved precisely by recurring to the capacity for rage.

In his program, the lynchpin for this retrieval is the notion of *thymos*, which he presents as the Greek term for the passionate part of the soul.

---

2   Citations from *Rage and Time* are from the English translation Sloterdijk (2010). The German original version was published in 2006. Translations from *Last Exit Indignation* are my own.

In his 2010 book *Rage and Time*, which was originally published in German in 2006, his overall diagnosis as to the current state of this human capacity was that of a "darkening of the thymotic dimension" caused by a "one-sided eroticization" (Sloterdijk 2010, 17) in modernity. However, in a later essay entitled *Last Exit Indignation*, his interpretation of the current age is less negative. Now he sees some of the "old" capacity of rage and indignation and interprets it as a force which motivates people to act against those tendencies which threaten democracy and citizen participation: "He is back, the citizen who retained his capacity of indignation, since he kept his sense of self-affirmation against all the attempts to reduce him to a container of libido, and who manifests these qualities by bringing his dissidence into the public sphere" (Sloterdijk 2015).

So, while the plot structure in *Rage and Time* was one of decline, *Last Exit Indignation* is characterized by a resurrection plot. By referring to the legend of *Lucretia*, the founding myth of the Roman republic, he also emphasizes that the motivational force of indignation is directly linked to the constitution of the political: After Lucretia was raped by the despotic king Tarquinius, she sacrificed herself instead of succumbing to the king's will to make her his wife. The king's arrogance and violence aroused the people's indignation, which in turn led to the foundation of the Roman republic. Sloterdijk makes it very clear that he sees this connection of indignation and political commitment as a source of hope for the present threats of "postdemocracy": "In moments like the present it does not harm to recall that the original res publica was itself derived from the psychopolitical primary affects pride and indignation" (Sloterdijk 2015).

Sloterdijk's praise of the indignant citizen who is moved to act against post-democratic threats by his rage was also explicitly directed against a critical portrait of the "raging citizen" ("Wutbürger") which was put forward in a widely read editorial by *Spiegel* journalist Dirk Kurbjuweit (Kurbjuweit 2010). Interestingly, the term was also appropriated by the Pegida movement and its supporters: In an article entitled *They question the system. Phenomenology of the new raging citizen* Pegida supporter Michael Paulwitz first lists the various references to the "raging" or "indignant" citizen, including the one to the middle-class opponent of infrastructure projects and the left-leaning exhortation to "be indignant" by Stéphane Hessel. He then goes on to argue that the anti-immigrant and anti-elite activists of Pegida are the *"real* raging citizens" in so far as they do not only protest against particular political projects but deny their support to the entire political class and the "media mainstream" and thereby "question the system" (Paulwitz 2015, emphasis added; Heins and Unrau 2020).

Mode

Apart from its motivating role, indignation is also recurred to as a mode of action and as a guiding principle. This is expressed by the Mexican *Zapatistas* in their Sixth Declaration, where they emphasize that instead of imposing certain decisions and coalitions with other social movements, their guideline is the existing indignation of their constituency. Thus "escuchar la indignación" – "listening to indignation" – is their motto (EZLN 2005). A similar use of the term is made by Hardt and Negri when they interpret their own task as

> to investigate the organizational framework of antagonist subjectivities that arise from below, based on the indignation expressed by subjects in the face of the unfreedoms and injustices of power, the severe forms of control and hierarchy, and the cruel forms of exploitation and expropriation in the disordered world of global governance. Indignation, as Spinoza notes, is the ground zero, the basic material from which movements of revolt and rebellion develop (Hardt and Negri 2009, 235).

Thus, they present the experience of indignation as the "basic material" of activism. What then arises as a question for them is in how far singular instances of indignation can be turned into a wider strategy: "Indignation is born always as a singular phenomenon, in response to a specific obstacle or violation. Is it possible, then, for there to be a strategy of indignation? Can indignation lead to a process of political self-determination?" (Hardt and Negri 2009, 236). They answer this question by pointing to the long history of spontaneous rebellions out of indignation, which they term *Jacqueries*, alluding to the French peasant rebellions of the fourteenth century. According to Hardt and Negri, in all those instances indignation never merely led to uncontrolled eruptions but targeted those symbols and objects of power which were "adequate" (Hardt and Negri 2009, 237) with regard to the respective grievance: While peasants targeted the riches of the aristocracy, workers rebellions were directed against machines as embodiments of capital and current rebellions (to which they also count the 2005 riots in the Banlieues) target the police, schools and means of transportation as symbols of the current "biopolitical" form of domination (Hardt and Negri 2009, 237). What concerns them is the fact that *Jacqueries* lack organizational structures, the ideation of which they see as part of their own task. Therefore, they conclude: "We remain convinced that the expression of indignation and revolt in jacqueries is essential for a process of transformation but that without organization they cannot achieve it. Jacqueries are not sufficient, in other words, but they are necessary" (Hardt and Negri 2009, 240).

By inscribing their own investigation in the history of *Jacqueries*, they show that there is a certain tradition of rebellions and disobedience born out of indignation. At the same time, they attest to the fact that not all of these rebellions had lasting effects and some lacked a "project", thereby ascribing to themselves the role of developing such a project for the current age of "Empire", in collaboration with the forces they identify as the "Multitude", composed of the global totality of marginalized, precarious, but nevertheless creative and powerful singularities.

If we look at the side of extreme right anti-globalization, we also find forms of sublimations of rage as a mode of action. The envisioned subjects, however, are not a wide and diverse coalition of indignant singularities, but an ethnocratically defined, exclusive collective of nationals. The "rage", in this case, is directed against a hostile world referred to as "the system", which is understood as an arrangement of "alien" dominant forces. Thus, in a song text of the neo-fascist rock band *Zetazeroalfa*, rage – translated into physical violence – is presented as a means of liberation:

It is growing and comes from below,
the metaphysics of the stone;
And I don't know if I can tell you: Aim high and jump over the ditch;
It is growing together with rage to destroy the cage;
And the window is breaking, there is someone who is crying now!"
(Zetazeroalfa 2010a) .

As is made clear in the last line, the form of action which follows from this rage is blind violence: the breaking of windows, which causes individual – but arbitrary – suffering: "Qualcuno", someone, that is anyone who is not part of the inner circle, is a representative of the "system" (see also the song *Mai come voi/Never like you*, Zetazeroalfa 2010b) and therefore made to cry.

While activists in extremist right-wing groups like *Casa Pound* see themselves as the subjects and the agents of rage – often engaging in and celebrating physical violence – right-wing populist politicians iden-tify as those who translate the "rage" of the people and bring it into the political system. One example is the public performance of Marine Le Pen, leader of the French populist right-wing party *Rassemblement Na-tional*. While she does not publicly endorse physical violence, her rhetoric deliberately transcends the boundaries of what is generally deemed ade-quate for the public debate. When criticized for her choice of words, she said she deliberately chose to challenge the "delicate ears" of those who are not used to such expressions, since she was the "porte-parole de la colère" (cited in Reuters 2017), i.e., "spokesperson of the rage" of the peo-ple vis-à-vis the powerful.

The question of indignation as a mode of political action is also discussed by political philosopher Peter Sloterdijk. In a deliberation which is reminiscent of Hardt's and Negri's argument about organiza-tional structures, Peter Sloterdijk turns to the political effectiveness of indignation and rage. With a view to historical episodes of what he calls "the project form of rage" (Sloterdijk 2010, 62), he comes to a different conclusion than the authors of the "Empire" trilogy:

Only when discrete energies are invested into superior projects and far-sighted, sufficiently calm, diabolic directors take care of administrating collective rage, can the many and isolated fire places become one single power plant. This plant could provide the energy for coordinated actions, up to the level of 'world politics' (Sloterdijk 2010, 63).

Goal of Action

The third type of invocations of indignation by activists of alter- and anti-globalization links it with goals of action: In various ways, activists express their surprise or anger at the fact that not everyone feels indignation in view of the grievances, injustices and sufferings of the present. For example, liberation theologist Jung Mo Sung emphasizes: "The founding experience, called by liberation theology the first moment, is [...] the experience of ethical indignation. Not everybody feels such indignation, no matter how grave the social problems are" (Sung 2005, 4). Implicitly, he calls for action to make other people feel the indignation which is adequate in view of the social problems he mentions. The direction of this action is alluded to in his diagnosis of the reason for this lack of indignation which – in his view – is pathological: According to his analysis, indignation in view of the inhumane treatment of the marginalized of the world is lacking because there is a deliberate effort of ideological construction (namely, neo-liberalism), according to which some sections of the global population are simply excluded from the circle of those who matter. In the name of macro-economic transformation – such as growth and privatization – the suffering of sections of the population is interpreted as a necessary evil which must be accepted in view of a higher overall goal. According to Sung, the success of this ideological endeavor is the result of a lack of indignation (Sung 2005, 5–9).

An alternative diagnosis for the same phenomenon – namely a lack of widespread indignation – is offered by sociologist Pierre Bourdieu. He takes issue with the way news are presented on TV, namely as an endless chain of threatening events without any distinction between problems caused by crime, natural catastrophes or unjust political actions (Bourdieu 1998, 83). And he concludes: "So a pessimist philosophy of history creeps in, one that invites to retreat and resignation rather than to revolt and indignation and, far from mobilizing and politicizing, can only contribute to the rise of xenophobic fears" (Bourdieu 1998, 83–84).

Thus, according to Bourdieu, television as a central medium of information for a large section of the population creates a mentality of retreat vis-à-vis a world which is perceived as senseless and threatening, it anaesthetizes people against what should trigger their indignation and their willingness to engage politically. By referring to xenophobic fears, Bourdieu also alludes to an alternative emotion which is triggered in many, one that he understands as equally inadequate as the lack of any emotional reaction caused by a general retreat from the world. So, the stimulation of indignation as an adequate reaction to the present injustices becomes the goal of political action, including the one he himself is engaging in by taking a public stance and analyzing patterns of the media field. Thereby, he also insinuates that the story of decline about an overwhelming amount of bad news leading to "fatalist disengagement" (Bourdieu 1998, 84) could be reversed.

A similar understanding can be found in the manifesto *Indignez-vous!*: What the appeal in the title suggests is that readers and listeners may not be indignant, but that they should be and the author will tell them why, reminding them of his specific legitimacy as a Résistance-fighter: "We, the veterans of the resistance movements and combat forces of Free France, we call on the young generation to live by, to transmit, the legacy of the Resistance and its ideals. We say to them: Take our place, 'Indignez-vous!' [Get angry! or Cry out!]" (Hessel 2011).

Sloterdijk, too, shares the goal of arousing passionate responses to the present, when he calls for an "intelligence which retrieves its thymotic motives" and envisions a "universe of energetic, thymotically irritable actors" (Sloterdijk 2010, 230).

While in *Last Exit Indignation*, the object of indignation is mainly the "neutralization of the citizen" in the sense of his marginalization from the political process, in *Rage and Time*, the calls for a thymotic culture remain rather vague in terms of their political implications. However, some remarks already point to a certain direction, such as ominous references to "potential genocides in the countries of the Near and Middle East and elsewhere, countries that are populated by angry young men" (Sloterdijk 2010, 42),[3] and more explicit warnings of an "approaching Muslim youth bulge, the most extensive wave of genocidal excesses of adolescent men in the history of mankind" (Sloterdijk 2010, 223).

When the German government decided not to close its borders to refugees who mainly arrived via the Balkan route in late summer 2015, Sloterdijk made it clear in several interviews that for him, the *thymos* he appealed to should be aroused by this arrival of refugees. For example, he claimed that Europe was rendered more fragile – using the psychotherapeutically connoted term "labil" – by the arrival of large numbers of refugees (Sloterdijk 2016).

This line of argument was taken up by Sloterdijk's disciple Marc Jongen, who abandoned his academic ambitions in order to become the chief rhetorician of the anti-immigrant and populist radical right party AfD. On several occasions, he drew a much clearer line from the celebration of thymotic rage to the "defence" of national identity against immigrants and new-comers. He diagnosed a "thymotic undersupply" (Bender and Bingener 2016) and declared that it was the goal of the AfD to "rise thymotic tension in Germany", in order to make it more "fortified" against more "robust characters", namely Muslim immigrants (Bender and Bingener 2016). This "self-confident voice" was immediately celebrated by right wing extremist intellectual Götz Kubitschek when he turned it into a "guideline for action" in his magazine *Sezession*: "Anything that serves the mobilization and heightening of thymotic tension, the big rage against the anti-German politics needs to be endorsed, bolstered and supported by us" (Kubitschek 2016, 10).

Ultimately, Jongen took the opportunity to present his theses on thymotic tension in person at the Winter Academy of the *Institut für Staat-*

---

3   The more drastic wording in the German original wording is "overpopulated": "die Neutralisierung der völkermörderischen Potentiale in den von zornigen jungen Männern übervölkerten Staaten des Nahen und Mittleren Orients und anderswo."

spolitik, the right-wing extremist think-tank co-founded by Kubitschek. In his speech, he called the situation caused by the alleged opening of the borders to refugees in Germany in 2015 a "prototypical cause of indignation". While he expressed his amazement at the fact that wide shares of the population did not feel this indignation, he also articulated a hope that the so-called "migration crisis" would lead to a "thymotic training", i.e., re-awakening of "thymotic tension" (Kanal Schnellroda 2017). Obviously, his own storytelling at this occasion and others can be interpreted as an attempt at reinforcing and accelerating this process.

5.   Making Sense: Reflecting on Indignation

As can be seen from this overview, references to indignation as motivation, mode and goal of political action can be found in both alter- and anti-globalist activism and idea production. Therefore, I suggest reflecting on these relationships between experience and action in order to move towards the development of a critical yardstick for the normative mobilization of this political emotion. These preliminary considerations might pave the way for what could be regarded as a critical assessment of indignation in the context of globalization.

Adequacy

If indignation is interpreted as a motivation for political action against the current form of world order, but also when it is set as a goal of action, then a first potential criterion to assess such a motivation is the *adequacy* of indignation. That this question is relevant for some of the protagonists of alter-globalism is attested to by Bourdieu's statement from the introduction of *Contre-feux*: On the one hand, he emphasizes that it was not just any form of rage which motivated his political commitment, but a "legitimate" one. On the other hand, he admits that this feeling might have been illusionary – "peut-être illusoire" – pointing to the dubious and transitory nature of emotions. Bourdieu thus interweaves certainty and doubt in an intricate way (Unrau 2018, 218–19). The use of the term "legitimate indignation" is not an isolated phenomenon: Similar expressions can be found in liberation theologian Yung Mo Sung, who speaks about "ethical indignation" (Sung 2005, 4), and in Leonardo Boff, who uses the term "iracundia sagrada" (holy rage, Boff 1993, 169). What these validating adjectives indicate is that these authors are aware that indignation per se does not suffice as the basis for a claim of legitimacy. Instead, it needs to be validated by some other source, notably other forms of experience.

As mentioned before, the question which criteria are apt to determine the adequacy of emotions like indignation was already discussed by Aristotle. While we may not agree with his specific criterion it is worth recalling that for Aristotle, the term indignation was reserved for adequate reactions to (political) injustices, and this adequacy could only be determined by recourse to practical reason. The validation of indignation through criteria which are set by practical reason is in line with philosopher Amartya Sen's view that injustice can be detected emotionally but that this emotional reaction must be subjected to "reasoned scrutiny" (Sen 200, viii, 39 ff.). As Matthias Iser puts it, "as a moral emotional reaction which claims to signal injustice, indignation requires an argumentative examination of its adequacy" (Iser 2008, 8). As potential criteria for such an examination he suggests Habermasian ethics of equal communication or Honneth's theory of recognition.

However, as the recent debate on the relevance of experience in Political Theory reminds us, there is a problematic element to this conviction that experiences of injustice can be easily divided into adequate and inadequate ones. For example, in her influential book *Faces of Injustice*, Judith Shklar calls for the recognition of the *subjective sense of injustice* as a valid element of any theory of justice since a simple comparison of expressions of indignation with the "known legal or ethical rule" (Shklar 1990, 49, 7) is not sufficient. Otherwise, any claim that exceeds these rules could be dismissed as inadequate. As she points out, important political victories, such as the ones won by the Women's and Civil Rights Movement, were only possible because people articulated their experiences of indignation, which, at the time of their struggle, went against the legal and ethical status quo. However, this welcome clarification does not amount to an obligation to accept any articulation of indignation as equally valid and politically relevant.

For example, empirical social research has shown that the activists and members of the Pegida movement have a clearly above-average level of formal education and income (Vorländer et al. 2017, 73–74). Of course, this socio-demographical fact alone does not warrant a denial of the adequacy of their indignation. However, it is an interesting entry point for a consideration of psychological mechanisms which account for particular mobilizations of indignation. In this context, the most relevant competitor to claims to indignation is probably not envy per se, as discussed by Aristotle, but a more complicated emotional disposition, namely *shame*.

With reference to the conceptual work by Turner (2007) and Scheff (1994), Salmala and Scheve argue that in case of right-wing populisms, what is expressed as indignation or anger is often a repressed form of (actual or anticipated) shame caused by a perceived threat to personal identity (Salmela and von Scheve 2017, 582). Shame – the loss of self-esteem which follows from the failure to fulfill internalized expectations (Salmela and von Scheve 2017, 582) – is a strong and negative emotion, which leads to its repression and, ultimately, its projection on minorities or members of cultural elites, who are constructed as "enemies of the precarious self" (Salmela and von Scheve 2017, 573).

While this argument contains an element of psychological speculation, a comparison between several European states in the aftermath of the 2008 financial crisis supports this line of thought. It suggests that left-wing populism has been more successful than right-wing populism in countries most affected by the 2008 financial crisis. If large portions of the population were affected by austerity cuts this led to a common awareness that individuals are not responsible for the loss of their jobs, salaries or pensions, which in turn makes it easier for them to self-identify as humiliated and blame unjust structures for their grievances. By contrast, in areas where the effects of neo-liberalism and austerity are less omnipresent, people are inclined to experience the consequences more individually, to tacitly accept responsibility for (potential) personal failure and thus develop the need of an externalized scapegoat (Salmela and von Scheve 2017, 574; della Porta 2015; Wacquant 2010).

The second crucial factor to explain the emergence of resentment against immigrants is a particular "ideology of exclusion" according to which "in times of scarce resources there would have to be a guarantee that immigrants were not to profit at the expense of the majority population of the social welfare state" (Flecker et al. 2007, 57; cited in Salmela/von Scheve 2017, 577). This shows that feelings such as indignation never take place in a vacuum. On the contrary, they are always already informed by (and in turn reinforce) ideological convictions.

Authenticity

The question of the adequacy of indignation is closely related to another challenge to assessing recourses to indignation, namely the relationship between an experience and its articulation, or the question of authenticity: The importance of this issue can be seen from the frequent reproach that manifestations are merely performances of indignation or stagings of rage – instead of genuine emotional expressions. Such reproaches can undermine both the claim to indignation as a motivation for action and the attempts at "educating others" by arousing indignation.

The background for this suspicion lies in a characteristic of emotional experience: Similarly to spirituality – and opposed to rationality – emotional experience is prone to invite such suspicion (Unrau 2018, 63). As Hannah Arendt (1963, 91) pointed out in a discussion about compassion and politics, this is because the human heart is "a place of darkness which, with certainty, no human eye can penetrate." According to her, the attempt to drag these motives into the public sphere lead to the dangerous atmosphere of suspicion which prevailed during the French revolution when everyone was suspected of being a hypocrite and failure to prove the opposite could lead to punishment on the guillotine.

However, instead of sharing her general suspicion against public displays of emotions, the expectation of "purity" with a view to articulations of emotional experience could be questioned. One way of doing so is by recognizing the important role of what Arlie Russell Hochschild has termed "feeling rules", i.e., "guidelines for the assessment of fits and misfits between feeling and situation" (Hochschild 1979, 564). They "reflect patterns of social membership" (Hochschild 1979, 564) and are susceptible to change over time (also Thoits 2004; von Scheve 2009, 293–94). Ultimately, the frequent recourse to indignation in progressive and backlash movements against the current world order can be seen as based on, and in turn contributing to the establishment of a feeling role of indignation. This makes it easy for right-wing anti-globalization actors to capitalize on a generalized understanding that indignation is an authentic and emancipatory reaction to an unjust world order. However, it makes a huge difference what and who is presented as a cause of indignation.

Effects

Besides the adequacy and authenticity of mobilizations of indignation, another criterion is on offer: The effect of the emotional experience of indignation. This is especially relevant when it comes to assessing indignation as a *mode* of action because this is where its effects both on the person experiencing it and on the outside world are most palpable.

One critique of indignation as a mode of political action is mentioned by the protagonists themselves, namely the possibility of it having no lasting effect at all for the political situation that caused it in the first place. Their response to this danger is the call to translate indignation into political projects. At the same time, some of the activists and authors also turn to the subjective effects of indignation. As can be seen from some of the quotations, they are aware of and celebrate the "liberating" effects of indignation on the experiencing subject but completely neglect the effects on the surrounding world. In the case of the neofascists of *Zetazeroalpha*, the suffering imposed on others is anticipated – "someone will cry now" – but it is not at all seen as a meaningful argument against violent action. In Hardt's and Negri's considerations on the meaning of what they call *Jacqueries*, they also do not take account of those against whom the discharge of indignation is directed.

While disregard for certain consequences of violent articulations of indignation may thus be found in both left-wing and right-wing activists and thinkers, there is a clear-cut difference with regard to who is the target of indignation: Right-wing, anti-immigrant and nationalist activists target alleged "enemies" of the self and associated groups, namely refugees, immigrants, the long-term unemployed, and political and cultural elites (Salmela and von Scheve 2017, 573). With progressive and left-wing activists, this is not the case. As noted above, it was suggested that one decisive factor in order to explain this difference is *repressed shame*: In a setting where economic failures and precariousness is individualized, real or anticipated shame for a loss of status is repressed and directed against minorities and elites.

This interpretation of what is invoked as indignation but is actually a transmuted expression of shame (as well as powerlessness and fear) also has important implications for an understanding of the subjective effects of the respective emotions. As pointed out by Salmela and von Scheve, the expressions of anger in the form of right-wing populism do not offer their adherents an "escape from shame" (2017, 586). Since the root causes for this complex emotional disposition are to be found in the combination of economic insecurity and an individualized interpretation of loss of status as personal failure, the threat of shame "either as present reality, or as an anticipated future scenario" (Salmela and von Scheve 2017, 586) will not be alleviated.

Another aspect of the subjective effect is suggested by philosophical anthropologist Max Scheler, who elaborated on Nietzsche's notion of resentment as born out of a feeling of powerlessness. According to Scheler, resentment is the result of a repression of primary emotions such as "revenge, hatred, malice, envy the impulse to detract, and spite" (Scheler 1998 [1915], 4), which cannot be lived out because the subject experiencing them feels powerless. As pointed out by Scheler, the French word *ressentiment* already indicates that the respective emotion is characterized by reiterated and perpetuated negative feelings, which never lead to action but rather to a "self-poisoning of the mind" (Scheler 1998 [1915], 4; Pulcini 2013). Such inhibiting consequences can be detected in the context of anti-immigrant movements. For example, in the case of Pegida, sociologist Hartmut Rosa diagnosed desperate attempts to "keep the world at bay" (Rosa 2016, 292). Instead of opening up to the world and welcoming the newly arrived refugees, anti-immigration activists like the ones from Pegida choose to withdraw into a fetishized community and try to isolate it against anything coming from outside, an attempt which is doomed to fail. They therefore also deprive themselves of new opportunities for encounters, exchange and personal growth (Heins and Unrau 2020).

Against this background, it is plausible to suggest that beyond the objective effects of certain forms of indignation, which can be criticized on the basis of ethical criteria, subjective effects of political indignation can be criticized as well. However, focusing on the subjective effects of indignation as a mode of action does not amount to assuming *pleasurable* political emotions indicate normative desirability. In fact, it is important to keep in mind that also indignation which is in line with emancipatory goals is not immune to becoming complacent or self-centered, reduced to "comfortable and fulfilling outrage which ultimately leaves untouched both subject and injustice alike" (Head 2020, 347).

6.   Concluding Remarks

This chapter started out from the observation that extremely different groups of activists and intellectuals recur to indignation in the context of globalization. In order to have a better grasp on these narrative and argumentative mobilizations of indignation, it gave an overview of these occurrences, which showed that in both progressive alter-globalization and far right anti-globalist activists and thinkers, indignation is referred to as a motivation for political action, as a mode and as a goal. The narrative analysis of these references to indignation showed that authors often presented themselves as exemplary "experiencers" when narrating their own personal or vicarious experiences of indignation. At the same time, they inscribed accounts of indignation into certain ideational traditions and historical directionalities, thereby nobilitating their own and others' experience of indignation. Through these narrative techniques, the respective texts, be they short manifestos or more elaborate philosophical considerations, unfold their own performativity. It includes an exhortation to not only take indignation as a serious signal of current pathologies of world order, but also as an appeal to the audience to allow for and cultivate these emotions.

The subsequent discussion examined three potential criteria for a critical evaluation of appeals to the emotion of indignation, namely adequacy, authenticity and effects. The questions of adequacy and authenticity turned out to be most relevant for assessing the mobilization of indignation as a motivation and a goal for action. The issue of subjective and objective effects, in turn, is most important for an evaluation of the role of indignation as a mode of action.

When looking at the three potential criteria for the assessment of claims to indignation, certain ambiguities and draw-backs come into view. Assessing *adequacy* might entail claiming an epistemically superior position and dismissing subjective experiences of indignation, which could amount to domination or discrimination. A validation based on the *authenticity* or alleged lack thereof in a given articulation of indignation might run the risk of exaggerated expectations of purity vis-à-vis emotional experiences which neglect the pivotal role of "feeling rules". The evaluation of the effect of invocations of indignation is certainly relevant but it can be regarded to move away from the actual focus on experience and its articulation.

Focusing on these ambiguities, however, does not mean that emotions and their narrative articulation cannot be critically assessed. Rather, they might point towards the relevance of an overarching criterion, namely *reflexivity*. Asking about the reflexivity of an invocation of indignation amounts to asking in how far the respective recourse to indignation already contains the possibility of critical introspection and – possibly – revision. Such a critical introspection might focus on the above-mentioned criteria of adequacy, authenticity and effects, or it might go beyond it. If the mental capacity in which such a reflexivity is grounded has to be identified as reason is an open question. In fact, there have been interesting discussions of "emotional reflexivity" (Flam 2010).

Thus, the mere invocation of indignation is neither reactionary nor progressive, neither emancipatory nor oppressive. A critical assessment of the recourse to indignation may reveal crucial differences regarding the mode and background of such an invocation. So even if the overview of narratives of indignation in alter- and anti-globalist thinkers exposed some structural similarities, the preliminary critical evaluation of different modes of narrative mobilizations of indignation points towards their differentiation.

The omnipresence of indignation in both alter- and anti-globalist storytelling attests not only to the emergence of a generalized feeling rule of rage and indignation. It also illustrates how far right anti-globalist actors and intellectuals appropriate and *re-semanticize* emotions and feeling rules that are generally associated with left wing politics (Freistein et al. 2022). This might also be one factor that contributes to its appeal. In other words, whenever there are calls for the "indignants of the world" to unite in the name of their indignation, questions of adequacy, authenticity and effect, as well as reflexivity, could be entry points for critique. If the indignants have *a world to win*, it is worth asking what kind of world this would be.

Works Cited

Abrahamsen, Rita, Jean-François Drolet, Alexandra Gheciu, Karin Narita, SrdjanVucetic and Michael Williams (2020) Confronting the International Political Sociology of the New Right. *International Political Sociology* 14(1), 94–107.

Antentas, Josp Maria (2015) Spain: The Indignados Rebellion of 2011 in Perspective. *Labor History* 56(2), 136–160.

Appadurai, Arjun (1996) *Modernity at Large: Cultural Dimensions of Globalization*. Minneapolis: University of Minnesota Press.

Arendt, Hannah (1963): *On revolution*. New York: Viking.

Aristotle (2020) *The Art of Rhetoric*. With an English translation by J.H. Freese, revised by Gisela Striker. Cambridge: Harvard University Press.

Bauman, Zygmunt (2000) *Globalization*. Cambridge: Polity Press.

Bauman, Zygmunt (2001) *The Individualized Society*. Cambridge: Polity Press.

Beck, Ulrich (1997) *Was ist Globalisierung? Irrtümer des Globalismus – Antworten auf Globalisierung*. Frankfurt am Main: Suhrkamp.

Bender, Justus and Reinhard Bingener (2016). Der Parteiphilosoph der AfD. *Frankfurter Allgemeine Zeitung* (15 January). Web: http://www.fa z.net/aktuell/politik/inland/marc-jongen-ist-afd-politiker-und-ph ilosoph-14005731.html#void.

Berlin, Isaiah (1978 [1961] Does Political Theory Still Exist? In: *Concepts and Categories. Selected Writings: Philosophical Essays*, ed. Henry Hardy, London: Hogarth, 143–172.

Boff, Leonardo (1993) *Ecologia, mundialização, espiritualidade. A emergência de um novo paradigma*. São Paulo : Ática.

Bourdieu, Pierre (1998) *Contre-feux. Propos pour servir à la résistance contre l'invasion néo-liberale*. Paris: Raisons d'agir.

Brecher, Jeremy, Tim Costello and Brendan Smith (2000) *Globalization from below: the power of solidarity*. Cambridge: South End Press.

Brighi, Elisabetta (2016) The Globalization of Resentment. Failure, Denial, and Violence in World Politics. *Millennium: Journal of International Studies* 44(3): 411–432.

Bringel, Breno and Geoffrey Pleyers (eds.) (2017) *Protesta e indignación global: Los movimientos sociales en el Nuevo orden mundial*. Buenos Aires / Rio de Janeiro : CLACSO & FAPERJ.

Bromell, Nick (2013) Democratic Indignation: Black American Thought and the Politics of Dignity. *Political Theory* 41(2), 285–311.

Campello, Filipe (2021) First- and Second-order Justice: Making Room for Affects in Social Critique. *Pragmatism Today* 12(1), 54–65.

Czarniawska, Barbara (2004) *Narratives in Social Science Research*. London: Sage.

della Porta, Donatella (2015): *Social Movements in Times of Austerity*. Cambridge: Polity Press.

della Porta, Donatella (ed.) (2007) *The Global Justice Movement. Cross-national and Transnational Perspectives*. Bolder and London: Paradigm.

Democracia Real Ya (2011) Manifiesto Democracia Real Ya. Web: http://www.democraciarealya.es/manifiesto-comun/.

Drolet, Jean-François and Michael C. Williams (2018) Radical conservatism and global order: International theory and the new right. *International Theory* 10(3), 285–313.

Drolet, Jean-François and Michael C. Williams (2022): From critique to reaction: The new right, critical theory and international relations. *Journal of International Political Theory* 18(1), 23–45.

EZLN (2005) Sexta Declaración de la Selva Lacandona. Web: http://enlac ezapatista.ezln.org.mx/sdsl-es/.

Flam, Helena (2010) Emotions, and the Silenced and Short-circuited Self. In: Archer, Margaret S. (ed.) *Conversations about Reflexivit*. Abingdon/New York: Routledge, 187–205.

Flecker, Jörg, Gudrun Hetges and Gabrielle Balazs (2007) Potentials of Political Subjectivity and the Various Approaches to the Extreme Right. Findings of the Qualitative Research. In: Jörg Flecker (ed.) *Changing Working Life and the Appeal of the Extreme Right*. Aldershot: Ashgate, 35–62.

Freistein, Katja and Frank Gadinger (2019) Populist Stories of Honest Men and Proud Mothers: A Visual Narrative Analysis of Right-Wing Populism. *Review of International Studies* 46(2), 217–236.

Freistein, Katja, Frank Gadinger, Frank and Christine Unrau (2022). It Just Feels Right. Visuality and Emotion Norms in Right-Wing Populist Storytelling, *International Political Sociology* 16 (4): 1–23.

Giddens, Anthony (1994) *Beyond Left and Right: The Future of Radical Politics*. Stanford: Stanford University Press.

Goodwin, Jeff, James E. Jasper and Francesca Polletta (2001) *Passionate Politics. Emotions and Social Movements*. Chicago: University of Chicago Press.

Griffin, Roger (2017) Interregnum or Endgame? The Radical Right in the 'Post-Fascist' Era. In: Mudde, Cas (ed.) *The Populist Radical Right. A Reader*. Abingdon: Routledge, 15–27.

Hardt, Michael and Antonio Negri (2009) *Commonwealth*. Cambridge (MA): The Belknap Press of Harvard University Press.

Head, Naomi (2020) Sentimental Politics or Structural Injustice? The Ambivalence of Emotions for Political Responsibility. *International Theory* 12, 337–357.

Heins, Volker and Christine Unrau (2020) Anti-immigrant movements and the self-poisoning of the civil sphere: The case of Germany. In: Alexander, Jeffrey C., Trevor Stack and Farhad Khosrokhavar (eds.) *Breaching the Civil Order: Radicalism and the Civil Sphere.* Cambridge: Cambridge University Press, 145–169.

Held, David and Anthony G. McGrew (2007) *Globalization/anti-globalization: Beyond the Great Divide.* Cambridge et al.: Polity Press.

Hessel, Stephane (2011) *Indignez-Vous. Get Angry! Cry Out.* English translation. Web: http://indignez-vous-indignacion.blogspot.com/p/english.html.

Hochschild, Arlie Russel (1979) Emotion Work, Feeling Rules, and Social Structure. *American Journal of Sociology* 85(3), 551–575.

Hoggett, Paul and Simon Thompson (2002): Toward a Democracy of the Emotions. *Constellations* 9(1), 106–126.

Homolar, Alexandra and Georg Löfflmann (2021) Populism and the Affective Politics of Humiliation Narratives. *Global Studies Quarterly* 1(1), 1–11.

Honneth, Axel (1992) Integrity and Disrespect: Principles of a Conception of Morality Based on the Theory of Recognition. *Political Theory* 20(2), 187–201.

Iser, Mattias (2008) *Empörung und Fortschritt. Grundlagen einer kritischen Theorie der Gesellschaft.* Frankfurt a. M.: Campus.

Jasper, James M. (2014) Constructing Indignation: Anger Dynamics in Protest Movements. *Emotion Review* 6(3), 208–213.

Jeffery, Renée (2011) Reason, Emotion, and the Problem of World Poverty: Moral Sentiment Theory and International Ethics. *International Theory* 3(1), 143–178.

Kanal Schnellroda (2017) Migration und Thymostraining – Dr. Marc Jongen beim IfS. Web: https://www.youtube.com/watch?v=cg_KuESI7rY.

Kubitschek, Götz (2016) Hygienefimmel und Thymos-Regulierung. *Sezession* 14(70), 10–13.

Kurbjuweit, Dirk (2010) Der Wutbürger. Stuttgart 21 und Sarrazin-Debatte: Warum die Deutschen so viel protestieren, *Der Spiegel* 41/2010, 26–27.

Lorde, Audre (1981) The Uses of Anger. *Women's Studies Quarterly*. 25 (1/2), 278–285.

Machiavelli, Niccolò (1996 [1531]) *Discorsi sopra la prima deca di Tito Livio*. Milan: Rizzoli.

Mayer, Frederick W. (2014) *Narrative Politics: Stories and Collective Action*. Oxford: Oxford University Press.

Míguez, Néstor, Jörg Rieger and Jung Mo Sung (2009) *Beyond the Spirit of Empire. Theology and Politics in a New Key*. London: SCM Press.

Nussbaum, Martha (2013) *Political Emotions. Why Love Matters for Justice*. Cambridge (MA) and London: The Belknap Press of Harvard University Press.

Orellana, Pablo de and Nicholas Michelsen (2019) Reactionary Internationals: The Philosophy of the New Right. *Review of International Studies* 45(5), 748–767.

Paulwitz, Michael (2015) Sie stellen die Systemfrage: Zur Phänomenologie des neuen Wutbürgers, *Junge Freiheit*. Web: https://phinau.de/jf-archiv/online-archiv/file.asp?Folder=15&File=201502010248.htm&STR1=pegida&STR2=&STR3=&STR4.

Pleyers, Geoffrey (2010) *Alter-Globalization: Becoming Actors in a Global Age*. Cambridge/Malden: Polity.

Pulcini, Elena (2013) Paura, risentimento, indignazione. Passioni e patologie dell'età globale. In: Cerulo, Massimo and Franco Crespi (eds.). *Emozioni e ragione nelle pratiche sociali*. Naples : Orthotes, 177–194.

Reuters (2017) Le Pen pose en porte-parole de la 'colère' face aux 'puissants'. *Reuters* (4 May). Web: https://www.reuters.com/article/franc e-presidentielle-le-pen-meeting-idFRKBN1802KI-OFRTP.

Rosa, Hartmut (2016) Der Versuch einer sklerotischen Gesellschaft, sich die Welt vom Leibe zu halten – und ein Vorschlag für einen Neuanfang. In: Rehberg, Karl-Siegbert, Franziska Kunz and Tino Schlinzig (eds.) *Rechtspopulismus zwischen Fremdenangst und "Wende" – Enttäuschung?: Analysen im Überblick*. Ed. Bielefeld: transcript, 289–296.

Roth, Gerhard (2003) *Fühlen, Denken, Handeln. Wie das Gehirn unser Verhalten steuert*. Frankfurt am Main: Suhrkamp.

Salmela Mikko and Christian von Scheve (2017) Emotional Roots of Right-wing Political Populism. *Social Science Information* 56(4), 567–595.

Scheff, Thomas J. (1994) *Bloody Revenge. Emotions, Nationalism, and War.* Lincoln: Authors Guild.

Scheler, Max (1998 [1915]) *Ressentiment (Das Ressentiment im Aufbau der Moralen).* Translated by Louis A. Coser. Milwaukie: Marquette University Press.

Schieder, Rolf (2020) The Political Theology of the New Right in Germany. In: *Religion and Neo-Nationalism in Europe.* Ed. Florian Höhne and Thorsten Meireis. Baden-Baden: Nomos.

Scholte, Jan Aart (2005) *Globalization. A Critical Introduction,* Basingstoke et al.: Palgrave.

Sen, Amatya (2009) *The Idea of Justice.* London: Penguin.

Shenhav, Shaul R (2015) *Analyzing Social Narratives.* New York: Routledge.

Shklar, Judith (1990) *Faces of Injustice.* New Haven (CT) and London: Yale University Press.

Sloterdijk, Peter (2006) *Zorn und Zeit. Politisch-psychologischer Versuch.* Frankfurt am Main: Suhrkamp.

Sloterdijk, Peter (2010) *Rage and Time. A psychopolitical investigation.* Translated by Mario Wenning. New York: Columbia University Press.

Sloterdijk, Peter (2015) Letzte Ausfahrt Empörung. Web: https://peter sloterdijk.net/2015/04/letzte-ausfahrt-empoerung/. (previously published under the title "Über die Ausschaltung der Bürger in Demokratien." *Der Spiegel* (8 November).

Sloterdijk, Peter (2016) Sloterdijk warnt vor "Überrollung". Philosoph attackiert Merkel und Flüchtlinge. *Cicero,* 29 January 2016.

Spinoza, Benedictus de (1994 [1677]) *Tractatus Politicus/Politischer Traktat.* Latin/German. Translated by Wolfgang Bartuschat, Hamburg: Meiner.

Sung, Jung Mo (2005) The Human Being as Subject. Defending the Victims. In: *Latin American Liberation Theology. The Next Generation.* Ed. Ivan Petrella, Maryknoll/New York: Orbis.

Taylor, Charles (1985) *Human agency and language. Philosophical papers.* Cambridge: Cambridge University Press.

Thoits, Peggy T. (2004) Emotion Norms, Emotion Work, and Social Order. In: *Feelings and Emotions. The Amsterdam Symposium.* Cambridge: Cambridge University Press, 359–378.

Turner, Jonathan (2007) Self, Emotions, and Extreme Violence: Extending Symbolic Interactionist Theorizing. *Symbolic Interaction* 30, 501–530.

Unrau, Christine (2018) *Erfahrung und Engagement: Motive, Formen und Ziele der Globalisierungskritik.* Bielefeld: transcript.

von Scheve, Christian (2009) *Emotionen und soziale Strukturen. Die affektiven Grundlagen sozialer Ordnung.* Frankfurt am Main/New York: Campus.

Vorländer, Hans, Maik Herold und Steven Schäller (2017) *PEGIDA and New Right-Wing Populism in Germany.* Basingstoke: Palgrave.

Wacquant, Loïc (2010) Crafting the Neoliberal state: Workfare, Prisonfare, and Social Insecurity. *Sociological Forum* 25, 197–220.

Walzer, Michael (2002) Passion and Politics. *Philosophy and Social Criticism* 28(6), 617–633.

Wodak, Ruth (2015) *The Politics of Fear. What Right-Wing Discourses Mean.* London: Sage.

Zetazeroalfa (2010a) Accademia della Sassaiola. Album: Disperato Amore. Web: https://zetazeroalfa.org/accademia-della-sassaiola/.

Zetazeroalfa (2010b) Mai come voi. Album: Italians do it better. Web: https://zetazeroalfa.org/mai-come-voi/.

Right-Wing Extremism and Ecology
Denial and Appropriation of the Climate Crisis by the Far Right

Daniela Gottschlich

Introduction[1]

The current mode of production and living standard causes existential ecological destruction. The current level of CO_2 emissions and release of synthetic substances set the stability of the Earth system at fundamental risk. Therefore, people all over the world are demanding political solution strategies for the serious environmental problems, especially for the climate crisis. The consequences of global warming such as droughts and extreme weather events are aggravating existing crises such as chronic and acute food and water shortages, species extinction, and climate-induced migration (IPCC 2007, 2021). People in the Global South bear the brunt of the climate crisis. The Movement for Climate Justice and Fridays for Future therefore call for a systems change instead of climate change (e.g., People's Demands for Climate Justice 2018; Thunberg 2018; Fridays for Future 2022). It is primarily young people who are taking to the streets and raising their voices against climate policies around the world that have been inadequate to date. Environmental issues are more politicized than they have been in a long time and

1   I sincerely thank Gesa Mackenthun for her valuable comments and Michelle Geiter for her help in preparing the English version of the text and in compiling the bibliography.

are receiving increasing social attention (Klein 2015; Almeida 2019). At the same time, the extreme right has grown in recent years. Authoritarian regimes, far-right networks, groups, and parties are gaining popularity worldwide (e.g., Rydgren 2008; Norris/Inglehart 2019). Antidemocratic positions are shared by an increasing number of people. While violent right-wing actors incite aggressiveness, intimidate antagonists, and commit murders, right-wing intellectuals are trying to take root in civil society. Positions, demands, and rhetorical strategies of the extreme right are partly adopted by other parties and thus move into the center of society – also in Germany (Zick, Küpper and Berghan 2019).

In my paper, I address the intersections of these developments. The paper was written in the context of the research project *"Rechte Landnahme (ReLa)"*, which was funded by the German Federal Environment Agency from July 2019 and carried out by the Institute for Diversity, Nature, Gender and Sustainability (diversu e.V.).[2] The starting point for the research project was the realization that ecological issues are increasingly taken up by the extreme right in times of social polarization. This happens in two ways: On the one hand, right-wing actors deny manmade climate change. On the other hand, environmental issues are used to spread *völkisch* (racial-nationalist) ideas. There now exist hardly any environmental and nature conservation issues that are not also occupied by anti-democratic forces. In particular, the climate crisis is being used to advance a *völkisch* project of protecting an imagined "white race" from the effects of that very crisis (Strobl 2022, 7). In my paper I will show that

---

2   Together with Christine Katz and Wiebke Schwandt, I investigated what experiences representatives of environmental and nature conservation associations have had so far with the exertion of influence by right-wing actors and how the associations have reacted to it so far. For this purpose, we conducted an online survey among the member associations of the Deutscher Naturschutzring DNR e.V. The results of this survey (Gottschlich, Katz & Schwandt 2020) as well as the strategy paper (Gottschlich & Katz 2020), which was prepared together with representatives from the environmental sector, are available at https://www.diversu.org/. In addition, we have prepared a handout "Right-wing populism/right-wing extremism and ecology" (diversu & FARN 2020), which also forms the background of my paper.

neo-Malthusian narratives ("There are too many people on the planet," "Fewer people – less ecological destruction") not only play into the hands of the ecofascist[3] project but can also be found at the center of the environmental movement. However, to effectively combat right-wing extremist ideologies in nature conservation and environmental protection, it is necessary to learn to identify what distinguishes emancipatory environmental protection from right-wing extremist environmental protection. A precise analysis is needed. This is because the underlying antidemocratic, inhuman and *völkisch* positions are not always visible at first glance.

1. Simultaneous Developments: Denial and Appropriation of the Climate Crisis Denial

The scientific and political preoccupation with climate change is described by a part of the extreme right as mere hysteria or as a big lie.[4] Accordingly, counterstrategies are not considered necessary. Even more: for climate deniers there is no reason to deal with the prevailing crisis-causing economic system in which a few live at the expense of nature, future generations, and most people in the Global South (Brand/Wissen 2017). Climate deniers, on the contrary, have an interest in keeping things the way they are. The following examples show that climate deniers defend their privileges through, first, policies of denial, banalization and relativization of the climate crisis; second, disparagement of climate justice activists; and third, exclusion and seclusion towards people who flee, not least due to the consequences of climate change.

---

3   I use the term ecofascism in reference to Sam Moore and Alex Roberts (2022).

4   Representative of this position is Fred Singer, who died in 2020. In 2007, Singer was involved in the founding of the Nongovernmental International Panel on Climate Change (NIPCC) – a climate skeptic response to the Intergovernmental Panel on Climate Change (IPCC). The AfD-affiliated association EIKE has published many of his works in German.

adelphi, an independent think-and-do tank on climate, environment, and development, studied the attitudes toward climate and energy policy of twenty-one right-wing populist/ extreme right-wing European parties (Schaller/Carius 2019). Election programs, statements and voting behavior were analyzed. The results show that in the European Parliament, half of all votes against resolutions on climate and energy come from the right-wing populist party spectrum. Two out of three right-wing populist members of parliament regularly vote against climate and energy policy measures. Climate protection is presented by right-wing populist parties as an elite project to be fought. Seven of twenty-one right-wing populist parties explicitly deny climate change, its man-made causes, and devastating consequences. These include the Dutch PVV of Geert Wilders or the FPÖ from Austria (Schaller/Carius 2019, 11). In Germany, the strategy of climate change denial is primarily advocated by the Alternative for Germany (AfD) and by actors close to them in the far right scene.

For an example, I will discuss below statements made by the environmental policy spokesman of the AfD parliamentary group Karsten Hilse,[5] which were examined by Konstantin Kopfmüller (2019). During a parliamentary debate on the federal government's climate protection program on September 26, 2019, Hilse first intervened with the following comment: "Climate change is a natural phenomenon. Humans with their CO_2 emissions do not contribute significantly to this climate change" (Hilse 2019, qt. Kopfmüller 2019, n.p.). In this way, the AfD politician ignores generally accepted scientific facts. To "prove" the thesis that there is no man-made climate change, Hilse in a second step presents the position of man-made climate change as controversial – which it is not in climate research. In his speech, Hilse cites, among other things, a letter to UN Secretary General António Guterres entitled "There is no climate emergency." This letter is said to have been signed by more than 500 scientists, contradicting the thesis of man-made climate change (Kopfmüller 2019).

---

5   Hilse is also a member of the Committee on the Environment, Nature Conservation and Nuclear Safety.

This letter does exist (Berkhout et al. 2019), but it does not deny the human influence on climate change. The signatories argue that science should be less political; climate policy, on the other hand, should be more science-based. Uncertainties and exaggerations in climate change predictions should be clearly stated. The strategy Hilse uses here is to twist statements by others in such a way that they supposedly support the AfD position (in this case, denial of man-made climate change). Usually, scientific studies are quoted selectively; or they are taken out of context; or correct and deliberately false statements are mixed.

Another example of such a mixture of correct and incorrect statements, which serves the purpose of denying or relativizing the human contribution to global warming, is also provided by the first basic program adopted by the AfD at its party conference in Stuttgart in spring 2016. The journalistic project klimafakten.de, which aims to contribute to a scientifically based debate on climate issues, fact-checked the AfD's program – based on the IPCC's publications. The authors of klimafakten.de conclude that the AfD's basic program contains almost no statement that is compatible with the state of research on climate and climate change. Instead, there are a considerable number of blatantly false and misleading statements.

One example: In chapter twelve on energy policy, the AfD's "climate protection policy" is presented on one page. It also contains the following paragraph: "In the 20th century, the global mean temperature rose by about 0.8 degrees. Since the end of the 1990s, however, there has been no further increase, in contradiction to IPCC forecasts, although CO_2 emissions have risen more than ever during this period" (AfD basic program, 2016, 79). Referring to the above quote, the authors of klimafakten.de conclude that only the first sentence correctly reflects the state of science: Between 1880 and 2012, the global mean temperature actually rose by about 0.85 °C, according to the IPCC report. However,

the claim that the earth has not warmed further since the 1990s is false. It is only true that after 1998 there was a phase during which air temperatures apparently rose more slowly. However, this is easily explained by natural fluctuations in the climate system. (Incidentally, in the oceans, which absorb much greater amounts of heat than the atmosphere, the temperature rise continued unabated.)

The years 2014 and 2015 then also brought new record values for globally averaged atmospheric temperatures. Therefore, there can be no talk of the warming having ended; at most, one could say that short-term, natural fluctuations have overlaid and at times obscured the long-term upward trend that continues to be observed. (klimafakten.de, n.d., n.p.; my translation)

The AfD sometimes also bases its own statements on the pseudo-scientific statements of the Jena-based association "EIKE – Europäisches Institut für Klima und Energie," which seeks to sow doubt about man-made climate change. Contrary to its name, EIKE is not a scientific institute, but a climate-denialist lobby association based in Jena. Its motto is: "It is not the climate that is threatened, but our freedom!" (ht tps://eike-klima-energie.eu). EIKE exists mainly as a website on which false reports can be found such as the claim that "worldwide weather services do not find trends towards more extreme weather" (https://eike -klima-energie.eu/die-mission/grundsatzpapier-klima/). From time to time the association organizes conferences with representatives of the American "Heartland Institute". One of its best-known representatives is the already mentioned climate denier Fred Singer, who died in 2020. The US-American institute was and is paid by the oil industry to carry out campaigns against the work of the Intergovernmental Panel on Climate Change. There can be no question of an ideology-free presentation of EIKE's energy and climate policy.[6]

---

6   See also https://www.klimaretter.info/forschung/hintergrund/10591-die-finan zierung-der-zweifel-am-klimawandel

2.   New Alliances: Climate Deniers and Opponents of Corona Measures

With the appearance of the COVID-19 pandemic in 2020, EIKE also began to spread doubt about the danger of the virus (Götze and Joeres 2021). Among the "freedom fighters" at so-called hygiene demos of the *Querdenker* movement, protesting the government's Covid measures, are vaccination opponents, but also right-wing extremists and climate deniers (Speit 2021). The common narrative of climate deniers and Covid skeptics is that "government regulation interferes with personal freedom" (Götze and Joeres 2021, 135). In addition to their aversion to state intervention, climate deniers and Covid skeptics are also united by a skepticism toward established science. In a remarkable study, Susanne Götze and Annika Joeres have demonstrated that many well-known climate deniers also raise their voices in social media or at demonstrations against the restrictive Covid measures – for example, the aforementioned Karsten Hilse:

> In the Bundestag, shortly after the attempted "attack" on the Reichs-stag building by "Querdenken" activists in the summer of 2020, he [Hilse] gives a speech – wearing a T-shirt of the movement. Publicly, he is taken away at an anti-Corona demonstration. Later, the Berlin police even investigated him on suspicion of a forged certificate that was supposed to exempt him from the mask requirement. (Götze and Joeres 2021, 138; my translation)

Another example of the intersection of climate and Covid denial is Heart-land Institute President James Taylor's claim that the computer models on Covid-19 were as wrong as those of the Intergovernmental Panel on Climate Change on global warming (Götze and Joeres 2021, 140).

Götze and Joeres identify yet another group that is decisively active in the scene of *Querdenker*: market-radical finance scientists who are both critical of Covid measures and hold inhumane positions regarding climate policy. For example, they cite Werner Müller, professor of ac-counting and controlling at Mainz University of Applied Sciences, who in spring 2020 coordinated a letter entitled "The damage of a therapy must not be greater than the damage of the disease," which served the AfD in the Bundestag as a template for a request to the federal government on the Covid measures. On his website, he had also referred to government politicians as "cattle" driven before the Covid crisis. Müller is also the author of a racist text on climate policy, in which he considers the return to colonialism to be suitable to better implement "German climate goals" in other parts of the world (qt. Götze and Joeres 2021, 138).

3. Climate Denial and Group-Based Misanthropy

The extreme right's reporting on climate-related issues is often accompanied by group-based misanthropy (FARN 2019). The concept of group-based misanthropy describes derogatory and exclusionary attitudes toward people based on their origin, sexuality, religion, or gender. This misanthropic attitude can be found, for example, in new-right magazines such as COMPACT,[7] which since 2015 has presented itself as the mouthpiece of the AfD and the islamophobic Pegida movement. The November 2019 issue of COMPACT is dedicated to the supposed climate delusion and the authors agitate against the Fridays for Future movement, against politicians of the Green party, migrants, and climate scientists. Repeatedly, especially the young well-known women of the climate justice movement like Greta Thunberg and Luisa Neubauer are exposed to sexist and insulting comments (Hoppenstedt 2020). In Facebook groups like "Fridays for Hubraum" privileged white men live out their murder and abuse fantasies against young female climate activists with impunity. In posts concerning the autistic Greta Thunberg, misogyny is paired with ableism. Matthias N. posted: "They put too many pills in the children's cereal," to which Stef I. replied: "As if she would come up with such a number on her own in her stupid autistic head. She belongs in psychiatric ward and locked away, the CO_2 bitch" (screenshot of Nicolaisen 2020). In addition, stickers are circulating on right-wing

---

7   COMPACT is published monthly. The editor-in-chief is Jürgen Elsässer.

websites showing Greta Thunberg being killed by a car. There is a call to place these stickers directly above the exhaust pipe. And on the Facebook page, Milan H. asks: "How much does a contract killing cost?" to which Maik W. responds: "We can put that together as a group, then it will be enough for the whole parliament" (screenshot of Nicolaisen 2020).

While the disregard for democracy and human rights is found among the actors of the extreme right who deny climate change and ecological limits, construct climate policy as a threat to freedom, and want to maintain the fossilistic system of capitalism, it also pervades the publications of those who, in the face of the climate crisis, now argue that existing security systems should be geared toward controlling the problems resulting from environmental degradation (for U.S. policy, see Moore and Roberts 2022, 65ff.). A solidarity-based management of the climate crisis is not envisaged by the extreme right. As a strategy, far-right ecologism pursues, among other things, a racialization of ecological problems: it is the "others" who are to blame for the crisis, an argument to be found in the demagogic discourse on population growth.

4.   Appropriation of the Climate Crisis

Already at the end of the 1990s, Oliver Geden (1999) warned against right-wing ecology and pointed out that it is often overlooked that a section of scientific ecology and the precursors of today's environmental movement have been historically entangled with a political strand that must be classified as right-wing. It may come as a surprise to many democratic, more left-wing nature conservationists and environmentalists that there is a connection between nature conservation and National Socialism, that antisemitic and *völkisch* ideologies have been used to enforce nature conservation goals, that racist continuities can be found in nature conservation and environmental protection, and that right-wing extremist actors are active against species extinction and for landscape and animal protection.

At present, there are hardly any environmental and nature conservation issues that are not also nominally occupied by anti-democratic forces. Right-wing extremists protest for example against genetic engineering, practice organic farming, are interested in sustainable energy and mobility concepts, vegan nutrition and demand regional economic cycles. To investigate the historical and current linkages of German nature conservation and environmental protection with extreme right-wing and current *völkisch* movements, the Fachstelle Radikalisierungsprävention und Engagement im Naturschutz – FARN for short – was founded in October 2017 by NaturFreunde Deutschlands and Naturfreundejugend Deutschlands.

Nature conservation as a discourse and field of action, then, is not being newly discovered by right-wing agitators but is rather being rediscovered by them. Right-wing extremist actors refer to the beginnings of nature conservation, which go back to the time of German Romanticism and have democratic as well as authoritarian-*völkisch* lines of tradition (Heinrich, Kaiser and Wiersbinski 2015, 7). In addition, environmental and nature conservation issues are interesting for right-wing groups because they promise an image gain. With them, right-wing extremist actors can gain sympathy and appear to be able to connect with important societal matters. Strategically, right-wing actors use nature and environmental protection issues to bring their racist and *völkisch* ideologies to the center of society. Through concrete engagement in local nature conservation initiatives and protest campaigns, right-wing actors can approach potential electoral groups through joint action.

Finally, *völkisch* settlers and right-wing ecologists "also want to practically live their *völkisch*-nationalist worldview with their families, educate their children in nature and in their spirit, reawaken customs and folklore, and often practice natural religiosity" (Röpke and Speit 2019, 7). Neo-Nazis in Wendland, for example, not only breed old animal breeds, but are also convinced that there are also human races, each of which is assigned to a specific habitat. For adherents of this ethnopluralist "blood and soil" ideology, who assume an organic unity between a racially defined body with its settlement area, it seems to be a compelling thought "that a healthy people [*Volk*] also needs a healthy nature"

(Melchert, qt. Staud 2015, n.p.; my translation). Nature conservation is thus seen as an instrument for preserving "the biological substance of the people [*Volk*]"; the slogan "nature conservation is homeland security" stands for the fight against everything supposedly foreign and fits into central right-wing narratives such as the "great population exchange" or "ethnopluralism".[8] In other words, when the extreme right advocates nature conservation and environmental protection out of conviction, it always conveys an image of society and mankind that is racist, anti-feminist and saturated with *völkisch* ideas. This far-right ecologism has been defined by Sam Moore and Alex Roberts as the "production and maintenance of racially defined hierarchies in and through nature" (Moore and Roberts 2022, 178).

In the following section, I will show how the debate around the climate crisis in the topic area of population growth is permeated by positions of such far right ecologism.

5.   Population Growth and Climate Crisis

Currently, 8 billion people live on earth (DSW 2022). In 1999, the figure was still 6 billion. Thus, the world population is still growing. According to the latest studies (Vollset et al. 2020), the population will continue to grow until the middle of the century. In 2064, due to the forecast, it will probably peak at around 9.7 billion people in the world. Globally, the number will start to decline again from the middle of the century, falling to around 8.8 billion people by 2100. That would be about two billion people fewer than some earlier UN estimates had suggested. Nevertheless, the growth of the world population is considered a central crisis factor in the discourse about the carrying capacity of the earth – at least since the book *The Population Bomb* by Paul Ehrlich (1968) and the report of the Club of Rome (Meadows et al. 1972) on the *Limits to Growth* famously made this argument. The scenarios of imminent collapse outlined therein are based on the thesis that, without population control, the population is

---

8   See the essay by Enrico Schlickeisen in this volume.

growing too fast or even exponentially and thus exceeding the limit of the carrying capacity of the earth. This had already been claimed by the British theologian and national economist Thomas R. Malthus at the end of the eighteenth century regarding the limits of food production. In his *An Essay on The Principle of Population*, published in 1798, Malthus argued that the fundamental scarcity of nature conflicted with a growing human population. He assumed that people reproduce in geometric series (1, 2, 4, 8, 16, …), while food could only be increased in arithmetic series (1, 2, 3, 4, 5 …). This would lead to a growing disparity between food supply and demand. Malthus used this "population law" to justify poverty, disease, slums, and the resulting social unrest in the major English cities of his time. To avert the imminent catastrophe of overpopulation, he recommended, among other things, sexual abstinence, late marriage, investment in education and the abolition of state welfare for the poor. Because of their "predisposed libidinousness", the poor were themselves to blame if they reproduce beyond their means. Wars, epidemics, famines, to which the poorest of the poor fall victim because they are unable to take care of themselves, would help regulate the population. "Referring to Malthus' thought", Moore and Roberts write,

> some argued against aid measures for the population of colonial Ireland during the Great Famine (1845–1852). Nassau William Senior, a contemporary Oxford economist, opposed government famine relief on the grounds that the root cause of the famine was an overly large rural population that the soil simply could not feed. The only solution, therefore, was a sharp drop in population and birth rates – which is what the famine eventually led to. (Moore and Roberts 2022, 34)

In the current debate about the deteriorating climate crisis, neo-Malthusian arguments are increasingly reinterated: population growth is blamed for climate change (see, e.g., Ripple et al. 2017). Anti-natalist measures are demanded to lower the birth rate of the poor so that it is lower than the death rate thus leading to population decrease. One of the arguments put forth is that savings in CO_2 emission can be achieved more cost-effectively by investing in family planning than by promoting renewable technologies (e.g., Müller-Jung 2018).[9]

6.   The Violence of Population Policy

Ignored in this debate about climate policy cost effectiveness is the fact that the history of population policy, especially anti-natalist policy, is full of examples of repressive measures; in the past fifty years critics have repeatedly pointed out the sexist, racist, and eugenic implications of anti-natalist population policy (e.g., Lindsay 1988; Wichterich 1988; Gottschlich 2000; Wilton 2013; Hartmann 2015; Murphy 2017). Examples can be found not only in China during the 35-year-long one-child policy, which relied on measures such as forced abortions up to the 7th and 8th month of pregnancy, forced adoptions abroad, sterilization, and fines, leading to infants abandoned out of desperation. Systematic forced sterilizations in India in the 1970s also became known. However, there were and are multiple other examples and a long history of forced sterilizations of Black, Indigenous, disabled, imprisoned or HIV-positive people in the Gobal North as well, as Susanne Schultz and I have pointed out elsewhere (Gottschlich and Schultz 2019). As recently as the late 1990s, a sterilization program in Peru sterilized about 300,000 people, the majority poor and indigenous women, within a few years. This often happened without their knowledge or consent. Some women were threatened that they would no longer receive food aid if they refused. Employees of the health system had to fulfill a certain number of sterilizations per month in order not to risk dismissal. Such quotas are typical of repressive population programs, as are "economic" incentive systems: in Bangladesh in the 1980s, women received boni for sterilizations that ensured the survival of the entire family for a few weeks. In

---

9   Joachim Müller-Jung refers to a study co-authored by John Bongaarts, a major representative of the U.S. population lobby. In it, the authors declare family planning to be one of the "most cost-effective" climate protection measures.

India, women in some regions still receive cash or non-cash boni if they undergo sterilization (Gottschlich and Schultz 2019).

7.   Entanglements of Climate Change and Population Growth Between Environmentalist and Far Right Discourses

In the discourse on sustainability in general and on the climate crisis in particular, feminist scholars have been warning for years against a revival of neo-Malthusian positions (see, for example, Gottschlich 2006; Hartmann and Barajas-Román 2009; Hendrixson and Hartmann 2018). The neo-Malthusian position that "population growth must be stopped" or that "a population decline is needed" and that "population policies are therefore necessary" can be found both among actors of the extreme right and in numerous scientific mainstream publications on the theme of sustainability, in positions of environmental associations, and among students of so-called green professions. This is what surveys and studies by diversu and FARN have shown. In the following section, I would like to discuss some of the results of this research in which I was involved and show that there are numerous interfaces in climate change policy for right-wing extremist strategies of appropriation.

Population growth is constructed in mainstream scientific discourse as one of the central environmental problems (see e.g. Ripple et al. 2017, 1026). It is claimed that it grew "uncontrolled" (Gesang 2014a, 13) like a "cancer cell" (Gesang 2014b, 19). We also find this construction among actors of the new right: for example, Felix Menzel[10] formulated the fol-

---

10   Journalist Felix Menzel is close to the far-right Institute for State Policy in Schnellroda, founded by Götz Kubitschek. He publishes in the Antaios Verlag, among others. He also founded the youth portal/magazine *Blaue Narzisse* in Chemnitz. *Blaue Narzisse* has been published since 2004 and has been supplemented by an Internet presence since 2006. The magazine is dedicated to youth topics as well as political content. According to its own statement, it takes a conservative stance. Political scientists regard *Blaue Narzisse* as belonging to the New Right.

lowing as the first of his seven theses for a conservative-ecological turn, published in the right-wing business magazine *Recherche Dresden*:

> Overpopulation is the mother of all environmental problems. The world population is heading for twelve billion people in the 22nd century. Against the gigantic increase in energy demand, renewable energies are therefore only a drop in the bucket. The ecosystem will hardly be able to cope with hundreds of millions of new meat eaters, hygiene product users, car drivers and smartphone owners. The world's population must therefore be stabilized at a lower level – otherwise there is a threat of irreversible eco-collapse (Menzel 2019, n.p.; my translation).

As a "solution" Menzel suggests linking German development aid to population reduction measures, especially in states that have "extreme youth surpluses" (Menzel 2019, n.p.; my translation). It is no coincidence that Menzel uses the term "overpopulation". Those who speak of "overpopulation" thereby claim that there are already too many people. But who are the supernumeraries at present? The speach of "overpopulation" pursues a purposeful *Othering*: it is the others who are redundant; it is the poor, the Black, the Indigenous, the migrant populations who are construed as "too many." However, the term "overpopulation" is also used in various contributions in the mainstream media. Representative here is the publication *Far too many people. How overpopulation could be slowed down* by the online news and knowledge portal Quarks.de directed especially at a young audience (Quarks.de 2021, n.p.). According to its own information, Quarks provides its readers and viewers with the "scientific classification, explanations and facts on current debates." The controversial and highly problematic thesis of "overpopulation" is presented as an indisputable fact. Even more: the term is constructed as "scientifically serious" by using it in the headline of an article of a widely circulated public science platform. Readers' comments below the article suggest active euthanasia, a one-child policy for the next thirty years, a reduction of child benefits, and a restriction of medical care – demanded also in the name of the environment. In the presence of such pervasive interfaces between environmentalist and demographic arguments, right-wing actors whose population policy follows a *völkisch* agenda have an easy time manipulating mainstream views.

The thesis that population growth is responsible for environmental problems is also reproduced to some extent in the environmental association scene und environmental movement (Gottschlich et al. 2020). It is shared by a majority of students of so-called "green professions", according to the results of a university survey conducted by the Fachstelle Radikalisierungsprävention und Engagement im Naturschutz (FARN 2022), in which 804 students across Germany participated from March to May 2021 and which was conducted in cooperation with the Institute for Diversity, Nature, Gender and Sustainability (diversu e.V.). The aim of the survey was to collect data on the current situation at universities concerning the historical and current linkages of German nature and environmental protection with nationalist, *völkisch* and racist currents in teaching, as well as students' knowledge of these topics. The evaluation of the survey shows that the crossovers between "nature conservation, environmental protection and right-wing extremism" have hardly been critically examined in university teaching to date. The vast majority of students support the democratic system, advocate the protection of minorities and reject authoritarian structures. Nevertheless, there is an openness to right-wing positions and models of thought in the surveyed group regarding their ecological stance. This applies not least to the issue of population policy. 55 percent of respondents agree with the statement that the causes of many environmental problems are to be seen in population development. In this context, almost one third of the students are in favor of anti-natalist measures in the Global South (FARN 2022). It can be assumed that most students are not aware of the neo-colonial thought patterns involved. Here, decolonial educational work is needed to make clear the consequences of a call for population policies. The call for population control policies in the Global South interferes with its inhabitants' rights for self-determination.

The fact that statements of the extreme right in the field of population policy cannot easily be distinguished from statements coming from the center of society or from the field of environmental protection has yet another effect. It leads to the fact that students who critically deal with population policy usually attribute racist statements to right-wing extremist actors – but not to actors from the environmental field. Asked to consider the political origins of the following quote, students in my seminars almost always assume that its author belongs to the far right:

> In view of the dramatic increase in population, we are faced with the dilemma that all nature conservation must inevitably end where the human avalanche overruns everything. [...] Only if this main concern of mankind, the stemming of the overpopulation flow, is ensured, will there be any meaningful prospect of building a thoroughly im-provable environment, of shaping our civilized landscapes so that they remain worthy of being called "home," of continuing to culti-vate our ancestral cultural values, and of surviving peacefully.

The astonishment is great when they learn that the sentences were writ-ten in 1964 by Helmut Weinzierl (1964/1993, quoted from Oliver Geden 1999, 228; my translation). Weinzierl was the federal chairman of the German section of Friends of the Earth (BUND) from 1983 to 1998. The fact that anti-humanist positions can also be found in nature conser-vation organizations baffles many of the younger environmentalists in particular, who associate environmental protection with emancipatory positions. Oliver Geden has examined Weinzierl's writings in detail and worked out the central importance that the assumed "population explosion" had for Weinzierl's view of the world and of nature (Geden 1999, 224ff.). Again and again, Weinzierl stirred up fears of people from the Global South with catastrophic images of "human avalanches" and of the "overpopulation current". Although Weinzierl is of the opinion that all world problems can be traced back to "overpopulation", he does not limit the problem to the Global South. Even Central Europe seems too densely populated to him as early as the mid-1980s, prompting him to ask, "Is nature conservation worthwhile here at all?" (Weinzierl 1985, 222; qt. Geden 1999, 227; my translation).

Right-wing extremists, on the other hand, apply double standards: on the one hand, they declare population growth in "emerging and developing countries" or in the Global South to be the biggest problem for environmental protection, warning of "refugee floods" and wanting to link "development aid" to strict population control policies. On the other hand, they demand for Germany "the consistent promotion of families with many children" in order to counteract the alleged "foreign infiltration" and to avert the "imminent death of the people." These voices, then, advocate anti-natalist measures for countries of the Global South and pro-natalist policies in Germany. Part of the AfD's pro-natalist policy, moreover, is decidedly against abortions in the domestic context but couples this campaign with anti-migration demands: election posters show pregnancy bellies with the slogan "New Germans? Let's do it ourselves!". On one of its latest posters, the AfD combines population policy demands with the rejection of anti-Covid measures in the form of slogans such as: "Lieber ohne Gummi als mit Maske. Yes to real family policy" (qt. Schäffer, 2021). Such racist and xenophobic statements are just as much part of ecofascist discourse as the obsession with "racial purity" as an indicator of an imagined "natural order" (Moore and Roberts 2022, 156).

Conclusion

Whereas man-made climate change was denied for years by large parts of the far right, the far right now also racializes the climate crisis and its effects by constructing population growth as the main cause of the global environmental problem. Right-wing propaganda displaces the serious issues of a global food crisis, fossil-based mobility and energy consumption, and the growing disparity between the propertied few and the dispossessed many on to a freak discussion about population distribution in which, bluntly speaking, the fertility and birth-rate of non-white women needs to be controlled. The intersectional critique of the underlying racist and social Darwinist assumptions of such a neo-colonial and neo-Malthusian perspective, as well as the inhumane implications of anti-natalist population policies, would have to be taken much more notice of in nature conservation and environmental protection debates. For neo-Malthusian positions are not only held by the extreme right but also by some environmentalists and climate scientists. What is needed is a general change of perspective in the debate on population development and the climate crisis, one that clearly abandons concepts of the planet's carrying capacity and that shifts attention from the individual to the structural level and thus to the real environmentally destructive consequences of the current global economic system (see also Hendrixson 2019).

Works Cited

AfD – Alternative für Deutschland (2016) *Programm für Deutschland: Das Grundsatzprogramm der Alternative für Deutschland*. Web: https://www .afd.de/wp-content/uploads/sites/111/2017/01/2016-06-27_afd-grun dsatzprogramm_web-version.pdf.

Almeida, Paul (2019) Climate justice and sustained transnational mobilization. *Globalizations* 16(7), 973–79.

Berkhout, Guus, Reynald du Berger, Terry Dunleavy, Viv Forbes, Jeffrey Foss, Morten Jødal, Rob Lemeire, Richard Lindzen, Ingemar Nordin, Jim O'Brian, Alberto Prestininzi, Benoît Rittaud, Fritz Vahrenholt and Monckton of Brenchley (2019) *There is no climate emergency*. Ed. by Clintel. Web: https://clintel.nl/wp-content/uploads/2019/09/ecd-let ter-to-un.pdf.

Brand, Ulrich and Markus Wissen (2017) *Imperiale Lebensweise: Zur Ausbeutung von Mensch und Natur im globalen Kapitalismus*. München: oekom.

diversu e.V. and FARN – Fachstelle Radikalisierungsprävention und Engagement im Naturschutz (2020) *Handreichung: Rechtspopulismus/ Rechtsextremismus und Ökologie. Zum Hintergrund. Weltweite Umweltproteste und antidemokratische Positionen*, ed. by DNR. Web: https://w ww.diversu.org/wp-content/uploads/2020/11/Handreichung_ReLa _2020.pdf.

DSW – Deutsche Stiftung Weltbevölkerung (2022) *7.990.978.118 Menschen leben auf der Erde*. Web: https://www.dsw.org.

Ehrlich, Paul R. (1968) *Population Control or Race to Oblivion? The Population Bomb.* New York: Ballantine Books.

FARN – Fachstelle Radikalisierungsprävention und Engagement im Naturschutz (ed.) (2019) *Aspekte Gruppenbezogener Menschenfeindlichkeit im Natur- und Umweltschutz. Eine Diskussion.* Berlin: FARN.

FARN – Fachstelle Radikalisierungsprävention und Engagement im Naturschutz in Kooperation mit diversu e.V. (ed.) (2022) *Ist-Analyse unter Studierenden der grünen Berufe hinsichtlich des Themenfelds "Natur-/Umweltschutz und Rechtsextremismus" Hochschulumfrage im Rahmen des "Demokratie leben!"- Modellprojekts NaturSchutzRaum.* Web: https://www.nf-farn.de/system/files/documents/farn-bericht-hochschulumfrage.pdf.

Fridays for Future (2022) *Promise.* Web: https://fridaysforfuture.org/fig htfor1point5/promise/.

Geden, Oliver (1999) *Rechte Ökologie. Umweltschutz zwischen Emanzipation und Faschismus.* Berlin: Elefanten Press.

Gesang, Bernward (2014b) Demokratie am Scheideweg. In: Gesang, Bernward (Ed.) *Kann Demokratie Nachhaltigkeit?.* Wiesbaden, Springer VS, 19–37.

Gesang, Bernward (2014a) Einleitung. In: Gesang, Bernward (ed.) *Kann Demokratie Nachhaltigkeit?.* Wiesbaden: Springer VS, 13–15.

Gottschlich, Daniela (2006) *Machtpolitik im grünen Kleid der Nachhaltigkeit. Feministische Kritik an ökologisch begründeter Bevölkerungspolitik.* Web: http://forumue.de/wp-content/uploads/2015/05/Demographischer_Wandel_AG-Frauen.pdf.

Gottschlich, Daniela and Christin Katz (2020) *Strategiepapier: Rechte Landnahme stoppen! Was Natur- und Umweltverbänden gegen Rechtsextreme Vereinnahmungen tun können,* ed. by diversu e.V. Web: https://www.diversu.org/wp-content/uploads/2020/09/Strategiepapier_ReL a_Version-1.pdf.

Gottschlich, Daniela and Susanne Schultz (2019) Weniger Klimawandel durch weniger Menschen? Feministische Kritik am neomalthusianischen Revival. In: FARN – Fachstelle Radikalisierungsprävention und Engagement im Naturschutz (ed.) *Aspekte Gruppenbezogener Men-*

schenfeindlichkeit im Natur- und Umweltschutz. Eine Diskussion. Berlin: FARN, 24–29.

Gottschlich, Daniela, Christin Katz, and Wiebke Schwandt – with the assistance of Simon Fritz (2020) Rechte Landnahme. Ergebnisse einer Online-Befragung von Natur- und Umweltschutzverbänden zur Einflussnahme durchrechte Akteur*innen und ihre Ideologien, ed. by diversu e. V. Web: https://www.diversu.org/wp-content/uploads/2020/06/Re La_Ergebnisse_Online-Befragung_Juni-2020.pdf.

Götze, Susanne and Annika Joeres (2021) Leugnerkabinett. Viele Klimaskeptiker bezweifeln auch die Coronagefahren. In: Kleffner, Heike and Matthias Meisner (eds.) Fehlender Mindestabstand. Die Coronakrise und die Netzwerke der Demokratiefeinde. Freiburg: Herder, 135–141.

Hartmann, Betsy (1995) Reproductive Rights and Wrongs. The Global Politics of Population Control. Boston: South End Press.

Hartmann, Betsy and Elizabeth Barajas-Roman (2009) The Population Bomb is Back – with a Global Warming Twist. Women in Action 2, 70–78.

Heinrich, Gudrun, Klaus-Dieter Kaiser and Norbert Wiersbinski (2015) Naturschutz und Rechtsradikalismus. Gegenwärtige Entwicklungen, Probleme, Abgrenzungen und Steuerungsmöglichkeiten. BfN-Skripten 394. Web: https://www.bfn.de/sites/default/files/BfN/service/Dokumen te/skripten/skript394.pdf.

Hendrixson, Anne (2019) A Renewed Call for Feminist Resistance to Population Control. DiffernTakes 94, 1–6. Web: https://sites.hampshire.e du/popdev/files/2019/11/DT-94.pdf.

Hendrixson, Anne, and Betsy Hartmann (2018) Threats and burdens: Challenging scarcity-driven narratives of "overpopulation". Geoforum. Web: doi:10.1016/j.geoforum.2018.08.009.

Hoppenstedt, Max (2020) Luisa Neubauer kämpft gegen Hatespeech in sozialen Medien. "Was über mich geschrieben wird, ist schon krass". Web: https://www.spiegel.de/netzwelt/netzpolitik/luisa-neubauer-uebe r-hatespeech-was-ueber-mich-geschrieben-wird-ist-schon-krass-a-19bd80bb-4fec-4fea-8e11-85b817c05bf3.

IPCC – Intergovernmental Panel on Climate Change (2007) Climate Change 2007. Synthesis Report. Contribution of Working Groups I, II and

III to the Fourth Assessment Report of the Intergovernmental Panel on Climate Change. Pachauri, Rajendra K and Andy Reisinger (eds). IPCC. Assessment Report 4.

IPCC – Intergovernmental Panel on Climate Change (2021) *Climate Change 2021. The Physical Science Basis. Contribution of Working Group I to the Sixth Assessment Report of the Intergovernmental Panel on Climate Change.* Masson-Delmotte, Valérie, et al. (eds.) IPCC. Assessment Report 6.

Klein, Naomi (2015) *Die Entscheidung. Kapitalismus vs. Klima.* Frankfurt a.M.: Fischer.

klimafakten.de (n.d.) *Was sagt die AfD zum Klimawandel? Was sagen andere Parteien? Und was ist der Stand der Wissenschaft? Ein Faktencheck zum Grundsatzprogramm der "Alternative für Deutschland".* Web: https://www.klimafakten.de/meldung/was-sagt-die-afd-zum-klimawandel-was-sagen-andere-parteien-und-was-ist-der-stand-der.

Kopfmüller, Konstantin (2019) *Falsches und Verdrehtes zum Klima.* Web: https://www.tagesschau.de/faktenfinder/afd-klima-101.html.

Lindsay, Jennie (1988) Südafrikanische Auslesepolitik in Namibia. In: Wichterich, Christa (ed.) *Zum Beispiel Bevölkerungspolitik.* Bornheim-Merten: Lamuv, 107–110.

Malthus, Thomas R. (1798) *An Essay on the Principle of Population, as it Affects the Future Improvement of Society. With Remarks on the Speculations of Mr. Godwin, M. Condorcet and Other Writers.* London: J. Johnson.

Meadows, Donella. H, Dennis L. Meadows, Jørgen Randers and William W. Behrens III (1972) *The Limits to Growth. A Report for the Club of Rome's Project on the Predicament of Mankind.* New York: Universe Books.

Moore, Sam and Alex Roberts (2022) *Außen grün, innen braun. Wie Rechtsextreme Klimakrise und Naturschutz für ihre Zwecke benutzen.* München: oekom.

Müller-Jung, Joachim (2018) *Ein Tabu brechen. Das schnelle Bevölkerungswachstum ist einer der großen Antriebe für den Klimawandel.* FAZ.net (14 September). Web: https://www.faz.net/aktuell/politik/mit-bevoelkerungspolitik-den-klimawandel-stoppen-15788619.html.

Murphy, Murphy (2017): *The economization of Life.* Durham: Duke University Press.

Nicolaisen, Lucas (2020) *Rechtsextremismus und Naturschutz.* [unpublished lecture].

Norris, Pippa and Ronald F. Inglehart (2019) *Cultural backlash: Trump, Brexit, and authoritarian populism.* Cambridge: Cambridge University Press.

People's Demands for Climate Justice (2018) *The People's Demands for Climate Justice.* Web: https://www.peoplesdemands.org/.

Quarks.de (2021) *Viel zu viele Menschen. Wie die Überbevölkerung gebremst werden könnte.* Web: https://www.quarks.de/gesellschaft/wie-die-ue berbevoelkerung-gebremst-werden-koennte/.

Ripple, William J., Chrisopher Wolf, Thomas M. Newsome, Mauro Galetti, Mohammed Alamgir, Eileen Crist, Mahmoud I Mahmoud, William F. Laurance and 15,364 scientist signatories from 184 countries (2017) Worlds Scientists' Warning to Humanity. *Bioscience* 67(12), 1026–1028. Web: doi:10.1093/biosci/bix125.

Röpke, Andrea and Andreas Speit (2019). *Völkische Landnahme. Alte Sippen, junge Siedler, rechte Ökos.* Berlin : Ch. Links Verlag.

Rydgren, Jens (2008) Immigration sceptics, xenophobes or racists? Radical right-wing voting in six West European countries. *European Journal of Political Research* 47(6), 737–765.

Schäffer, Mona (2021) *Neues AfD Wahlplakat mit absurder Forderung – Zurück ins Mittelalter.* Web: https://www.wmn.de/buzz/afd-wahlplakat -absurd-id275181.

Schaller, Stella and Alexander Carius (2019) *Convenient Truths. Mapping climate agendas of right-wing populist parties in Europe.* Berlin: adelphi.

Speit, Andreas (2021) *Verqueres Denken. Gefährliche Weltbilder in alternativen Milieus.* Berlin: Ch. Links Verlag.

Staud, Toralf (2015) *Grüne Braune.* Web: http://www.bpb.de/politik/extr emismus/rechtsextremismus/211922/gruene-braune.

Strobl, Natascha (2022) Vorwort. In: Moore, Sam and Alex Roberts (2022). *Außen grün, innen braun. Wie Rechtsextreme Klimakrise und Naturschutz für ihre Zwecke benutzen.* München, oekom, 7–10.

Thunberg, Greta (2018) *COP24 Speech.* Web: https://www.youtube.com/ watch?v=qB8jXY5uWaI&feature=emb_rel_end.

Vollset, Stein E., et al. (2020). Fertility, mortality, migration, and population scenarios for 195 countries and territories from 2017 to 2100:
a forecasting analysis for the Global Burden of Disease Study. *Lancet*
396: 1285–1306. Web: https://www.thelancet.com/journals/lancet/ar
ticle/PIIS0140-6736(20)30677-2/fulltext.

Wang, Nanfu, Zhang, Jialing (2019) *Land der Einzelkinder*. Documentary.
First screening ARTE (October 10). Web: https://www.youtube.com
/watch?v=gMcJVoLwyDo.

Wichterich, Christra (1988) (Ed.) *Zum Beispiel Bevölkerungspolitik*. Bornheim-Merten: Lamuv.

Wilson, Kalpana (2015) The "New" Global Population Control Policies:
Fuelling India's Sterilization Atrocities *DifferenTakes* 87. Web: https:/
/dspace.hampshire.edu/bitstream/10009/940/1/popdev_differenta
kes_087.pdf.

Wilton, Katelin (2013) "Double stigma": Forced sterilization of women
living with HIV in Kenya and Namibia. *DifferenTakes* 80. Web: https:
//dspace.hampshire.edu/bitstream/10009/934/1/popdev_differenta
kes_080.pdf.

Zick, Andreas, Beate Küpper and Wilhelm Berghan (2019) *Verlorene
Mitte – feindselige Zustände: Rechtsextreme Einstellungen in Deutschland
2018/19*. Bonn: Dietz.

Planters of Doom and Playful Gardeners
Determinist and Possibilist Narratives of Mankind

Gesa Mackenthun

I dedicate this essay to Marina Ovsyannikova, whose courageous action of speaking truth to power on 15 March, 2022 proves that humans have free will.[1]

Introduction

The global economic crisis of the early 2000s marks the beginning of a rush of one-volume "big" histories of "mankind." Offering compact and complete knowledge about the history of the world to be absorbed within the length of an intercontinental flight, these airport bestsellers address an educated and itinerant non-expert audience grateful for having their lives explained as being the meaningful result of a logical and continuous historical development. Following the model of books like Jared Diamond's *Guns, Germs and Steel: A Short History of Everybody for the Last 13000 Years* (1997/2017), these popular historical narratives have titles like *A Short History of the World. The Story of Mankind from Prehistory to the Modern Day* (Alex Woolf, 2008); *Origin Story. A Big History of Everything* (David Christian, 2018); *History: From the Dawn of Civilization to the Present Day* (Dorling Kindersley/"DK," 2015); *Big History. From the Big Bang to the*

---

1 'They're lying to you': Russian TV employee interrupts news broadcast | Russia | The Guardian

Present (Cynthia Stokes Brown, 2007); *Applied Big History. Guide for Entrepreneurs, Investors and Other Living Things* (William Grassie, 2018); Adam Rutherford's volumes *A Brief History of Everyone Who Ever Lived. The Story of Our Genes* (2016) and *The Book of Humans. The Story of How We Became Us* (2018); and Bill Bryson's, *A Short History of Nearly Everything* (2003). Next to the anglophone volumes there are also German ones, such as *Die kürzeste Geschichte allen Lebens. Eine Reportage über 13,7 Milliarden Jahre Werden und Vergehen* by Harald Lesch and Harald Zaun (2008). The seriously meant stories of planetary becoming have generated parodies such as Tom Phillips's delightful *Humans: A Brief History of How We F*cked It All Up* (2019). Together, these books offer their readers compact, entertaining, and not too complex reports on how humanity ended up in the bliss, or mess, in which it currently finds itself. They are the jet setter's equivalent to their grandparents' *Readers Digest* volumes, showing how far we have come in the skillful consumer-friendly packaging of world history. What's more, while classic accounts of world history hardly ever got beyond Eurocentric narratives of the period between Greek antiquity and the modern period, today's airport histories cover the whole of mankind's presence on this planet. Their Western-masculinist "we-ism" comes at the sacrifice of the ideals of diversity, complexity, and comprehensiveness.

While the planet heads toward climate catastrophe, then, its mobile cultural elite consumes texts offering a long backward glance at the beginnings of the world, or of the Anthropocene, most of which explain the present disruptive episode of earth history as the result of a long series of unavoidable events. The usual prognosticated future of this deterministic master narrative is doom. Even a book resisting narratives of impending extinction, Robert Kelly's *The Fifth Beginning*, is inappropriately translated as *Warum es normal ist, dass die Welt untergeht* ("Why it is normal that the world goes down") (Kelly 2020). Kelly's argument, formulated on the ground of deep archaeological knowledge, is not that the world will end soon but rather the contrary: that human societies have reached a period of great cultural potential for *beginning* a period of global networking and peace. The mistranslation shows that "deep" historical narratives planting the story of civilizational doom not only enjoy high currency but have developed an ideological pull difficult to resist. They also contribute to a fatalistic mentality of leaving things as they are. It's easier for these texts and readers to imagine doom than to imagine humans engaged in change.[2]

These histories are not narrative chronicles of pre-human and human events but more or less philosophical reflections on mankind at the point of the "sixth" massive species extinction (Kolbert 2014), enriched with anecdotal information that seemingly confirms the depressing thesis. Most of these "big" narratives follow the logic of the Biblical master narrative of man's fall from divine grace and his subsequent suffering the sad consequences of what is known as the Neolithic "revolutions": the introduction of agriculture and the domestication of animals. They also frequently use a narrative mode which Foucault referred to as the history of the present, offering nostalgic views on the deep past (with the earth as pristine, beautiful, and empty) and dystopian future from an explicitly present perspective.

The interest in the early history of mankind is necessarily coupled with a conspicuous amount of speculation as the documentary record for that period is particularly scattered and fragmentary. Much better documented times such as colonial expansion, industrialization, and the Enlightenment, which we should assume to be much more responsible for the present predicament, receive much less attention in these accounts. This asymmetry between bold speculative assertions and the fragmentariness of evidence may cause suspicion. What, we may wonder, is the ideological work of such big histories at the present historical conjunction? This essay interrogates two of these works with a view to their semantic productiveness, and ideological "subversiveness": the first one is Yuval Noah Harari's bestselling *Sapiens. A Brief History of Mankind* (2011) – both the original book and its two graphic versions, called "graphic history" in English while the German translation is announced as "graphic novel." The master narrative used by Harari and most other named writers has recently received a substantial critique from anthropologist David Graeber and archaeologist David Wengrow.

---

2   See Mackenthun 2021a for a more elaborate discussion of this narrative mode.

The Dawn of Everything: A New History of Humanity (2021), which will be my second example, is a counternarrative to the hegemonic narrative of doom. *Sapiens* and *Dawn*, though explicitly reviewing the deep past from a present perspective, use different forms of emplotment: while Harari's books aim at infotainment and wildly mix different times and geographical scenes, Graeber/Wengrow offer a more scholarly historical-critical analysis but avoid narrative necessity and closure. In fact, both Harari and the two Davids employ a semantics of *play* that is reinforced by the structure of their texts, but to vastly different ends: while Harari presents human history as an inconsequential postmodernist tale, Graeber and Wengrow are strongly committed to a philosophy of political change. Harari's playfulness is that of a gambler seducing his readers into believing a particular neoliberal version of history while Graeber and Wengrow use "play" conceptually as a space of intellectual freedom from an ideology of inevitability and its hegemonic master narratives. Harari can be seen to subvert the semantics of humanism and political liberalism promoting a libertarian stance, while *Dawn* subverts both the semantics and the narrative structure of *Sapiens*'s historical master narrative. This has significant consequences for each narrative's interpretive power.

1.   Determinist and Possibilist Pasts

Harari's original book *Sapiens* (2011, engl. 2014) promises to answer mankind's most pressing questions: where do humans come from? How do humans differ from other animals, i.e. how did consciousness and cognition develop? Are humans originally good or bad, peaceful or fatally aggressive? Did "stone age" humans have more fun and freedom than neolithic ones burdened by agricultural labor? Do humans benefit from cooperativeness? Are our decisions the result of ideas and historical choice or rather conditioned by biological laws? Trained as a military historian with a specialization in the medieval period, Harari assumes expertise as a global *savant* with a very particular message: because of genetic mutations and environmental challenges that happened to

humans in the distant past, social inequality and the impending destruction of life on earth are inevitable. Human life will eventually merge
into a digital existence (similar to Zuckerberg's Metaverse) where the
world will be reigned by inorganic algorithms while a small human elite
will become godlike, as Harari promises in *Homo Deus*. The majority of
mankind, however, will continue to wallow in poverty (Harari 2017, 64).

Barack Obama promoted *Sapiens* just like Mark Zuckerberg and Bill
Gates; Ridley Scott wanted to turn it into a TV series and there is a *Sapiens*
museum in Israel. Harari himself started a social-impact company called
Sapienship in 2019, whose function is to increase the distribution of his
globally successful story to future decision makers.[3] All of this suggests
that Harari's version of world history is striving to become the hegemonic historical narrative for decades to come. With the graphic versions and a version for children it will enter the reading lists of schools.
Sapiens is the brand name for an educational product whose impact will
have to be reckoned with.

Harari's condemnation of agriculture was preceded by other popular "big" historical narratives by Jared Diamond, William Ruddiman,
and James Scott which present mankind as having lapsed from a state
of original hunter and gatherer bliss to sedentary squalor as a consequence of the Neolithic "revolutions" (Keeler 2021). In *Guns, Germs, and
Steel* (1997) Jared Diamond uses a geographical-deterministic framework
to explain the inequality between the societies around the world – not
as a consequence of colonial and imperial impact but of environmental
milieu.[4] Social inequality, rather than being the result of war and con-

---

3   One of Sapienship's aims is to "learn to distinguish reality from illusions." As the
     books explain, such "illusions" include the belief in free will and democracy. ht
     tps://www.sapienship.co.

4   Diamond begins his study with a conversation between himself and an inhab-
     itant of New Guinea who asks him to explain the inequality between their so-
     cieties since their encounter about 500 years ago. In his answer he reaches out
     into the poorly documented distant Neolithic past, suggesting that inequality
     is produced by difference in environmental placement rather than European
     imperial aggression. Harari follows the same strategy of using "big" history to
     avoid sustained analysis of the more recent colonial past.

quest, is presented as natural destiny. Both Diamond and Harari offer a crypto-biblical story of a fall from the Garden of Eden all the way to impending apocalypse. The general narrative frame inspiring their accounts is the nineteenth-century story of a linear-teleological cultural development. In different versions – from the Scottish Enlightenment philosophers to the American natural philosopher Lewis Henry Morgan – this model views humanity to have developed in stages usually beginning with the savage stage, progressing to barbarism and pastoralism and then to urban civilization. Later versions of this stadialist model add industrialization and, in Harari's case, digitalization. This master narrative has greatly shaped historical thinking, including Karl Marx's political-historical account of a progression from feudalism to capitalism to socialism. The archaeological timeline invented in Denmark in the mid-nineteenth century, which viewed mankind moving from simple to more complex technological stages (from stone to bronze to iron age), follows the same universalist and unilinear logic. From its beginnings, the optimistic narrative coexisted with a story of decline, inspired by Edward Gibbon's classic account of the decline and fall of the Roman Empire. When Enlightenment optimism waned under the impact of increasing economic and social inequality, the narrative of cultural decline culminated in what we may call a naturalistic turn: some human groups, it was now promoted, just were not fit enough for joining the common train of progress. This was explained by way of "natural" racial differences and the "natural" inclination of certain "races" to degenerate and to become extinct.

Building on the power of this social-Darwinist master narrative, Harari, as others before him, claims that the growth of communities and increasing social complexity, caused by the introduction of agriculture, inevitably led to inequality and social hierarchies. Like Diamond, he does not dwell on the historical agency of feudalism or colonialism. He rather, as we shall see, regards wheat itself as the originator of inequality. In his sustained critique of Harari's work, Phil Deloria expresses justified doubt about such selective use of historical facts: "There is an obvious danger in widening the chronological frame to the point that human action becomes structural, abstract, and socially meaningless – even as the supposed lesson remains socially meaningful in the *now*" (Deloria 2021, 234). The philosophy of the *Sapiens* volumes is indeed unresponsive to social questions, as humans are regarded as the result of neurological and chemical processes. Sociality as a realm distinct from nature and its implication of human agency are foreign to Harari's ideological set-up. "Free will" for him is not a reality but a mere "myth" (Harari 2018). In his denial of the "reality" of free will, he does not explain why modern, extremely complex states, global institutions and NGOs came into being and why humans constantly respond creatively to sociopolitical conditions, thereby effecting change. That part of human history is only used for ornamental purposes in a narrative asserting the essential difference between humans while also claiming that "we" did not change significantly since "our" hunter-gatherer state. In fact, the "we"-ism of Harari's and other "big" historians' books denies the significant diversity between human societies and civilizations and their histories. The deceptive collective pronoun also suggests that *all* humans were collectively responsible for the destruction of more-than-human life, such as "our" contribution to species extinctions, climate change, and environmental degradation.

Other recent versions of the doom narrative add an anthropogenic twist to the crypto-biblical narrative, claiming, in the words of Kyle Keeler, that humans have bred greed, created "catastrophic climate change," caused a separation of humanity from nonhuman beings through domination, and fostered "conditions responsible for future Anthropocene markers." This narrative, then, "creates a deterministic worldview that ties agriculture to the conception of private property through subduing the Earth" (Keeler 2021, 5). It arises as the question of the responsibility for climate change takes root in deep history discourse. Tim Beach of Austin University hypothesizes that Maya agriculture may have significantly contributed to global warming (Conellan 2019), while others stress the cooling effects of the massive loss of life in America resulting from the colonial encounter (Koch et al. 2019). In other words, the deepening of the time scale allows for downplaying the historically recent agency of industrial-extractive colonialism while establishing a link between precolonial carbon emissions and Indigenous lives: the fewer Native farmers the better for the climate. Dead Indians are good Indians once again. These deep historiographical constructions confirm Philip Deloria's suspicion that large-scale narratives of the human past tend to create more "harm" to Indigenous people (whose ancestors are featured as unecological mass-murderers and destroyers) than explaining through which agency, human and other, climate change and the present loss of biodiversity primarily came into the world (Deloria 2021, 243).

However, Harari's, Diamond's and other determinists' master narrative of agricultural doom does not remain uncontested. Most reviewers and expert scholars regard Harari's books as instances of popular history whose assumptions have long been rejected, all the way down to schoolbook level. Yet the biologist-determinist narrative continues to thrive in the demi-monde of pop science, as a convenient naturalization of the neoliberal economy's tolerance of inequality, by demonstrating its inevitability with a series of illustrious and out-of-context examples from the deep historical past – preferably those periods for which little documentation exists. With the timely publication of David Graeber and David Wengrow's *The Dawn of Everything*,[5] *Sapiens* and companion volumes have now received a serious rival.

The narrative of *Dawn* contradicts the basic assumption that human history moved from a period of initial hunter and gatherer innocence to a period of endless drudgery as the result of man's fatal turn to agriculture. It also denies the thesis that the existence of social hierarchies was purely imaginary and a matter of "chance" and "accident," as Harari

---

5   "Timely" not only because of the urgency of a forceful objection to the raconteurs of doom but also because one of its authors, David Graeber, died suddenly just a few weeks after finishing the book at the age of 59. *The Dawn of Everything* is part of his intellectual legacy, after his earlier appraised critiques of neoliberalist capitalism. Graeber was one of the spokespersons of the Occupy movement; his books on debt and "bullshit jobs" have had a huge impact on intellectual debate worldwide. Although *Dawn* deals mostly with the period between the Neolithic Age and early colonial America, Graeber's critique of finance capitalism, cancerous bureaucracy, and widespread intellectual illiberalism pulses throughout the pages of his last, co-authored, book.

writes (Harari et al. 2021, 187, 206).[6] Quite to the contrary, Graeber and Wengrow argue, the archaeological record and anthropological knowledge show that humans at all times took advantage of their faculty of creatively shaping their environment, learning from mistakes, and avoiding the social consequences of an unequal distribution of power and wealth. The history of mankind, they show, did not follow a predetermined teleology but consists of endless variation and experiment. They identify the biblical origins of the determinist master narrative and its reiterations first in Enlightenment stadialism, then social Darwinist racial evolutionism, and the modern imperial developmentalism, to be a powerful construct whose interpretive effectiveness consists in its repetitiveness and its explanatory power for global social inequality. Referring to the arbitrariness of that narrative, they also critique the pop historians' reiteration of anthropological dualisms which have long been abolished by the sciences themselves. They find abundant evidence for human societies and economies having been much more flexible than the dualist doctrine of hunter-gatherer societies vs. sedentary agricultural societies, once established under the impact of Victorian-imperial science, is ready to concede.[7] In other words, Graeber and

---

6   Racial law in the US is the result of "a bunch of random factors," as Harari's figure Dr. Fiction explains, preceded by the old adage that transatlantic slavery developed out of preexisting African slavery (Harari et al. 2021, 196–97, 206). Confusingly, "economic self-interest" is mentioned as another reason for American slavery in this book of contradictions (197). From an anti-humanist perspective, "self-interest" is probably a random fact.

7   In his book on "the foraging spectrum," the renowned anthropologist Robert Kelly relates the emergence of US anthropology's focus on hunting/gathering and foraging to the 1966 Chicago conference *Man the Hunter* (Kelly 1995, 9). Kelly's discriminating social analysis of foraging societies does not explore to what extent those foraging practices coexisted with horticultural or agricultural ones. But he offers a sustained critique of the theoretical hegemony of the concept of "foraging" as a scientific paradigm preventing more intense study of the murky in-betweenness of "foraging" groups also practicing gardening and field farming. This hegemony must be seen as a late effect of the nineteenth-century (Victorian) reign of the dichotomy of nomadic "foragers" on the one side and sedentary agricultural societies on the other, which is now slowly erod-

Wengrow contest the linear-determinist narrative and dualist semantics both by providing massive counter-evidence and by historicizing
the ideological contexts from which these hegemonic narratives and
semantics derive: in most cases, the context of late nineteenth-century
colonial and imperial science. Unlike Harari's books, *Dawn* views the
present predicament of global inequality as a result of colonial capitalism which also produced Harari's own narrative frame. It responds to
Harari's individualist libertarianism by pointing out humans' capacity
for mutual aid and for saying "no" to authoritarian power, or slipping
away from it. Graeber and Wengrow's possibilist message is that, even
today, another world is possible if people would just take up action.[8]
Indebted to possibilist thinking, *Dawn* does not deny the shaping impact
of the environment on human action. But it does not regard humans as
being "trapped" by their environment, least of all a grass called wheat
(Wengrow 2021).

---

ing. Wengrow and Graeber's book contributes to that necessary erosion, empirically supported by ever more refined bioarchaeological methods and more
attentive re-readings of historical documents, which show mixtures between
hunting, gathering, and various forms of plant management having been the
rule rather than the exception (Graeber/Wengrow 2021, chapters 6 and 11; Safier
2015; Doolittle 2000; Mt. Pleasant/Burt 2010).

8   Introduced by the French geographer Paul Vidal de la Blache (1845–1918), possibilism is a principle of human geography that holds that the geological environment, rather than Naturalism's milieu and heredity, sets "natural" limits to human activity. As history shows, humans have used their creative force to shape
the earth since the introduction of agriculture and increasingly since the beginnings of industrialization and extractive capitalism. In emphasizing human
creativity, inventiveness, and freedom of choice, possibilism explicitly refutes
the geographical determinism of Friedrich Ratzel, who, in accordance with the
doctrines of Naturalism and Social Darwinism, regarded human action as being
severely inhibited by the natural milieu. Possibilist thinking formed the basis
of the field of cultural ecology initiated by Carl Ortwin Sauer and continued by
Lucien Febvre and Marshall Sahlins, one of Graeber's teachers (Heineberg 2003:
23–24; Hanks 2011: 83, 262).

2.   Planting Doom. Subversive Determinism in Constructions of the Agricultural Past

In my following comparison of Harari's and Graeber/Wengrow's deep histories of the present I will concentrate on Harari's graphic versions, written for an unidentified age group probably ranging from eighth grade to young adult – that age group most likely interested in wooly mammoths and super(wo)men. The cartoon versions are part of a campaign for epistemic hegemony. *Sapiens. A Graphic History. The Birth of Humankind* (Harari et al. 2020) and *Sapiens. A Graphic History. The Pillars of Civilization* (Harari et al. 2021) greatly benefit from Harari's collaboration with the French illustrator Daniel Casanave and the Belgian scriptwriter David Vandermeulen. The graphics facilitate reception and seem to explicitly appeal to young readers, but they also add multiple intertextual layers not available to young adults, thus addressing a mixed-generational, but certainly western-educated, readership.

Sapiens. A Graphic History. The Birth of Humankind presents itself as a story told by Uncle Harari who tells the story of Homo Sapiens to his niece Zoe with the help of various experts and interlocutors: the London-based classification biologist Arya Saraswati, the French-German Benedictine friar and archaeologist Father Klüg, and the superwoman figure Dr. Fiction. The narratives of the *Sapiens* graphic volumes intersect with numerous intertexts such as the story of Prehistoric Bill, a skinny version of the famous US cartoon figure Fred Flintstone: they both drive around in cars (made of stone or trees) and have nuclear families behaving like modern American families. Presented as fictions within the story, the Prehistoric Bill stories are nevertheless used to explain Neolithic reality.

The first graphic book ends with a highly dramatic, and rather silly, criminal investigation and court trial against "Sapiens" for having exterminated all the charismatic Ice Age megafauna. This story is based on a narrative as empirically weak as it is resistant to scientific counter-evidence, initiated in the late sixties and since continued by popular science books and blogs. In spite of major temporal inconsistencies, the Pleistocene overkill hypothesis argues that the first human populations of Australia and America were responsible for the rapid extinction of these two continents' megafauna (Martin 1967; Diamond 1987). It dismisses the impact of other factors like climate change. There is little hard evidence for such a "blitzkrieg" (as it is called), and the scientific narrative is silent about the fact that mammoths and giant sloths became extinct around the world: the impact of Eurasian hunters did not trigger a similar story of human misdemeanor. The first *Sapiens* graphic volume greatly elaborates on this problematic hypothesis, bringing a "Sapiens" couple to court for their "crime" across many pages while retaining the geographical focus on the two continents whose Indigenous populations later became themselves subjects to extinction policies (Harari 2011, chapter 4; Harari et al. 2021, 224–43). While nominally charging *all* of humankind with the slaughter of Pleistocene megafauna, the brief mention of this mega event in both volumes' initial timeline is reduced to paleo-Australians and paleo-Americans.[9] The effect is twofold: present-day assertions of a heightened Indigenous "ecological" consciousness are weakened by references to the ecocidal behavior of Indigenous ancestors. And it is suggested that, in Vine Deloria, Jr.'s words, "at *no* time were human beings careful of the lands upon which they lived" (Deloria 1997, 97), rendering futile all attempts to mobilize against this human "nature" – be it by fighting the effects of climate change or those of environmental degradation in the present.

For my discussion I will select two historical themes that seem particularly important to Harari: (1) his claim that the agricultural "revolution" imposed a "trap" on humans leading directly to social and material inequality; and (2) his claim that democracy, human equality, and "free will" were politically imposed fictions without any foundation in the real world. In Harari's version of human evolution, the event that decided the triumph of Homo Sapiens over against other early homo groups is what he calls the cognitive revolution or the "Tree of Knowledge mutation," caused by a spontaneous genetic mutation about 70,000 years ago (Harari 2011, 23–24; Harari et al. 2020, 101). Three more revolutions followed on the way to modern man: the Neolithic revolutions in-

---

9   See Mackenthun 2021b, chapter 1, and Philip Deloria 2021 for discussions of the colonial subtext of the Pleistocene overkill hypothesis.

troducing sedentary agriculture and the domestication of animals; the scientific revolution c. 500 years ago (discovery of America); and finally the industrial revolution. The graphic versions do not represent this narrative as one linear account; instead they mix the characters' conversations about distant historical events (or theories thereof) with present-day scenes typical of a global-itinerant social elite –visits to the London zoo, to a fancy conference compound, and to the archaeological site of Lascaux in the Dordogne. Figures discuss the history of Sapiens during a performance of *Faust*, undertake an extended trip to Philadelphia (where they discuss the Declaration of Independence with the Founding Fathers) and shorter ones to Paris, New York and Ibiza. The present-day city- and landscapes are blended with historical ones, dependent on the erratic flow of their conversation. The graphics brim with delightful intertextual and intermedial allusions. The storytelling situation is established in the first panel of volume 1, with Uncle Harari lecturing from his armchair. Dr. Fiction delivers lengthy additional lectures on the fictionality of history, adding another postmodernist twist.

The introduction of agriculture was, according to Harari, a "trap" causing human misery and social inequality. Volume 2 of the graphic *Sapiens* begins with Harari and his friends visiting a performance of Goethe' *Faust*. Mephistopheles is dancing on a medievalist stage singing his "little ditty 'Little Crop of Horrors'." The scene merges into his delightfully illustrated retelling of his major triumph about 12,000 years ago when he succeeded to convince "a poor sapiens called Faustus" into adopting agriculture (Harari et al. 2021, 12, 14). (Fig. 1). The serpent of Paradise was in reality an ear of wheat, the story suggests, forcing Faustus and his whole species into the "agricultural revolution" (17). In one of many parallactical leaps (connecting the Neolithic with contemporary events), the Mephistophelian wheat connects the Faustian beginnings with present-day industrial wheat farming (19), triumphantly exclaiming that all of this was the result of the satanic Wheat's original plot. Man's tragic mistake was to exchange the freedom of a hunter-gathering life for the drudgery of farming which, Harari claims as he continues his story, led to a poorer diet, physical ailments and, as the embedded adventures of the Prehistoric Bill characters suggest, violence and social inequality (Harari et al. 2021, 28–30).

Fig. 1: A Mephistophelian grain of wheat laying the agricultural trap for Faustus.

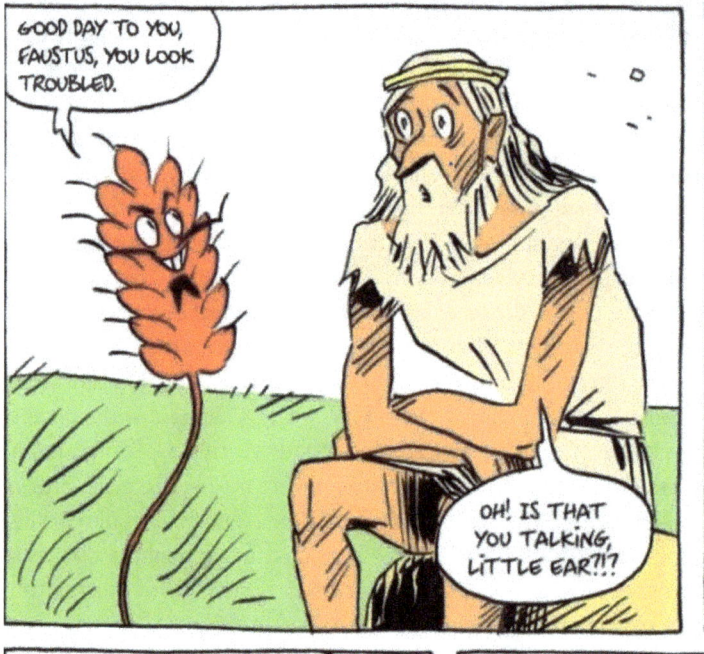

Harari, Yuval Noah, David Vandermeulen, and Daniel Casanave (2021). *Sapiens. A Graphic History, Vol. 2. The Pillars of Civilization.* London: Jonathan Cape. P. 15.

After planting in readers' minds anthropomorphized Wheat's colorful story of its exceptional historical seduction of Sapiens – a remarkable agency considering that wheat is genetically a mere grass while Sapiens had already been cognitively revolutionized 60,000 years prior to that fateful event –, Harari has Prof. Saraswati explain to his niece that the agricultural revolution was no single or sudden event but "took thou-

sands of years" (Harari et al. 2021, 25). Yet elsewhere the same figure explains, "Over time, a lot of small changes accumulated into a big revolution" (33). Such temporal-terminological haziness and semantic uncertainties abound in the graphic books, giving them the character of fictional stories, not graphic "histories," as the English versions contend.

All three books are strongly dedicated to a roundabout dismissal of
agricultural society which Harari regards as "history's biggest fraud"
(Harari 2011, chapter 11). Asked whether he thinks that hunter-gatherers
had a more comfortable and gratifying life than farmers, "Harari" answers: "Most people who 'came after them' were impoverished peasants
rather than people like us flying to conferences and eating in snazzy
restaurants" (Harari et al. 2020, 155). There are several problems with this
sweeping claim: (1) Harari gives no systematic account of how Sapiens
developed from freedom-loving "foragers" to impoverished peasants
to the jet-setting "us" of his frame narrative; (2) he does not elaborate
the real reasons why most peasants were (and still are) so poor; (3) he
insinuates that the societies of the present are no longer agricultural:
the wholesome food served in his "snazzy restaurants" is not traced
back to its human producers. The snobbish cartoon discussion about
the deficient nutritious value of their pasta dishes, combined with their
similarly simplistic discussion of man as the slave of a plant, disguises
the real – both historical and contemporary – reasons for peasant
poverty. The most recent chapter of that real-life story can presently
be observed in India where farmers were killed in violent opposition
to a corporatization of agriculture destroying their markets,[10] or the
United States where farmers are "trapped" by the GMO industry and
opiods. One does not have to be an expert in agricultural history to
know that peasant poverty was and is less the result of field labor than
of feudal slavery and, since the beginnings of the twentieth century,
of farmers' dependency on big corporate landowners and chemical
companies which are indeed depriving them of any agency – even the
freedom to choose their own seeds. In spite of its nominal emphasis on

---

10   See the very detailed Wikipedia entry: 2020–2021 Indian farmers' protest - Wi
      kipedia. The harmful farm laws were repealed in December 2021.

agriculture, the second graphic volume skips the history of feudalism and agricultural corporatism and the social inequality they involve.

As other adherents of biodeterminist big histories, Harari looks at the Neolithic period for answers about man's essential "character" as needed for grasping, or legitimizing, the present socio-economic conjunction. Aided by the popular graphic genre, *Sapiens* does not present a social-economic history connecting the Neolithic with our own time. In its longue durée perspective, colonial capitalism is an insignificant episode, as it is in most other big historical accountsn-made past. A second effect of the "big" picture is that it downplays, or altogether eliminates, human diversity – a problem that also frequently occurs in discussions about the Anthropocene. As several scholars have emphasized, not "man" or "Sapiens" in general are responsible for the present precarity but identifiable groups of humans involved in establishing, shaping, and defending the existing global constellation marked by growing social inequality and environmental degradation.

Agriculture, Harari's story goes, forced humans to live in settlements, causing human inequality, a poorer diet (too much gluten: one delightful panel shows the devilish wheat head jump, snakelike, from Zoe's pasta dish), an increase of epidemics, and general misery (Harari 2021 et al., 27–39). His hostility to agriculture can in part be explained by his condemnation of modern industrialized meat production, the abuse and pain imposed on "farmyard" animals.[11] But the volumes also contain a fair amount of paleo-hunter-gatherer nostalgia – at least as long as the hunters are not indigenous to Australia or the Americas.

In his *second* overall argument, Harari precludes the expectable humanist objection to his bio-determinist theory – proof of human agency throughout modern history – by making extensive claims about the *fictionality of equality* and of human rights. Human rights, democracy, and other liberal values are claimed to be mere fictions and "myths."

---

11   The original book contains a photo of a calf separated from its mother and bound for slaughter, looking into the camera with doleful eyes (Harari 2011, 108). Here indeed might rest the serious core of Harari's nihilist cynicism: a vegetarian's deep compassion for the captive fellow creature.

In his graphic versions he introduces a specific character to promote that message, a superwoman figure called Dr. Fiction. Using the same irresistible didactic tone as "Uncle Harari," Dr. Fiction presents the radical constructivist thesis that psychologically, humans have not changed much since the early days of mankind: they are still more or less gullible primitives capable of cognition but easily manipulated by fancy fictions – QED, we have to admit with a view to *Sapiens'* publishing success. As most commentators of the books note, their biologism amounts to a complete dismissal of humanism, the Enlightenment, the innovations they produced, and social theories built on them – most importantly the conviction of human beings' ability to intellectual growth if exposed to a feasible education. Mankind for Harari consists of smart elites telling the less educated population what to believe – a thesis reminiscent of Arnold Toynbee's old theory of a charismatic "intelligentsia" manipulating the "internal proletariat" of force-assimilated societies, keeping the uneducated masses in awe with their stories.[12] The imagined communication situation he describes resembles what Eric Cheyfitz calls a "scene of primal education," by which a colonial power imagines superimposing its "superior" values on another culture, thereby explaining and promoting social inequality (Cheyfitz 1991, 113). Colonial realities were often less didactically refined.

In addition to her theory about manipulating gullible majorities, Dr. Fiction and the Indian biologist Prof. Saraswati join forces in explaining to the stunned American Founding Fathers that their Declaration of Independence was no more than a list of fictions. Over ten pages, Harari's friends explain that men were not "created equal," that they there were not endowed with any rights by a "creator," and that in effect the DI is indistinguishable from the old-testamentarian lex talionis of the brutal Babylonian ruler Hammurabi in claiming universally valid applicability. While Hammurabi's code fixed punishments for the destruction of property, including slaves and women, the DI and the US Constitution exclude these groups from the defined rights. In fact, they were still regarded as property at the time these documents were drafted (Harari

---

12   Toynbee calls this enforced mission civilisatrice "mimesis" (Toynbee 1939).

et al. 2021, 92–101).[13] A philosophical statement of political revolution against authoritarian rule is compared with a criminal code of just such a tyrannical rule. The Declaration of Independence is misrepresented as a scientific definition of the human species rather than a statement of political will.[14] Harari's denial of the "biological" existence of equality caters to the idea that social inequality is naturally determined and therefore unavoidable. Madame Saraswati's "scientific", i.e. biologist, mutilation of the DI has its humorous effects,[15] but the consequence of her deconstruction is to invite a willing and politically naive readership to a position that denies the efficacy of the principles of human rights, rule of law, and a state striving for social equity – the moral foundation of modern democratic states. Both figures, Saraswati the biologist and Dr. Fiction the radical constructivist, function to convince readers that such statements of political will are insubstantial fictions. In spite of the leisure-

---

13   Volume 2 also contains a long treatment of American slavery, which it downplays to a mere "bunch of random factors" – joining the reactionary historical claim that the transatlantic slave-based system, which produced the foundation of Europe's and America's present wealth, was the accidental continuation of preexisting African human trafficking (Harari et al. 2021, 197, 206). Harari's declaration of slavery as a "chance historical event" raises the suspicion that "chance" and "mutation" are always evoked when historical explanation is too difficult or inconvenient.

14   The historical context of the DI is ignored, as is the extended critical literature on the document, whose spirit has since influenced all modern democratic-republican constitutions worldwide (including the Universal Declaration of Human Rights).

15   Including the vicious-malicious comparison of the development of inequality between humans with the lengthening of the necks of giraffes (Harari et al. 2021, 97). Yet, there are no short-necked giraffes; and their long necks have developed over millennia. In addition to the fake comparison, humans possess the power of reason enabling them to avoid social inequality. The *Sapiens* volumes deny that ability. They are saturated with similar limping comparisons which certainly find their adherents among readers who, like Andrew Carnegie, are grateful for great inequality among men because it is "essential for the future progress of the race" to have clearly separated classes of rulers and laborers (Carnegie 2006, 3).

liness with which Harari's figures travel through the world, the books' message is that humanist idealism is a dispensable lie.[16]

Later, Dr. Fiction intervenes into a sixteenth-century Spanish inquisition court at Valladolid by charging both inquisitor and victim with being blinded by fictions. With apodictic certainty – "no human society has ever cornered the market on absolute truth" – she sweeps away all hermeneutic struggle about *relative* truths as well. The impressed torture victim wonders whether Dr. Fiction's statement was not itself "some new revelation." Leaving through the window, the superwoman figure exclaims that truth and "identities" are constantly changing, depending on the "stories" which people believe (Harari et al. 2021, 242–43).

Valladolid was the place where Bartolomé de las Casas defended the human rights of Indigenous Americans against the fundamentalist cynic Luís de Sepúlveda in 1550–51. This was a major intellectual event during the early phase of European imperial expansion which shaped later discourses on international law (Hanke 1965). A sad result of Las Casas' activism was that Africans were used instead of Native Americans as plantation slaves. But the widespread claim that he was responsible for slavery itself is as cynical as Dr. Fiction's nihilism because it shows a similar

---

16   Having "deconstructed" the political-philosophical principle of universal human rights, *Sapiens* offer an extended series of statements on the need for an ideology (called "imagined orders," "beliefs" or "fictions"). "Gravity will still be there tomorrow morning, but human rights and the dollar, who knows…," we read, followed by the assertion that it often takes armies and police to force people into complying with the imagined order. But for "some people" more than violence is required to sustain an imagined order; they "have to really believe in it." Even "the elite" have to believe in "something" to be able to cooperate, like "God, money, … or honor, patriotism, manliness." These sociologically sloppy statements merge into an appreciation of cynicism as a general position, as "real cynics" rarely ever try to "reach the top" of a society. "Empires", Uncle Harari lectures to his smart niece (who indeed does believe that cynics can take power), "are far more likely to be built by true believers than cynics" (Harari et al. 2021, 104–5). The formulation is for once precise: the "builders" of empires are indeed often common laborers blinded by the named ideologies; their leaders, as innumerable examples show, are often cynics only interested in their own power.

resistance toward historical analysis of the political and discursive forces at play during that formative period.[17]

With the foundations of humanist legal thought being reduced to a vapid fantasy, the biologist narrative reigns supreme. The Valladolid scene is followed by a silly conversation between Margaret Thatcher and John Lennon on the beach if Ibiza about the existence of contradictory stories without any mature reflection on the relationship between stories and the real.[18] The plausibility of the theory that the majority of humans react to the stories of convincing elites finally dissolves when Dr. Fiction turns her previous assertion upside-down, now claiming that "the world isn't inevitable, you can change the story. It's up to you" (Harari et al. 2021, 251). Banks, religions and governments are indeed not the work of nature, heaven, or biology but just "human inventions". This final subversion is itself merely the last statement in a confusing, and – for those enjoying the spread of confusion – delightful shadow play about truth and fiction, to be continued in two more volumes promising to explain, as the preview announces, the historical interactions between money, empire, and religion (Harari et al. 2021, 251–53).

Harari's books expose their readers to stunningly contradictory positions, reiterating the epistemic and intellectual confusion currently at large in the social media and beyond, amplified by the intentional spread

---

17   Spanish jurists laid the basis for modern international law, in the Valladolid debates and other debates to follow. No contemporary English or US court or law faculty ever went to any lengths to determine the legality of colonial activities in America before the Marshall Court of the Removal era.

18   The bottom line is that stories are created for "people" (by whom?) to manipulate them. Harari suggests the existence of a conscious apparatus for the dissemination of state ideologies, e.g. through the educational system, architecture, images and the like (Harari et al. 2021, 108, 187–93). This simple cybernetic model of the authoritarian implantation of beliefs cannot readily explain social and political change. For Dr. Fiction, change – such as the "feminist revolution" – comes about because someone decided to change the story (Harari et al. 2021, 249), without adding which power position ascertains the success of such interventions. Essential questions about cultural communication, the dissemination of ideology, and the emergence of counterdiscourses remain unresolved.

of fake "truths" and "alternative facts". Certainly, at the end of the second graphic volume, all claims to historical truth have evaporated: historiography is merely a colorful story, told by Uncle Harari from his armchair. It is not a responsible and pedagogically useful approximation of the truth about the past. *Sapiens* owes its popularity to its intelligent use of implicit knowledge and beliefs, expressed in the form of postmodern play and pastiche. Its narrative creatively employs various fallacies, such as confusing correlation with causation, anachronistic representation, generalization, logical monocausality, and an anecdotal-parallactical method linking its modern humans with decontextualized fictional scenes from much earlier times without accounting for the historical process of centuries and millennia. There is especially little mention of the history of colonial capitalism immediately preceding, and indeed continuing in, the present period. The books' argument builds on the fact that our access to the real is regulated by ideology and belief systems imposed by an intelligent elite on the less intelligent majority. Their own position is an amoral one: that of the cynical and mentally superior observer of the affairs of the human rabble with their actions unredeemably trapped by petty beliefs. In other words, it is based on dividing "Sapiens" into the many who go about their daily work and the few who can afford to look down upon them, arranging the figures of world history as in a sideshow for their entertainment. Harari's superior observer in fact occupies a god-like position, *Homo Deus* being one of his titles declaring the elite's future state. Or that of the devil, as the case may be.[19] For an Americanist reader, Uncle Harari is reminiscent of Mark Twain's mysterious stranger, who calls himself "Satan" and visits Earth to entertain three Austrian boys by creating five hundred miniature people whom he then kills off at his pleasure in wars and catastrophes. While snuffing out a peasant's life, he comforts the boys not to worry: "they were of no consequence, and we could make more, some time or other, if we needed them" (Twain 1980, 173). In terms of the little value attributed to common humanity, "homo deus" becomes indistinguishable from "homo diaboli".

---

19   After all, "homo deus" – the promise to become godlike – is the serpent's promise to Adam and Eve (Genesis 3, 5).

3.   Sedentariness Without Social Hierarchy

Next to the drudgery of a sedentary lifestyle, agriculture, according to the biodeterminist narrative promoted by Harari, also brought about social inequality and an increase of human violence. Then again even the mass killings of the twentieth century seem statistically small compared to the percentage of violent deaths found in selected ancient graves (Harari et al. 2020, 184–88).[20] As David Graeber and David Wengrow remind us, the argument that agriculture brought about social inequality and a raise of human violence can be traced back to Jean-Jacques Rousseau's *Discours sur les origines et les fondements de l'inégalité parmi les hommes* (1755; Graeber/Wengrow 2021, 27–28; 63–67). However, it is by no means clear that Rousseau draws a causal connection between agriculture and inequality:

> The first man who, having fenced off a plot of land, thought of saying 'This is mine' and found people simple enough to believe him was the real founder of civil society. How many crimes, wars, murders, how many miseries and horrors might the human race have been spared by the one who, upon pulling up the stakes or filling in the ditch, had shouted to his fellow men 'Beware of listening to this impostor, you are lost, *if you forget that the fruits of the earth belong to all and that the earth belongs to no one.'* But by that time, things had very probably already come to the point where they could no longer go on as they were, for this idea of property*, depending upon many prior ideas which could only have arisen successively, *did not suddenly take shape in the human

---

20   In a breathtaking arithmetic tour de force, the first graphic "history" calculates, on the basis of scant finds in ancient graves and a lot of speculation, that "forager" societies were probably less violent than sedentary ones. The calculations are methodically questionable, as in the statement "So ancient Kentucky may have been as violent as the 20th century!" (Harari et al. 2020, 185). The absurdity of such a comparison (we have a handful of skulls from the archaeological site of Indian Knoll, Kentucky, but hard evidence of the violence of the whole last century) gets lost in assertive self-praise on having "explained all that so clearly" (186) although "we really don't know much about the lives of ancient foragers" (187).

mind. It was necessary to make much progress, to acquire considerable ingenuity and knowledge, and to transmit and increase them
from age to age, before arriving at this last stage of the *state of nature*. (Rousseau 1988, 34; emphasis added)

If I read him correctly, Rousseau here regards the invention of private property as occurring at the last stage of the state of nature, later
extending to the privatization of land, which was formerly used in
common ("the fruit of the earth" belonging "to all"). The fence comes to
represent the beginnings of private property rather than the beginnings
of agriculture: Rousseau distinguishes between the dividing up of land
in consequence of its cultivation and the emergence of private property:
"From the cultivation of lands necessarily followed their division, and
from property, once recognized, the first rules of justice," he writes,
followed by a confirmation of John Locke's theory of property by labor
(Rousseau 1988, 41). The *Discours*, which is a piece of political theory
rather than a historically precise account of the emergence of agriculture, assumes a concurrence of land cultivation and private property,
without claiming a causality. Rousseau's reflections must have been
inspired by observing the fencing off of common land and its transformation into private property, which he would have been able to witness
in Europe at the time: the violent enclosure of land and its transfer into
private manorial estates. Less interested in farming than in the sociological causes of inequality and moral decline, Rousseau stresses the
presence, or lack of, "talent" and "ambition" to increase wealth among
men as a decisive factor rather than agricultural practices (Rousseau
1988, 41, 42).[21]

Graeber and Wengrow spend a large part of their book demonstrating, on the basis of archaeological reconstruction and anthropological

---

21   I find confirmation for my reading from Kyle Keeler who critiques what he calls
      the Early Anthropocene Narrative. Agriculture, greed, "and eventually private
      property", Keeler writes, "do not follow one another in a linear fashion. Instead,
      commodified land and private property arise from colonialism rather than agri-
      culture" (Keeler 2021).

field study, that agricultural-sedentary societies were not inevitably hierarchical, just as non-agricultural societies can be shown to have hierarchical structures responsible for social inequality. The standard historical narrative that regards the introduction of agriculture, rather than the introduction of private property, as the beginning of inequality, is to them unfeasible. They regard agriculture as a matter of human choice, to be adopted and later neglected for long periods of time. Instead of speaking of a monolithic concept they regard agriculture as a vast spectrum of activities, knowledge, and skills developed over many centuries – knowledges and inventions that "we are likely to be benefiting from" and are grateful for every morning when "we sit down to breakfast" (Graeber/ Wengrow 2021, 499). *The Dawn of Everything*, subtitled "A New History of Humanity," is both a history of mankind and a historically substantiated assessment of human agency and creativity. It is also a counterhistory to the biologist-determinist historical narrative discussed above. *Dawn* confronts that narrative on many grounds, of which I would like to focus on those two examples already selected for my reading of *Sapiens*: the role of cognition and of agriculture, subject to Harari's two "revolutions".

There was no agricultural revolution, Graeber and Wegrow argue. For many centuries, if not millennia, as they demonstrate, agricultural practices were included by human groups in their portfolio of food production, without replacing hunting and gathering practices, and without forcing humans into permanent settlement. In addition, their book contains a running critique of the stadialist-developmentalist narrative (described above), whose teleology they find to be incompatible with historical evidence, and of the colonial-capitalist economic structure that produced both the technocratic-Enlightenment narrative of progress and the well-known semantics of cultural inequality explaining particular human groups' success and other groups' disaster. At the same time, the humanist-Enlightenment ideals of human rights, deliberative democracy, and altruistic reciprocity, they argue, are at least partially indebted to the cultural encounter in the Americas. This is not a new argument, of course, and the authors may be charged with a too indiscriminate reading of the semantically complex colonial sources (seventeenth- and eighteenth-century accounts of Jesuits and travelers

like the Baron de Lahontan).[22] However, it is indisputable that the encounter between critical European intellectuals and Indigenous peoples
did cause a process of intellectual alternation and that Enlightenment,
and especially Romantic thinking was influenced by these epistemic exchanges.[23] Plant knowledge is only one of many transcultural epistemic
contact zones between European and American societies. For reasons
deserving further analysis, this botanical transculturation is still only
partially understood.[24]

David Wengrow and David Graeber offer a richly researched synthesis of the past decades' research into Neolithic and Indigenous
societies, which forcefully demonstrates that the simplistic dualism
between "hunter-gatherer" or "foraging" societies on the one hand and
"agricultural" societies on the other is not tenable. According to their
evidence, humans were much more flexible than the dichotomy allows,
adjusting their mode of production according to environmental and
social needs. Historical societies' flexibility, *Dawn* shows, confounds the
determinist narratives' smooth assertions. Rather than being sullenly

---

22   They do refer to Anthony Pagden's important essay on the philosophical fig-
      ure of the "savage critic" in which Pagden argues that narratives of encounters
      with wise representatives of Indigenous people, whether partially or fully fic-
      tional, served above all rhetorical purposes (Pagden 1983). Based on several ex-
      tended encounters between Lahontan and the Wendat (Huron) leader Kandi-
      aronk (Adario), Lahontan's conversations are semi-fictional, heteroglossic texts
      not easily available as factual historical evidence.

23   I'm borrowing Jack Goody's term "alternation". In *Theft of History*, Goody makes a
      similar argument about the influence of Oriental thought on classical Mediter-
      ranean philosophy and critiques the erasure of that indebtedness by Western
      historiography (Goody 2006).

24   There is a massive literature on botanical exchange during the expansion of Eu-
      rope (e.g. Drayton 2005; Schiebinger 2007). But there is very little analysis of
      the interactions between settlers and Indigenous agriculturalists and garden-
      ers. This is in part owing to the fact that destruction of crops was part of colonial
      warfare, that Indigenous agriculture was ideologically incompatible with Eu-
      ropean constructions of cultural identity and alterity (thus rendered invisible),
      and that in the United States the eastern, agricultural tribes were forcefully re-
      moved in the 1830s.

driven by conditions not of their making, Wengrow and Graeber show in an impressive number of cases, our ancestors have always made choices, responded intelligently and creatively to changing situations, and, if the social structure became too hierarchical or too centrist, "walked away". Neither were humans cognitively incapable of making at times radical changes. This insight, well known from the study of recent history but here demonstrated for pre-modern societies, is confirmed by innumerable cases of colonized societies which show(ed) incredible resilience in securing their survival in spite of dispossession, deculturation, and the destruction of their natural source of subsistence.

While for Harari free will is a myth, then, Graeber and Wengrow regard the "agricultural revolution" and the denial of human choice as a myth. Human beings had "tens of thousands of years to experiment with different ways of life, long before any of them turned their hands to agriculture" (Graeber/Wengrow 2021, 140). In fact, they claim, the "Agricultural Argument' … has played a major role in the displacement of untold thousands of indigenous peoples from ancestral land in Australia, New Zealand, sub-Saharan Africa and the Americas." The assertion that the people to be dispossessed lacked knowledge of agriculture formed the legal basis for dispossession (Graeber/Wengrow 2021, 148–49). They present overwhelming evidence that because Indigenous ways of land use differed from European-style farming they were invisible to the newcomers: what "to a settler's eye seemed savage, untouched wilderness usually turns out to be landscapes actively managed by indigenous populations for thousands of years" (Graeber/Wengrow 2021, 150). What differed was the concept of land ownership informing human relations to the earth, with the European, Lockean, concept of property being of a relatively recent date and extremely narrow in its admission of different kinds of labor (Graeber/Wengrow 2021, 149). Ultimately, this concept of property stems from Roman Law and its tripartite definition of property as *usus*, *fructus*, and *abusus*, with only those enjoying all three rights being regarded as true legal proprietors. Usufruct alone did not provide absolute property. "The defining feature of true legal property, then, is that one has the option of *not* taking care of it, or even destroying it at will" (Graeber/Wengrow 2021, 161). The *right to destroy* land (*abusus*) gave absolute property according to Roman Law, not skillful and creative land stewardship.

In the chapter "The Gardens of Adonis", Wengrow and Graeber make an impressive, richly documented case for the coexistence of agricultural and non-agricultural practices of food production in the ancient Fertile Crescent. They report scientific evidence for humans living in areas of annual flooding to having been employed in various mixtures of food production. The fact that it took at least three millennia for humans to become fully sedentary confounds Harari's and other popular historians' thesis of an agricultural revolution, no matter how flippantly "Professor Saraswati" deals with long time sequences (Graeber/Wengrow 2021, 233).

As in the Fertile Crescent, according to *Dawn* and other expert studies, agricultural food production in different parts of the world coexisted with other forms both on a seasonal level or as a mixed economy. Similar kinds of "play farming" have been reconstructed by archaeobotanists, e.g. for the Amazon Basin (Graeber/Wengrow 2021, 266–72; Safier 2021). The thesis of the very gradual and slow transition toward more and more solid forms of plant cultivation is supported by archaeological evidence on the emergence of agricultural practices in America. In *Children of Ataentsic*, Bruce Trigger reconstructs the period leading to the formation of both the Haudenosaunee (Iroquois) and Wendat (Huron) confederacies before or around AD 1500. A gradual shift toward sedentary horticulture and then agriculture, Trigger assumes, already began around AD 500 (Trigger 1987, 131). For the Late Owasco phase, from c. AD 1230 to AD 1375, there is evidence of a hybrid form of food production, including the cultivation of corn, beans and squash (the Three Sisters) (Graeber/Wengrow 2021, 487). A warmer stretch of the climate, Trigger assumes, might have encouraged the adoption of corn and beans even in this northern latitude around Lake Ontario. There is no evidence of an increase of social conflict as a result of agriculture; rather, growing population numbers were concurrent with the formation of peace alliances. Trigger makes a case for greater social density having been desired by those people, who preferred to spend more time together in the plant growing season while moving apart for the hunting season after the harvest was brought in (Trigger 1987, 133–34).

There is good evidence that the proto-Iroquoians took the advantage of horticulture, which enabled them to stay together all year round, because they actually valued sociability. Trigger's argument is a complete inversion of Harari's who assumes that population density inevitably leads to conflict. The reason for the difference is that Trigger, Graeber and Wengrow go about scientifically: they find evidence for a tribal kinship structure quite unlike that assumed by Harari, who projects a modern competitive nuclear family structure on to "prehistorical" times ("Prehistoric Bill"). The experts thus differ from Harari both in their assessment of the historical practice of plant cultivation and in their emphasis on humans' desire for mutual aid and cooperation. *Sapiens* suggests that cooperation was coercive practice; it favors competition as the natural form of social interaction (e.g., Harari 2021, 29, 65–76, 86). Graeber, Wengrow, and Trigger find that cooperativeness and alliance-making were actively sought.

Just like Graeber and Wengrow, Bruce Trigger finds evidence for the emergence of matrilineality and a strengthening of women's social roles as a consequence of sedentariness, as life was increasingly organized around female horticultural work groups (Trigger 1987, 135). In one of their rare direct critiques of the narrative of agriculture as trap, Graeber and Wengrow ask the question of who precisely domesticated whom or what. The flippant thesis that humans were domesticated by wheat, they write, obscures the view of who actually did "all the intellectual and practical work of manipulating wild plants: exploring their properties in different soils and water regimes, experimenting with harvesting techniques, accumulating observations about the effects these all have on growth, reproduction and nutrition; debating the social implications … Consciously or not, it is the contributions of women that get written out of such accounts" (Graeber/Wengrow 2021, 236–37). They call attention to the "gendered assumptions" (Graeber/Wengrow 2021, 238) behind dominant concepts of agriculture, domestication, and cultivation – epitomized in the term "husbandry". They refer to the neglect of women's work, especially their artificial and often temporary creation of garden plots: "Instead of fixed fields," these female gardeners "exploited alluvial soils on the margins of lakes and springs, which shifted location from year to year. And instead of hewing wood, tilling fields and carrying water," Graeber and Wengrow write, "they found ways of 'persuading' nature to do much of this labor for them. Theirs was not a science of domination and classification, but one of bending and coaxing, nurturing and cajoling, or even tricking the forces of nature." They find evidence for the high social standing of women, based on their horticultural and soil expertise, in female figurines and statues found at Neolithic sites (Graeber/Wengrow 2021, 239–40).

Other scholars confirm the distinction between two forms of agricultural practice along gender differences. This distinction, as Kyle Keeler writes in his critique of the agricultural "trap" narrative, is one between an extractive, "masculine" agricultural practice, and a relational, "feminine" "system of partnerships between humans and other-than-human beings over centuries" (Keeler 2021, 1). His assessment is confirmed by Indigenous scholars like Robin Wall Kimmerer who stresses the symbiotic partnership between Indigenous planters and their food plants (Kimmerer 2013, 139–40). Innovation in early agricultural societies, Graber and Wengrow concur, was not based on "some male genius realizing his solitary vision" but rather "on a collective body of knowledge accumulated over centuries, largely by women, in an endless series of apparently humble but in fact enormously significant discoveries" (Graeber/Wengrow 2021, 499).

The story that emerges from these studies is that of a non-extractive but rather companion species-oriented practice of plant cultivation that developed in the Americas and elsewhere in conjunction with more or less sedentary forms of social organization. Instead of a vicious agricultural "trap", the scholars observe an increase of female social status. Graeber and Wengrow give other examples of the well-known prestige of women in Iroquoian societies, including the Wendat which they particularly studied. In addition, they produce evidence for Indigenous Americans' ability to escape from situations of political centralization, hierarchy, and inequality. For example, they argue that the formation of confederacies by both the Haudenosaunee and Wendat may be a late lesson from the collective historical experience of the flowering and decline of Cahokia (c. AD 1050–1350), one of the cultural centers on the banks

of the Mississippi. That metropole's maximum population size is calcu-
lated to have been 15,000, with a peak around 40,000 for the surrounding
area called the American Bottom (Graeber/Wengrow 2021, 452, 465). After the decline of Cahokia, the cultivated area up the Ohio River became
a depopulated zone – a "haunted wilderness of overgrown pyramids,"
as the two Davids romanticize the demographic vacuum. They assume
that the experience of Cahokia's disintegration left "extremely unpleas-
ant [collective] memories" which may have "erased" it from "oral tradition" yet left an impact on social practice. For centuries to come and over a
large geographical area extending from the Ohio to Ontario,[25] they spec-
ulate, future communities sought to avoid the trap of social inequality
(Graeber/Wengrow 2021, 468). When European settlers arrived in Iro-
quoia and Huronia, they encountered societies acting on their knowledge of their own political history, who "saw their own social orders as
self-conscious creations, designed as a barrier against all that Cahokia
might have represented – or indeed, all those qualities they were later to
find so objectionable in the French" (Graeber/Wengrow 2021, 482). The
European newcomers encountered peoples who had learned their historical lesson.

4.   Social and Communicative Competence

This is an admittedly speculative account,[26] but a more plausible and
evidence-based one than the popular imperial narratives of imploding
ancient American civilizations, or their destruction by intruding enemies. Ancient settlements, in Wengrow and Graeber's reading, rather
dissolved gradually for ecological or sociological reasons or both. Those
who "walked away" from Tikal and Cahokia did not disappear; they just

---

25   This would make its geography to roughly coincide with the earlier Hopewell
Interaction Sphere c. 100 BC – AD 500.

26   Graeber and Wengrow also pussyfoot around the excessive violence between
the Haudenosaunee and the Wendat, which led to the latter confederacy's disintegration under the pressure of European settlement.

left no archaeological trace.[27] The dissolution of these states confirms evolutionary theory's thesis of nature's, and thus humans', power of adaptation as a prerequisite of survival – a knowledge that fits into no linear, developmental, or teleological narrative. That narrative is a human invention rather than a fact of nature.[28] The narratives of hostile destruction are most likely projections of the displacement which imperial nations themselves enacted upon the descendants of the ancient populations. They derive their plausibility from the knowledge of more

---

27   I adopt Graeber and Wengrow's use of the semantics of "walking away", which is influenced by Ursula Le Guin's short story "The Ones Who Walk Away from Omelas" (1973). The metaphor of walking away continues to enjoy literary popularity, e.g. in Cory Doctorow's novel *Walkaway* (2017) whose sympathetic urbanite group walk away from an increasingly oppressive state starting their own communities with the help of digital inventions. Graeber and Wengrow explicitly refer to Ursula Le Guin's tale (Graeber/Wengrow 2021, 290), a bleak ethnographic parable of a fictional society whose comfort and joy is dependent on the living sacrifice of a child scapegoat. The fictional population is not without knowledge or compassion for the terrible suffering of the child, but it sadly accepts it as inevitable: "Yet it is their tears and anger, the trying of their generosity and the acceptance of their helplessness, which are perhaps the true source of the splendor of their lives. Theirs is no vapid, irresponsible happiness. They know that they, like the child, are not free. They know compassion. It is the existence of the child, and their knowledge of its existence, that makes possible the nobility of their architecture, the poignancy of their music, the profundity of their science" (Le Guin 1973, 283). Inspired by a conversation in Fjodor Dostyevsky's *The Brothers Karamasov* (1880), it is Le Guin's version of the Christian sacrifice ethic, as well as of Walter Benjamin's famous phrase that there is no document of civilization which is not at the same time a document of barbarism. But every now and then, the story continues, individual members of the imaginative city leave, never to return. We do not learn where they go or whether they will start a community of their own. Le Guin's resistance to simple utopianism is idiosyncratic: it breathes ethnographic and psychological wisdom but is deeply discomforting.

28   It is well to remember Johannes Fabian's splendid critique of the superimposition of the imperial narrative of development onto Darwin's theory (Fabian 2002, chapter 1). Time itself is as irrelevant to the theory of evolutionary adaptation as narrative.

recent imperial routines which they naturalize, not from the scientific analysis of the archaeological and anthropological evidence.

To read the forging of political federations as a response to the failures of earlier social formations is to regard Indigenous Americans to be as capable as seemingly more "civilized" people of learning from past mistakes and preferring peaceful interaction to warfare, democracy to authoritarian rule, freedom of will to tyranny. In fact, as Keeler argues following Daniel Wildcat, the ability to learn from mistakes is uppermost among social qualities in Native American cultures, as is testified in Indigenous story traditions (Keeler 2021, 7). In their similar emphasis on the social and pedagogical competence of Indigenous Americans (Graeber/Wengrow 2021, 45–48), Wengrow and Graeber contest the romantic colonial celebration of Indigenous eloquence as merely ornamental and as remaining blind to the implications: indeed, Indigenous enthusiasm for extensive oral communication is an indicator of what we call deliberative democracy. A result not of genetic essence but of training and patient practice, the competence to communicate has proven the only feasible means of conflict solution.

The existence of large ancient settlements – Teotihuacan in the Valley of Mexico and the Trypillian mega-sites in today's Ukraine and Moldova – suggest that sedentariness did not automatically lead to conflict and inequality (Graeber/Wengrow 2021, 328–45; 288–94). As archaeological analysis suggests, these large urban centers were organized around "flat" political and administrative structures. Building on earlier readings of these "invisible cities", Wengrow and Graeber show their settlement patterns to lack all evidence of centralization or a social elite (like palaces) while showing remnants of neighborhoods with homes organized around larger meeting places not unlike the longhouses of Native North America. Agriculture in these societies was not responsible for inequality. Consequently, the source of inequality must be sought in the social and property structures of societies, not their food economy.

5.   On Cognitive Freedom

Wengrow and Graeber's book, then, is a full-fledged subversion of the imperial providential-determinist narrative. Human history in their account is not moving along an arrow of time from savagism to perfection and off into the posthumanoid metaverse but is rather the result of constant negotiation and adaptation, trial and error. *Dawn* regards human events and human interactions with the more-than-human world as evolutionary in that term's original meaning, formulated as a law of adaptation by Charles Darwin – not evolutionist as in social Darwinism, which integrated Darwin's theory into the existing linear-determinist plot. This tragic crypto-biblical narrative of man's fall from Paradise is the real trap, not least because of its popularity with billionaires (Graeber/Wengrow 2021, 493). While the doom narrative semantically adheres to the suspense-driven plot of Aristotelian tragedy with its very strong sense of closure, *Dawn* promotes an open-ended historical narrative by insisting on the indeterminacy of events. It also *performs* that episodic and indeterminate plot form by engaging the reader in a cyclical narrative that runs its main arguments through a series of empirical scenarios.[29]

In other words, *Dawn* radically contradicts *Sapiens*'s assertion of humans' cognitive captivity and susceptibility to elite fictions. Against the pervasive neoliberal dogma that populations are easily nudged into all kinds of beliefs and ideologies, Graeber and Wengrow make a forceful argument for humans' ability for intellectual freedom.[30] People are capable of listening to other humans' fictions, their book suggests; but they are just as capable of rejecting them. Both *Sapiens* and *Dawn* attempt to find an answer to the question why humanity ended up in the mess in

---

29   The plot structure of tragedy is well known; my understanding of episodic plot rests on Lawrence Sterne's *Tristram Shandy* (1759–67), whose narrator at one point sketches for his readers the chaotic plot structure of the novel.

30   Harari's sweeping claim of cognitive unfreedom is probably more dangerous than his particular constructions of the distant past.

which it presently finds itself – with itself and the rest of creation threatened by mass extinctions and climate change, and increasingly threatened by authoritarian regimes ready to bomb their own populations and their neighbors back into the stone age. Wengrow and Graeber suspect a causality between this self-destructiveness and the imaginative incompetence of too many humans: "If something did go terribly wrong in human history – and given the current state of the world, it's hard to deny something did – then perhaps it began to go wrong precisely when people started losing that freedom to imagine and enact other forms of social existence," together with the memory of that loss (Graeber/Wengrow 2021, 502). Collective amnesia and an extremely narrow conception of the past, after all, are the foundation of an increasingly privatized and consumerized educational system.

In claiming history to be messy and open-ended and the human mind to be flexible and adaptable, Wengrow and Graeber subvert Harari's subversions of humans as an unthinking crowd marching to its predetermined end. They counter a pop history of common humanity's doom and godlike elite with a historical narrative of possibility and repair; and a "history" based on the imagined agency of wheat with a history of human agency and companion-species resilience. Human inequality, in this reading, is not the inevitable result of a process of civilization (or cultivation) but of a very particular kind of civilization, one based on the irresponsible and profitable extraction of nature and other humans.

6.   Romantic Foraging and Invisible Gardens

Sapiens and *Dawn* conspicuously differ in their use of visuals. While Harari fully exploits the potential of graphic images by hiring two excellent cartoon artists, Graeber and Wengrow are puritanically abstinent when it comes to visuals. The graphics of the illustrated *Sapiens* volumes deserve appreciation in their own right for their intelligent metaleptical intertextuality, mixing the disappearance of the Neanderthals with *Guernica*, illustrating a discussion on the ills of modern society with the iconic image of Charlie Chaplin being machine-fed in *Modern Times*, or integrating Franz Kafka's absurd experiences with modern bureaucracy into the narrative. The image of the Faustian wheat is very funny and therefore effective. But the historical messages of such extravagances mostly remain unclear. A sketch of Harari as Caspar David Friedrich's wanderer in the mountains – the last man? – reveals a trace of self-irony. The impressive Dordogne landscapes devoid of human inhabitants imitate colonial travelers' "discoveries" in empty lands (Figure 2). The figures are presented as romantic foragers in pristine landscapes, enjoying the imperial dream of being alone in the world and having it laid out before them. *Dawn*, conversely, demonstrates an almost ghostly resistance to images. The map of one of the reconstructed ancient Ukrainian settlements (Figure 3) can be read as a statement *against* nonverbal representation, underscoring the scientific rigor used in the volume.[31]

But visibility features on a second level as well. In reconstructing ancient agriculture, Graeber and Wengrow provide an explanation for the invisibility of gardens as a form of food production: they were predominantly worked by women, a group of "Sapiens" that hardly features in Western patriarchal historiography. This principal sociological invisibility, however, is reinforced by the material transience of gardens, which, unlike larger fields, hardly leave a lasting geomorphological trace (Doolittle 2000, 82–117).[32] *Dawn*'s refutation of the pop narrative, then, is also a refutation of an illustrated and essentially masculine story, which they replace with a much more sober reconstruction of the emergence of agriculture as a very complex and longue durée process which significantly involved the intellectual and creative input of women.

---

31   Visual reproductions of these sites do exist; see, e.g. this popular-scientific one: The Cucuteni-Trypillian culture and the mysterious burning of the buildings | Ancient Origins (ancient-origins.net).

32   William Doolittle exemplifies the ideological invisibility of female-run gardens by referring to an archaeological report's silence about gardens in a Mississippi site while the report's title page artwork clearly shows three gardens (Doolittle 2000, 102).

Fig. 2: Pleistocene Dordogne landscape.

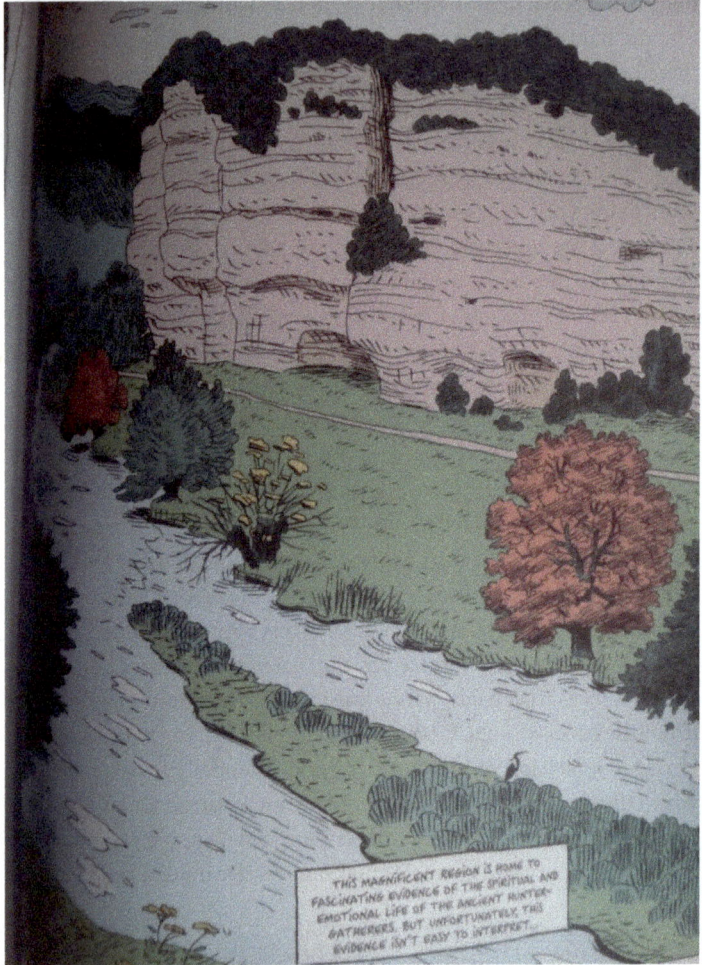

Harari, Yuval Noah, David Vandermeulen, and Daniel Casanave (2020). *Sapiens. A Graphic History. The Birth of Humankind.* London: Jonathan Cape. P. 167

Fig 3: Reconstruction of the ancient (c. 5000 BC) settlement of Maidanetske, Ukraine.

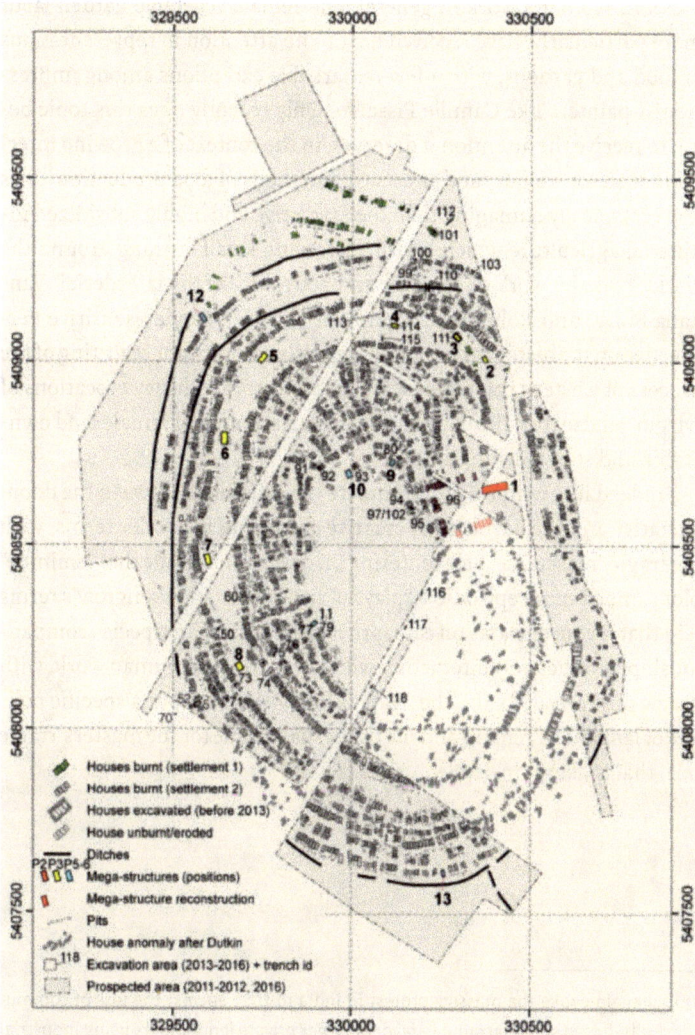

Credit: Robert Hofmann. Institute of Pre- and Protohistoric Archaeology, Kiel University (Hofmann et al. 2019).

The process of invisibilization which *Dawn* discloses and verbally "repairs" is indeed pervasive in Western discourse about female food production. Women's work in general, and female vegetable garden labor more particularly, have received next to no attention in representations of food and gardens, with a few remarkable exceptions among impressionist painters like Camille Pissarro. Only recently does this topic begin to receive the attention it deserves, in the context of a growing interest in food sovereignty and alternative methods of food production, ones less ecologically damaging than the extractive and highly subsidized industrial agriculture which is still destroying small farming around the world.[33] As the work of scholars and activists like Silvia Federici, Vandana Shiva, and Robin Wall Kimmerer shows, a gender-sensitive perspective on the history of agriculture entails a significant rewriting of the process of western colonialism, whose testosterone-heavy evocations of "virgin" landscapes all but obscure the displacement of female land ownership and stewardship.

Indeed it is tempting to formulate the difference between the doom narrative and the narrative of creative gardening in gender terms, with the tragic "masculine" plot centering on destruction while the "feminine" plot is much more episodic – "playful" in Graeber and Wengrow's terms – in that it concentrates on care, procreation, and transspecies companionship, productively interacting with the more-than human world with a view to survival. Again, the "trap" is not agriculture but a specific politics of land management and the tragic master tale (or the masters' tragic tale) that makes it invisible.

---

33   I again evoke the massive protest in India in 2021 against the loss of community-based small farming in favor of larger private landholders using industrial methods. The enclosure policy, which started in Europe in the late Middle Ages, has never really ended; it continues today in the global south, especially India, Africa, and Latin America.

7.   Thomas Cole's Barbarians

Speaking of visibility. The narrative of progress was subverted by Romantic intellectuals right at its inception. In his painting cycle *The Course of Empire* (1833–36), inspired by Edward Gibbon's classic *The Decline and Fall of the Roman Empire* (1776), the British-American painter Thomas Cole gave aesthetic expression to the first three stages of "civilization" – in his version the savage stage, the pastoral or arcadian stage, and what Cole calls "Consummation": a Mediterranean-style imperial city; the foreground shows a triumphal march of a conqueror returning with foreign spoil and captives. But in the last two paintings his visual narrative shifts direction: the empire is destroyed by barbarian hordes (then the common view of the end of ancient Rome), and in the last painting all traces of any human presence are gone. Nature has repossessed the monumental ruins, and a bird has built its nest on top of one of the triumphal pillars. This is not the end of the world; only the end of humanity. Contrary to more recent re-inscriptors of the stadialist narrative (the planters of doom and/or the metaverse), Cole also names the real force of misery: not "nature" but "empire". The greatest leap in his cycle is between the second and third painting: while the pastoral or arcadian stage is modeled on romantic views of Greek antiquity and includes a farmer pushing an oxen-drawn plow over a field, "Consummation" surprises the viewer who may wonder how this triumphant empire – both its arts and architecture and its foreign aggressiveness – was able to leap into being.

Cole's empire cycle subverts his contemporaries' optimistic narrative of empire in a way that still resonates with our own time. In his romantic critique, modern civilization is built on inequality and exploitation, and therefore doomed. Although he could not have anticipated climate change and species extinction, Cole's cycle is a cautionary tale that subverts the American national narrative of Manifest Destiny. It would be interesting to know more about Cole's barbarians: perhaps some of them were playful gardeners providing the urban elite with tasty vegetables while being held in social dependency and having their fields trampled over by imperial armies. Destroying crops and harvests in addition to all other life, after all, is what imperial armies prided themselves with throughout human history.

Conclusion

Sapiens and *Dawn of Everything* share a strong desire to explain current human affairs as resulting from the long durée of human history. Yet they represent two irreconcilable views on history and human nature: the first as biologically determined and illiberal; the second as open and intellectually flexible.[34] The popular master narrative of agricultural doom is grafted on earlier narratives – the providential-apocalyptic narrative of Christianity, the optimistic narrative of progress and successive stages, and the social Darwinist narrative of "natural" selection developed in response to the incompatibility of capitalism with the humanistic ideal of social equality. This biodeterminist version, popularized among that part of humanity benefitting from being born into the right milieu, combines a disdain for the non-elite producers of food with a denial of their intellectual equality.[35] It ultimately reiterates the Aristotelian position that humanity is divided into born masters and born slaves. Next to its protean quality – its shapeshifting adoption of various disguises throughout modern Western intellectual history – it is also Panglossian in its narrow and simplistic message that the world "we" inhabit is the best of all possible worlds. With its charismatic presentation it *performs* its semantic message of the impressionability of humans to the fictions of their mental superiors. In fact, it *produces* the non-thinking human beings which it claims already exist. As humanity embarks on probably its most ambitious collective effort to save both

---

34 They are also widely divergent concerning the depth of scholarship: *Dawn* has a 63-page bibliography and 83 pages of notes; *Sapiens* has a meager thirteen pages of notes.

35 Another essay could be written on the pervasive mode of contempt and ridicule used with reference to agricultural laborers – those who bend their backs and dirty their hands to produce our food.

humanity and the planet itself, as even the global elite congregating at Davos has accepted this truth, the Panglossian tale's denial of humans' power to effect such change already appears out of date – a perverse reminder of a neoliberalist doctrine proven wrong by the course of events. *Dawn*'s response to this gamble is to emphasize the human power of creative "play" – quite in the sense of Friedrich Schiller and Johan Huizinga – as that which makes humans truly human (Lewis 2021). In Graeber and Wengrow's hands, "play", a force they associate with carnival, stands for the freedom to relocate, the freedom to disobey commands, and "to shape entirely new social realities" (Graeber/Wengrow 2021, 117, 503) – in other words the power to imagine a world beyond the confines of the present social, economic, and cultural constellation.

Fig. 4

Harari, Yuval Noah, David Vandermeulen, and Daniel Casanave (2021) *Sapiens. A Graphic History, Vol. 2. The Pillars of Civilization*. London: Jonathan Cape. P. 115.

"It would take a superhuman effort to free my personal desires from the imagined order," Yuval Harari speaks, dividing the lines of a bar code as if spreading the curtain of a theater stage, or the bars of a prison window (Figure 4). "And if I did succeed, I'm just this one person" (Harari et al. 2021, 115). The "one person" story is one of capitalism's most successful traps – evoking mythical tales of heroism while denying the effects of individual and collective agency. Graeber and Wengrow confront this inherently contradictory position with innumerable examples of individuals and groups of humans having done just that: walk away from monocultural prison-houses physically and intellectually – to find out that they were not alone.

Works Cited

Carnegie, Andrew (2006) The Gospel of Wealth. 1889. The *"Gospel of Wealth" Essays and Other Writings*. New York: Penguin, 1–12.

Cheyfitz, Eric (1991) *The Poetics of Imperialism. Translation and Colonization from* The Tempest *to Tarzan*. Oxford University Press.

Conellan, Ian (2019) More Fuel for Early Anthropocene. *Cosmos* (7 October). Web: https://cosmosmagazine.com/history/civilisations/more-fuel-for-early-anthropocene/.

Deloria Jr., Vine (1997) *Red Earth – White Lies. Native Americans and the Myth of Scientific Fact*. Golden: Fulcrum.

Deloria, Philip (2021) Red Earth, White Lies, Sapiens, and the Deep Politics of Knowledge. In: Mackenthun, Gesa and Christen Mucher (eds.) *Decolonizing "Prehistory" Deep Time and Indigenous Knowledges in North America*. Tucson: University of Arizona Press, 231–48.

Diamond, Jared (1987) The American Blitzkrieg: A Mammoth Undertaking. *Discover*, 82–88.

Diamond, Jared (1997) *Guns, Germs and Steel: A Short History of Everybody for the Last 13000 Years*. London: Vintage.

Doctorow, Cory (2017) *Walkaway*. London: Head of Zeus.

Doolittle, William E. (2000) *Cultivated Landscapes of Native North America*. Oxford University Press.

Drayton, Richard (2005) *Nature's Government. Science, Imperial Britain, and the 'Improvement' of the World*. Delhi: Orient Longman.

Durant, Will and Ariel (1935–75) *Story of Civilization*. 11 vols. New York: Simon & Schuster.

Fabian, Johannes (2002) *Time and the Other. How Anthropology Makes Its Object*. Orig. 1983. New York: Columbia University Press.

Federici, Silvia (2019) *Re-Enchanting the World. Feminism and the Politics of the Commons.* Oakland: PM Press.

Foucault, Michel (1972) *The Archaeology of Knowledge.* New York: Pantheon.

Fritz, Gayle J. (2019) *Feeding Cahokia. Early Agriculture in the North American Heartland.* University of Alabama Press.

Goody, Jack (2006) *The Theft of History.* Cambridge University Press.

Graeber, David and David Wengrow (2021) *The Dawn of Everything: A New History of Humanity.* New York: Farrar, Straus, and Giroux.

Hanke, Lewis (1965) *The Spanish Struggle for Justice in the conquest of America.* Orig. 1947. Boston: Little, Brown and Company.

Hanks, Reuel R. (2011) *Encyclopedia of Geography, Terms, Themes, and Concepts.* Santa Barbara: ABC Clio.

Harari, Yuval Noah (2011). *Sapiens. A Brief History of Humankind.* London: Vintage.

Harari, Yuval Noah (2017) *Homo Deus. A Brief History of Tomorrow.* London: Vintage.

Harari, Yuval Noah (2018) The Myth of Freedom. *The Guardian* (14 September). Web: https://www.theguardian.com/books/2018/sep/1 4/yuval-noah-harari-the-new-threat-to-liberal-democracy?source =Snapzu.

Harari, Yuval Noah, David Vandermeulen, and Daniel Casanave (2020) *Sapiens. A Graphic History. The Birth of Humankind.* London: Jonathan Cape.

Harari, Yuval Noah, David Vandermeulen, and Daniel Casanave (2021) *Sapiens. A Graphic History, Vol. 2. The Pillars of Civilization.* London: Jonathan Cape.

Heineberg, Heinz (2003) *Einführung in die Anthropogeographie/Humangeographie.* Paderborn: Ferdinand Schöning.

Hofmann, Robert et al. (2019) Governing Tripolye: Integrative Architecture in Tripolye Settlements. *PLos ONE* 14,9. Web: https://doi.org/10 .1371/journal.pone.0222243.

Keeler, Kyle (2021) Before Colonization (BC) and After Decolonization (AD): The Early Anthropocene, the Biblical Fall, and Relational Pasts, Presents, and Futures. *EPE: Nature and Space* (21 August). Web: https ://journals.sagepub.com/doi/full/10.1177/25148486211033087.

Kelly, Robert L. (1995) *The Lifeways of Hunter-Gatherers. The Foraging Spectrum*. Cambridge University Press.

Kelly, Robert L. (2016) *The Fifth Beginning. What Six Million Years of Human History Can Tell Us About Our Future*. Berkeley: University of California Press.

Kelly, Robert L. (2020) *Warum es normal ist, dass die Welt untergeht*. Darmstadt: Theiss.

Kimmerer, Robin Wall (2013) *Braiding Sweetgrass. Indigenous Wisdom, Scientific Knowledge, and the Teaching of Plants*. Minneapolis: Milkwee.

Koch, Alexander, Chris Brierley, et al. (2019) Earth System Impacts of the European Arrival and Great Dying in the Americas After 1492. *Quaternary Science Reviews* 207: 13–36. Web: https://doi.org/10.1016/j.quascirev.2018.12.004.

Le Guin, Ursula (1987) The Ones Who Walk Away From Omelas. 1973. Repr. *The Wind's Twelve Quarters*. New York: Morrow/Harpercollins. 275–84.

Lewis, Zach (2021) Possible Worlds. The Broad Thinking of David Graeber and David Wengrow. *The Quietus* (18 December). Web: https://thequietus.com/articles/30965-david-graeber-david-wengrow-the-dawn-of-everything-review.

Mackenthun, Gesa (2021a) Sustainable Stories. Managing Climate Change With Literature. *Sustainability* 13(7). Web: https://www.mdpi.com/2071-1050/13/7/4049/htm.

Mackenthun, Gesa (2021b) *Embattled Excavations. Colonial and Transcultural Constructions of the American Deep Past*. Münster: Waxmann.

Martin, Paul S. (1967) Prehistoric Overkill. *Pleistocene Extinctions*. Paul S. Martin and Herbert E. Wright (eds.). New Haven: Yale UP, 75–120.

Mt. Pleasant, Jane and Robert F. Burt (2010) Estimating Productivity of Traditional Iroquoian Cropping Systems From Field Experiments and Historical Literature. *Journal of Ethnobiology* 30(1), 52–79.

Pagden, Anthony (1983) The Savage Critic. Some European Images of the Primitive. *Yearbook of English Studies* 13, 32–45.

Rousseau, Jean-Jacques (1988) Discourse on the Origins and Foundations of Inequality Among Men. 1755. In: Ritter, Alan and Julia Conway Bondanella (eds.). *Rousseau's Political Writings*. New York: Norton, 3–57.

Safier, Neil (2015) Fugitive El Dorado: The Early History of an Amazonian Myth *Fugitive Knowledge. The Loss and Preservation of Knowledge in Cultural Contact Zones*. Andreas Beer and Gesa Mackenthun (eds.). Münster: Waxmann, 51–62.

Schiebinger, Londa (2007) *Plants and Empire. Colonial Bioprospecting in the Atlantic World*. Harvard University Press.

Shiva, Vandana (2016) *Who Really Feeds the World? The Failures of Agribusiness and the Promise of Agroecology*. Berkeley: Atlantic Books.

Toynbee, Arnold (1939) *The Study of History*. Vol. VI "The Disintegration of Civilizations." Oxford: Oxford University Press.

Trigger, Bruce (1987) *Children of Aataentsic. A History of the Huron People to 1660*. Montreal: McGill-Queen's University Press.

Twain, Mark (1980) The Mysterious Stranger. 1916. Repr. *The Mysterious Stranger and Other Stories*. Signet, 161–253.

Wengrow, David (2021) Humanity is not Trapped in a Deadly Game with the Earth – there are Ways out. *Guardian* (31 October). Web: https://www.theguardian.com/commentisfree/2021/oct/31/man-not-trapped-in-deadly-game-with-earth-there-are-ways-out?msclkid=af740 630b10511ec8d84b0866e5a8689.

Contested Nationhood in the United States of America

Susanne Lachenicht

1.   Introduction

Article 1 of the purposes of the United Nations states that the UN are to "develop friendly relations among nations based on respect for the principle of equal rights and self-determination of peoples" (UN Charter, Article 1). Who is a sovereign nation, though? Are indigenous peoples sovereign nations?

In September 2007, after thirty years of debates, conflicts, civil rights movements, and negotiations, the United Nations General Assembly adopted the UN Declaration on the Rights of Indigenous Peoples with an overwhelming majority. It recognizes that indigenous peoples do have *collective* human rights including the rights to self-determination, spirituality, lands, territories, and natural resources (UNDRIPS 2007). While in 2007, the United States, Canada, New Zealand, and Australia had initially opposed the UN Declaration on the Rights of Indigenous Peoples, New Zealand and Australia reversed their positions in 2009, Canada and the U.S. in 2010.

The *United Nations Department of Economic and Social Affairs, Indigenous Peoples* (UNDRIP) holds that this document is "the most comprehensive international instrument on the rights of indigenous peoples. It establishes a universal framework of minimum standards for the survival, dignity, and well-being of the indigenous peoples of the world and it elaborates on existing human rights standards and fundamental freedoms as they apply to the specific situation of indigenous peoples" (UN-DRIP 2020). However, as a UN General Assembly Declaration, UNDRIP is not a legally binding instrument under international law. In addition, at UN and many states' level, indigenous peoples are mostly treated as non-government organizations (NGOs), not as sovereign nations with an autonomous government and sovereignty over their territories and resources.

In contrast to this general view of the rights of indigenous peoples vis-à-vis national governments, Native Americans in the United States of America have claimed for centuries to be treated as sovereign nations. With this, they have drawn on concepts of nationhood that Europeans developed from the fifteenth century onwards. Indigenous peoples thus inscribe themselves into fractured continuities (Lachenicht 2018), with regard to concepts of *the nation* and *nationhood*. Up to the present day, they try to (re-)negotiate their sovereignty rights, at times within the framework of the United States of America, sometimes outside or in between – in a Third Space, as Kevin Bruyneel put it (Bruyneel 2007, xi). Native Americans claim some form of postcolonial sovereign status, that is sovereignty rights within the modern United States of America. For the latter, this threatens its very integrity and sovereignty. Nationhood always implies the potential of resistance, subversion, rebellion, and revolution. Denying peoples nationhood or autonomous government has often been, and still is, a sign of subjugation, dispossession, and a strategy of extinction.

While classic theories on nationhood and nationalism suggest that "the nation" only became important from the later eighteenth century onward, that is with the Age of Revolution, research on the later Middle Ages and the early modern period suggests that nationhood has been a central category of belonging ever since (see below and literature quoted in Lachenicht 2022). Modern notions of the nation and nationhood grew out of these older, early modern ones. Since the Age of Revolution, some nations such as the French and U.S. American ones have been understood as nation states (*Staatsnationen*). Others such as Italians, Poles, or Germans, are defined as cultural nations (*Kulturnationen*), i.e., as nations having inhabited their territories since times immemorial, as sharing a common history, language, artefacts, and literatures. For quite some time, civilization and modernization theories required that nations had to form a nation state, as nations came to be considered the sole source of legitimate political power. Nations thus had the right and duty to determine themselves in a nation state. Nations which lacked these capacities were to be civilized by others. While most of these notions came with essentialist understandings of nationhood, the year 1983 brought a decisive turn for our understanding of nationhood and nationalisms: it saw the publication of Ernest Gellner's *Nations and Nationalism*, Eric Hobsbawm's and Terrence Ranger's *The Invention of Tradition*, and Benedict Anderson's *Imagined Communities*. These works took the inventedness of nations as "imagined political communities" as a point of analytical departure. They identified nations and nationalisms as the result of meaning-making activities, of performative acts that created the idea of nation in the first place. This so-called anthropological turn in nationalism theory thus problematizes essentializing concepts of ethnicity, nation, and nationhood. It also sheds light on the many varieties of nationhood, the fuzziness and ambivalence of the semantics of "the nation," and opens up horizons for nationhood beyond western ideals (Depkat and Lachenicht 2022).

This chapter tells the story of how European colonists in North America, and after 1776 the United States of America, on the one hand, and Native Americans on the other, made use of European notions of nationhood in the process of colonization, both with subversive intentions and effects, as we shall see. The essay will do so for the sixteenth to the early twenty-first century, zooming into specific moments in this process. The paragraphs will show how and in which periods it was useful for American Indians to appropriate the politically "subversive" elements of the concept of the nation, and when and why colonial governments started denying Native American nationhood.

The chapter starts out with a brief survey of colonial discourse on indigenous nationhood and sovereignty from the sixteenth to the eighteenth century. It will then move to the game-changing Peace of Paris of 1763 and the Early Republic. The major focus of this chapter is on the period of treaty-making with Native Americans in the United States between the later eighteenth and nineteenth centuries: how did Native Americans try to negotiate their nationhood and sovereignty rights in what some authors have described as the period of new colonialism (Wunder 1994, 27)? I will then look into the politics of removal and termination. The chapter ends with examples from the United States of America today, to analyze how American Indians use present concepts of nationhood and sovereignty in subversive ways to empower themselves as sovereign political entities.

2.   Colonial Discourse and Indigenous Nationhood

There has been some debate on indigenous nationhood and sovereignty in the early modern period. Before we look into this specific aspect of colonial discourse, it might be worthwhile to briefly address early modern concepts of nationhood.

In the early modern period, not only the French, English, Spanish, and Irish were addressed as nations but also Native Americans. In theory, all nations were equal. They were all subject to natural law and as such invested with common sovereignty rights. At the same time, all nations had and developed in history. In early modern times, the term *"nation"* comes with a variety of often entangled meanings: it referred to the same (mythical) origin, the same territory, which had been inhabited by the nation since times immemorial. In many instances, *"nation"* is tied to territory. Be it the English nation, the French, the Spanish or indigenous nations in the Americas: *the nation* is about territorial belonging, territorial and genealogical ancestry, climate, food, bodies, language, and history. Territorial ancestry, that is the idea of having inhabited a given space since times immemorial, meant that the nation united the "natural inhabitants" of a given territory and that those natural inhabitants were its "owners". Not only European but also indigenous people in the Americas could thus lay claim to being "natural inhabitants" – as among many others Charles de Rochefort writes in his 1681 *Histoire naturelle & morale des iles Antilles de l'Amérique* (Rochefort 1681, 6–7, 9, 11, 39; Labat 1722, vol.1, 60, 227). Ancestry entitled indigenous nations to sovereignty, to governing their ancestral territory. The *development in history*, however, was a trickier element: Europeans considered some nations "less developed" than others, "less civilized." From this perspective, the latter needed to be subjected and governed by "more superior nations" (Labat 1722, 135, 209–210; on the concept of early modern nationhood see Lachenicht 2022, Depkat and Lachenicht 2022).

Against this background, colonial discourse of Native American nationhood and sovereignty developed a number of somehow contradictory elements: in early seventeenth-century England, some doubted the lawfulness of colonization. Others held that just wars came with a right of conquest that included rights to seize and subdue land and people. Many colonial charters of the seventeenth and eighteenth centuries show that the respective European crown was thought to be entitled to issue patents to discover, subdue, and own land and people. As Christian rulers, they thought they were summoned to take the land of Native Americans. Conquest, in this reading, was the necessary prerequisite for Christianization and civilization (Banner 2005, 6–8, 10–48).

At times, we find these varied and somehow contradicting *topoi* in one and the same source, such as in André Thevet's (1516 – 1590) *Singularitez de la France Antarctique* of 1558. Thevet was a French Franciscan friar, explorer and cosmographer who travelled to the Eastern Mediterranean and Brazil. As many other travel accounts, the *Singularitez* are concerned with Europeans "discovering", gathering, and cultivating the riches of "new lands" which are described as abundant and invaluable. While Thevet concedes that the land belongs to the "savages," he judges the latter not to be "numerous enough to *properly* cultivate their land." Europeans are therefore required to take the newly found land from the "savages," to cultivate it and to thus take indigenous peoples out of barbarism and guide them into more civilized ways of life. The land of plenty, in today's Brazil, therefore, is in "the wrong hands" – according to de Thevet, a narrative which became a *topos* in European colonial discourse (Thevet 1558, 2, 14, 51).

In many other European texts of the mid-sixteenth to the early eighteenth century, American Indians are viewed as the natural inhabitants of the Americas who had lived there since times immemorial and who own the land – as we can see from Jean-Baptiste Labat's *Nouveau voyage aux isles de l'Amérique* of 1722, Charles de Rochefort's 1681 edition of his *Histoire naturelle & morale des iles Antilles de l'Amérique* and Thomas de Raynal's famous *Histoire des deux Indes* in its edition of 1780 (Labat 1722, 227; Raynal 1780, vol.1, 226; Rochefort 1681, 6, 9, 11, 39). In some passages, especially those that describe indigenous planting and farming, Native American nationhood and sovereignty rights over lands and territories are not being contested. In other chapters of the same texts, however, referring to social organization, religion, customs, and habits, the Caribs are represented as uncivilized people subject to colonial control. Their land has, as Labat writes in his *Nouveau voyage*, "no proper master," somehow echoing Thevet, John Winthrop, and other writers who held that the land was too vast to be only populated by a few "Indians" (who had been decimated by European disease). According to many of these authors, European kings needed to take possession of the Caribbean islands and other parts of the *New World* (Thevet 1558, 135). In other words, only if Europeans/Christians took possession of the land would there be full because "civil" sovereignty over these territories.

Colonial discourse on indigenous nationhood and sovereignty thus oscillates between an early modern understanding of nationhood and sovereignty that fully included Native American nations possessing property rights on the one hand and justifications for conquest, land grabbing and, later, subjugation based on the denial of such rights on the other. Both reasonings frequently appear in the same texts.

For a long time, however, the discursive assumption of ownership heavily contrasted with realities on the ground: during the "old period" of colonization in North America, that is up to the late eighteenth century, Europeans were often too weak to subjugate and govern vast Native American territories. Instead, Europeans were dependent on Native Americans and their knowledge of the land and its resources, as Captain John Smith, among others, readily conceded (Smith 1612). For a rather long period in the history of North America, "taking" American Indian land therefore meant that Europeans purchased land from American Indians and thus entered into treaties with these sovereign nations. These treaties not only regulated the purchase of land but also alliances, trade, jurisdictions, and territorial boundaries. They formally and legally recognized Native Americans as sovereign nations, with their own governments, territorial boundaries, laws, and jurisdictions (Konkle 2004, 2–3; Hoxie 1994, 87; Harring 1995, 14–15).

Between the seventeenth and the late eighteenth centuries, Native Americans used the language of nationhood and sovereignty in negotiations, conflicts, and treaty-making with Europeans. Native Americans drew on genealogies, ancestry, notions of having inhabited territories since times immemorial, and of related sovereignty rights in their dealings with Europeans. They understood themselves and acted as sovereign nations (Konkle, 2004, 2). Notions of nationhood and sovereignty, adopted from Europeans and transformed *mutatis mutandis*, left Native Americans with some room for interpretation and maneuvering for their survival and their own developing national discourse. They adapted to negotiate in a Third Space, as we shall see.

3.   The Peace of Paris (1763)

The fourth French and Indian War ended with the Peace of Paris in 1763. Huge landmasses, or, as Francis Parkman wrote, "half a continent" (Parkman 1905, 526), changed their "proprietors": French territories east of the Mississippi River and in Canada went to Britain – at least from a European perspective. From the perspective of Native Americans, France had sold their territories to Britain, without asking the land's original and sovereign owners (Calloway 2006, 66). This peace treaty proved to be more than dramatic in its consequences, in particular, as, nominally, Britain became the sole imperial power in the northeastern parts of North America. It was from now on the only power with which Native Americans in these regions had to negotiate their sovereignty rights. With France leaving behind much of mainland North America, Native Americans could no longer play off the two competing imperial states.

During the French and Indian War, American Indians had mostly fought on the French side, to get rid of British settlers menacing their lands. In 1763, however, the latter had come out as victors. To avoid bloodshed, some British colonial authorities meant to separate Native Americans and white settlers: they made attempts to keep "Indian country" clear of European settlements. In many instances, British colonial authorities continued to recognize that, in principle, the land was Native American land and concluded treaties with American Indians as sovereign nations. Newly arriving white settlers, however, increasingly disputed American Indian land and sovereignty rights, often against the colonial authorities' will (Calloway 2006, 48–55).

From a Native American perspective, the Treaty of Paris of 1763, in which they had not been included as allies and sovereign nations, was no peace treaty but a declaration of war by British colonial authorities and white settlers alike. In addition, the British did not continue diplomatic relations with American Indian nations, as the French had done before. Inspired by the Delaware prophet Neolin's vision, Pontiac's war broke out in 1763, the first Native American war of independence – as American Indians later put it. It was a pan-Indian movement against British colonialism, uniting a number of indigenous nations: Ottawa, Potawatomis, Ojibwas, Wyandots, and other. Their united forces tried to take Detroit, laid siege to the town for six months and took a number of British forts between the Appalachian Mountains, the Great Lakes and the Mississippi regions. When a peace treaty was signed in 1764, Native Americans had not driven the British from their lands. However, they had received concessions from the British: the latter had to ask for passports to cross "Indian country"; for rights to erect or maintain forts they had to accept local tribes as equal partners – at least from Native American perspectives (Calloway 2006, 66–91). From a British colonial perspective, establishing a clear border between "Indian" and British territory, as King George III did with his proclamation of 1763, was to establish peace. It was not quite clear whether this proclamation established Native Americans and British colonizers on an equal footing, whether it safeguarded Native American sovereignty or land rights, or whether American Indians had come under British dominion (Calloway 2006, 96). From a Native

American perspective, the proclamation was and still is understood as their Bill of Rights. Especially in Canada, it became a major instrument in land disputes in the centuries to come.

4.   The New Republic

With the American War of Independence, Native Americans were in many instances forced to negotiate sovereignty over their land with the United States of America, a newly emerging empire which succeeded Britain without feeling any obligation to further respect the Royal Proclamation of 1763. While the U.S. claimed sovereignty over the territories "acquired" from the British, the federal and the state governments were by no means able to control these territories. In practice, U.S. American sovereignty was limited; the middle ground was still there (White 2010). US Americans had to continue to treat Native Americans as sovereign nations with whom treaties were to be made on an equal footing, that is as sovereign nations with autonomous governments (Gould 2012, 1–4; Konkle 2004, 14–15).

The U.S. constitution of 1787 recognizes Native Americans as separate political entities. At the time, it was not quite clear, however, whether indigenous nations were to be treated as foreign nations, that is as sovereign states outside the United States of America and beyond its political boundaries, or as the several states of the U.S. Congress became the very institution entitled to deal with foreign nations and the several states. While, in theory, notions prevailed that saw Native Americans as different, primitive, and less civilized than other societies, the colonial practice of treaty-making continued. To some extent, this continuous practice re-established Native American nations on an equal footing with the U.S. American nation (Bruyneel 2007, 11; Konkle 2004, 8–9; Hoxie 1994, 90, 92, 97). With the westward expansion of the United States of America, "fulfilling" its "manifest destiny", this ambiguity became more and more complex and complicated.

5.   Treaties and Removal

After 1787, the colonial traditions of treaty-making prevailed. Many of
the more than 500 treaties between American Indians and the United
States government, concluded between 1778 and 1871, still have legal effect today. From 1778 to 1831/32, the majority of these treaties was mainly
negotiated to establish new borders between indigenous and U.S. American territories, including the necessity to hold a passport when crossing
American Indian territory. To some extent, these treaties resembled in
their structure, concepts, and stipulations international treaties of alliance between European powers.

One good example is the Treaty with the Delawares, signed in Fort
Pitt on 17 September 1778. It was the first written treaty concluded
between the young and, in this case the (Delaware). It was essentially
a formal treaty of alliance allowing U.S. Americans to travel through
Delaware territory. From the Delaware or Lenape perspective, as Dan
Richter has pointed out in *Facing East from Indian Country*, the agreement
was considered as allowing the free passage of revolutionary troops and
the building of a protective fort for defending white settlers (Richter
2001). The treaty spoke of the Delaware as a sovereign nation (Treaty
with the Delaware 1778, art. III). It recognized their sovereignty rights
and encouraged other Ohio Country Indian tribes, friendly to the United
States, to form a state headed by the Lenape, with representation in the
Continental Congress. It has been suggested that this stipulation had
been inserted on request of the Lenape chief, White Eyes, who proposed
the measure in the hope that the Lenape and other tribes might become
the fourteenth state of the United States. In any case, it was never acted
upon by either the United States of America or the Lenape Indians
(Treaty with the Delawares 1778).

At the same time, colonial discourse on the state of nature of Native
Americans sharpened. It continued with some of the early modern *topoi*,
inherited from the "old colonial period": "Indians" were represented as
being different from Europeans or Americans of European descent. The
former were unable to rise from their state of nature, were morally de-
praved, did not want to improve themselves, had no notion of property,

and did not properly cultivate their land. "Indians" had thus to be excluded from the universal human. From this colonial perspective, natural law did not apply to Native Americans. Instead, they were considered to be incapable of forming their own governments (Konkle 2004, 10–11). The US American government was thus trying to use the subversive semantics of "civilization" within the semantic field of "the nation" to deprive Native Americans of their rights as nations. As Frank Kelderman states:

> This paradox of indigenous sovereignty shaped the workings of Indian diplomacy in the nineteenth century. On the one hand, by making treaties Indian nations reaffirmed their inherent sovereign status as nations external to the United States. On the other hand, the American government recognized indigenous sovereignty only within the context of the colonial relationship between Native people and the United States: for instance, it did not recognize Indian nations as sovereign powers that could engage in formal diplomatic relations with other foreign powers. (Kelderman 2019, 19)

From the early 1800s, the treaty-making practice between the United States and Native American tribes was increasingly inspired by the perceived necessity of removing indigenous inhabitants from areas east of the Mississippi. In 1830 this new policy ushered in the Indian Removal Act under President Andrew Jackson. The Jacksonian era has frequently been described as the very years when the US American empire shifted the balance of power from indigenous to settler dominance (Snyder 2017, 16). The U.S. federal legal rhetoric on American Indians now turned from "sovereign nations" into "domestic dependent nations," or later "domestic, dependent tribes" in relation to the U.S. American federal state – a development against which many American Indian nations tried to push back (Kelderman 2019, 5–6). Despite these efforts, the treatment of Indian Affairs moved in 1849 from the U.S. department of War, dealing with international relations, to the Department of the Interior. In terms of the political executive, Indian Affairs thus became part of U.S. American domestic affairs, notwithstanding the legal ambivalence of the Removal era Supreme Court decisions. The Civil War Period and the re-consolidation of the United States of America after 1865 further pushed towards the end of treaty-making. Increasingly, Native Americans were no longer viewed as independent, foreign entities but rather as a domestic problem – as "domestic dependent nations" or as "domestic traitors" (Bruyneel 2007, 5). In 1871, the House of Representatives decided that the House would no longer recognize individual tribes within the U.S. as independent nations with whom the United States could contract by treaty. All of this put an end to more than one hundred years of treatymaking between the United States of America and American Indian nations. It enhanced what some have called the end of "Old Colonialism" and the beginning of "New Colonialism" (Wunder 1994, 27).

From the U.S. American colonial perspective, Native American leaders tried to use the semantics of nationhood, civilization, and sovereignty in subversive ways to uphold and renegotiate their rights. In his reassessment of American Indian literatures, Frank Kelderman has shown for the nineteenth century how Native American leaders and writers "were apt readers of institutional networks and discourses" (Kelderman 2019, 6). They brought their tribal, national, and international understandings of sovereignty and landownership to the table to negotiate with an empire increasingly hungry for other sovereign nations' land. Through the use of the expanding print culture in nineteenth century North America, Native Americans published their understandings of sovereignty and nationhood in their own newspapers but also used the well-known newspapers of settler society to argue their causes (Kelderman 2019, 6–7).

The Cherokee nation is a good example for these endeavors. Already in 1794, the Cherokee nation, with its territories in today's Georgia, founded a National Council. In 1808, the Cherokee codified their laws in the English language and declared themselves to be a republic in 1817. This was followed by the foundation of New Echota as the Cherokee's republic capital city, and the call for a constitutional convention in 1827. It brought about a government and constitution with a bicameral national council, courts and one principal chief, at that time John Ross.

The Cherokee held that as a "modernizing nation," they had to be considered a "civilized tribe" (Konkle 2004, 49) and therefore recognized as a sovereign nation.

In 1818, the Cherokee nation was close to being removed from its ancestral homes in Georgia. Nancy Ward (1738–1822), a Cherokee elder, drafted her petition to the Cherokee National Council. She held:

> We have heard with painful feelings that the bounds of the land we now possess are to be drawn into very narrow limits. The land was given by the Great Spirit above as our common right, to raise our children upon & to make support for our rising generations. We therefore humbly petition our beloved children, the head men, and warriors, to hold out to the last in support of our common rights, as the Cherokee nation have been the first settlers of this land; we therefore claim the right of the soil ... Our Father the President advised us to become farmers to this advice we have attended in every thing as far as we are able. Now the thought of being compelled to remove to the other side of the Mississippi is dreadful to us, because it appears that we shall be brought to a savage state again. (Cherokee 2000, 29–30).

Nancy Ward made use of the concept of the "civilizing mission", arguing that the Cherokee used their land "properly", were therefore "civilized" and as such, according to European-American logics or the semantics of the concept of the nation, not to be removed from their ancestral land. Other Cherokee leaders, such as Elias Boudinot, John Ridge or John Ross, also emphasized the civilized nature of the Cherokee, as a literate and Christianized nation, with a government based on republican principles, a nation that was in a process of "improving" itself through its own schools and imported farming techniques. Cherokee writers and political leaders insisted that the era of treaty-making had proven the Cherokee nation to be sovereign, that natural law and the rights of nations to autonomy and sovereignty, and therefore to form their own government, had to be applied in their case, especially as they had lived on their lands since times immemorial. They also insisted that they had history, that as a nation they were developing in history. *Cherokee Nation v. Geor-*

gia (1831) and *Worcester v. Georgia* (1832) show impressively how this battle for sovereign nationhood failed. It was followed by the Cherokee removal treaty in 1835 and the Trail of Tears in 1838 (Konkle 2004, 17, 20, 36–37, 42–96).

During and after the Civil War, the Cherokee nation was divided on the question how they should deal with the reinforced efforts of the U.S. federal state to "domesticate" Native Americans. The Cherokee nation now lived in the Indian Territory. The territory was governed by American Indian nations who had been resettled, in particular the Cherokee, Choctaw, Chickasaw, Creek and Seminole nations. In this context, the Cherokee became divided into a northern (full-blood) and a southern (mixed-blood) Cherokee nation. While the northern section under the leadership of John Ross wanted to "secure Cherokee autonomy in the 'third space' between domestic and foreign status" (Bruyneel 2007, 47), the southern section of the Cherokee led by Stand Waitie, which had sided with the Confederate States of America during the Civil War, wanted to disunite the Cherokee nation and was ready to agree to the conditions of the colonial U.S. settler state. In the end, the treaty of 1866 secured the Cherokees' needs as a nation: up to 1898, they became exempt from the land allotment policy in Indian Territory, but only for one year, up to 1898 (Bruyneel 2007, 29, 47–53, 63–65). Other Native American nations had used a language of subordination much earlier than the southern part of the Cherokee nation: in the 1818 Pawnee treaty, Pawnee nations declared themselves "under the protection of the United States of America, and of no other nation, power and sovereign, whatsoever" (Treaty with the Great Pawnee 1818, 156–7).

Up to 1832, many land cession treaties use the language of *nation* and *sovereign nation* with regard to their American Indian treaty partners, even in removal treaties such as the *Treaty of Dancing Rabbit Creek* which was signed on 27 September 1830 between the "Choctaw nation" and the U.S. government in today's state of Mississippi. It is considered to be the first removal treaty carried into effect under the Indian Removal Act, ceding 45,000 square km of Choctaw nation territory to the U.S. government in exchange for about 61,000 square km in the Indian Territory, that is today's state of Oklahoma. While the Choctaw are still approached as a sovereign nation, "forever exempt from laws of any U.S. state," the latter serves the Choctaws as a protectorate state. Also, the U.S. negotiated that it would be allowed to establish post-offices, military posts, and roads in the Choctaws' territory, which meant the implementation of U.S. state institutions and U.S. infrastructure in Native American territory (Treaty of Dancing Rabbit Creek, 1830).

In more and more instances, the United States of America ignored or denied that American Indians made "proper use" of their land. From the colonial settler state's perspective, American Indians therefore only had temporary titles to their lands and needed to be replaced by "civilized" white settlers. In addition, Native Americans were now described as vulnerable people who had to be removed from white settler societies for their own protection and benefit (Kelderman 2019, 59). This last addition to colonial rhetoric on Native American land titles slowly turned American Indians into domestic dependent nations. In their publications and oratory, Native Americans objected to this status of "vulnerable people" who were on their way to natural "extinction". Furthermore, some Native American diplomats, somehow echoing the Cherokee nation's arguments, claimed their readiness to implement "western civilization", however on their own terms (Kelderman 2019, 64–66, 69, 93).

With the process of removal continuing, American Indian nations lost their status as sovereign nations as the treaties of the 1850s to 1870s show. For instance, the *Treaty of Traverse des Sioux*, signed on 23 July 1851 between the U.S. government and Sioux Indians, regulating land cessions in today's Iowa and Minnesota, no longer used the term *nation* for the American Indian treaty "partners", as most treaties had done prior to the 1850s. American Indians were now approached as "bands", or "tribes".

With or during their removal, some American Indian nations, or more precisely, some of their leaders, such as Peter Pitchlynn (1806–1881), or Hatchoctucknee, of the Choctaw nation, tried to renegotiate, or as he put it, "rebuild" the Choctaw nation. The latter was like the Cherokee part of the "Five Civilized Tribes", together with the Chickasaw, Creek, and Seminole nations. European-American colonists classified these "tribes" as "civilized" as they had adopted Christianity, centralized governments, written constitutions, literacy, nineteenth century market economies which included European forms of agriculture and plantation slavery. Pitchlynn, with a mixed background and coming out of the landed Choctaw elite, attempted to assimilate to U.S. American narratives of nationbuilding: Pitchlynn's aim was the educational, governmental, and economic reorganization of the Choctaw nation, along the lines of modern nation-building, as promoted by U.S. American institutions in the mid-nineteenth century. His endeavor, however, was to have the Choctaw nation do it on its own, not guided by U.S. American institutions but rather by the Choctaw elite. Through "modernization" efforts, that is drafting a constitution, building institutions, law-making in written form, an educational system, establishing social rules for marriage and other, Pitchlynn sought to regain control over his nation's future, to undertake these steps towards "modernity" on its own, without colonial control (Snyder 2019, 124–131, 145, 165). Pitchlynn's nationalism did not build on Choctaw traditions and ancestry but aimed at the building of a "modern" Choctaw nation in Indian Territory. This nation, however, did not consist of equal and free members but was divided into unfree and free, into different social strata, invested with class privileges (Kelderman 2019, 147). As other American Indian nations' leaders, Pitchlynn also adopted the Western concept of civilization: as the Choctaw nation was willing to become "civilized", they also had more/better claims to Indian Territory than other American Indian nations who were – according to European-Americans – on a lower level of civilization (Snyder 2017, 131). Pitchlynn thus readily took on a narrative of white settler exceptionalism, by using it for to the "civilized" Choctaw nation (Kelderman 2019, 137). According to this narrative, Indian Territory was "vacant", or only populated by "non-civilized", "barbarian" nations.

Some Native Americans took a different line of argument. A number of chiefs and diplomats saw the frontier, quite contrary to Frederick Jackson Turner's interpretation in "The Significance of the Frontier in American History" (1893), not as separating "wilderness" from "civilization", but rather as two differing economic systems that needed to be reconciled (Kelderman 2019, 102–103). Much of this reasoning still informs Native American claims to sovereignty over land and their forms of land usage today.

6.   Extinction and Termination

After 1871, U.S. politics and that of the Bureau of Indian Affairs in particular turned to "assimilation", to the "extinction" of American Indian nationhood, self-government, and culture. Among many other measures, boarding schools were established, where American Indian children were separated from their families, often abused, and even killed. In addition, these institutions prohibited Native Americans from using their languages, practices, and cultures. From 1887, the allotment era, land was distributed among individual tribal members, which virtually abolished the collective ownership of land by "tribes". In 1924, Congress unilaterally declared all Native Americans as citizens of the United States of America. All of this culminated in the Indian termination policies of the United States from the mid-1940s, with the Indian Termination Act in 1953. Its purpose was to end the existence of Native American nations and their governments and to turn all Native Americans into assimilated U.S. citizens. The Termination policy thus nominally abolished the remnants of the U.S. government's recognition of the sovereignty of American Indian nations and the U.S. trusteeship over Indian reservations. For Native Americans, however, it did not end the legal significance of the treaty-making period.

This clashed with American Indian aspirations to more collective rights and to their reinvigoration as sovereign or semi-sovereign nations with land titles and extensive rights to self-government within their reservations. Again, Native Americans used arguments from the "old colonial period": that the British and later the United States federal government had recognized Native Americans as sovereign nations through the politics of treaty-making. These treaties, though broken, were still legally binding, the tribes claimed.

The U.S. Termination policies started changing in the 1960s. Rising American Indian activism resulted in the coming decades in claims for the restoration of Native American rights. According to Tóth, referring to the work of Benedict Anderson, nationhood is not natural but *performed* in cultural representations, government policy, and international diplomacy. Indian diplomacy thus increasingly became "the performance of the nation through 'representation' – the standing in of an individual or a team for the interests and positions of a larger 'imagined community'" (Tóth 2016, 15). Performing the sovereign nation, both in the U.S. and in Canada, culminated in *cross-border* initiatives, with the Trail of Broken Treaties in 1972 as one of the most visible endeavors to push for a renewed negotiation of treaties and the enforcement of treaty rights (with the occupation of the Department of Interior headquarters from November 3 to 9, 1972). With regard to the U.S. government (Nixon was on the verge of being re-elected), the aim of the movement's *Twenty-Point Position Paper* was to re-establish and legally protect American Indian sovereignty rights, which meant to abolish the 1871 Act and to reinvigorate *Indian Nations'* power (so the position paper went) to contract treaties with the U.S. as *other foreign powers* would (Deloria 1998, 25–31). Among many other related stipulations, the position paper asked the U.S. government to restore by 4 July 1976 a permanent Native American land area of no less than 450,000 square kilometers. This area was meant to be perpetually non-taxable by the federal and state governments and exempt from U.S. federal law. In addition, the petition demanded that the Termination Acts of the 1950s and 1960s be repealed, and the Bureau of Indian Affairs dismantled by 1976 with the purpose of establishing a new institution governing American Indian-U.S. federal relations at an equal level with international relations. While the American Indian Movement activated the language of nationhood, sovereignty, and equality, the language used on part of the United States Congress and the Bureau of Indian Affairs preferred the term "tribes" to "nations." This unilateral definition notwithstanding, Native Americans were seeking no less than full decolonization and independence from the United States of America, as according to Vine Deloria Jr. and others, American Indians had never ceased to be sovereign nations (Deloria 1988, 38). The declaration of the Independent Oglala Nation at Wounded Knee in 1973 was meant to re-establish political sovereignty beyond the legal framework of the United

States, recognized by other nation-states. It was a clear act of re-territorialization, accompanied and followed by multiple processes of nation-(re-)building throughout North America. As much as other political performances, the militant takeover was meant to force the United States of America to treat Native Americans again as independent nations and to recognize treaties as international treaties. In the mid-1970s, these initiatives resulted in Native Americans and Canada's First Nations gaining NGO-status with the United Nations (Tóth 2016, 6, 34, 39, 46–47, 50–52).

7.   Subversive Semantics since the 1970s

Today, indigenous peoples in the United States of America draw on modern critical interpretations of colonial treaty-making in the eighteenth and nineteenth centuries. They try to negotiate their rights as sovereign nations between the federal state, the individual states, and their own territories, moving – as Kevin Bruyneel put it – on the spatial and temporal boundaries set by the colonial state. The conflicting parties operate not only with different notions of sovereignty but also with different notions of spatial and temporal boundaries. Indigenous nations in the U.S. claim that their rights as nations and as such their sovereignty rights do not stem from the colonial powers but can be traced to times immemorial. They thus draw on early modern European notions of legitimizing nationhood and national sovereignty, also claiming that the treaty agreements of the eighteenth and nineteenth centuries were still in place. They thus adopt a concept of nationhood that is close to that of the *Kulturnation*. While this can indeed be derived from the acceptance of those agreements in the U.S. constitution, the Marshall Supreme Court rulings and subsequent laws have left Native Americans legally in a Third Space, not fully inside and not fully outside of the U.S. American federal state. From Native American perspectives, this uncertainty with regard to their rights as sovereign nations is interpreted as the colonial state, the U.S., holding them back from advancement, from moving forward in time. It is thus the colonizer who is "holding back", who is static, not the to be colonized, quite contrary to colonial notions of time with regard to the "static" indigenous people (Bruyneel 2007, XI-XVII, 1–2).

Indigenous sovereignty claims from the 1970s to the 1990s sought support in a transnational perspective. American Indians were supported by Central European peace, environmental, anti-nuclear and Marxist movements west and east of the Iron Curtain, national liberation, and decolonization activists on a global scale. In forging diplomatic relations with other NGOs, Indigenous Americans performed as sovereign nations. The International Indian Treaty Council was highly successful with its petitions to the United Nations, through its correspondence networks, mass media, political and cultural actions, seeking recognition that they alone, and not the United States of America, were entitled to represent Native Americans as sovereign nations among other nations. Aiming to move from NGOs to sovereign nations with their own territory deeply challenged what the U.S. Government thought to be the integrity of the nation-state and their full sovereignty rights over territory and people (Tóth 2016, 1–6, 149–152, 155–167).

In other colonial states, such as Canada, this language of *nation* and *nationhood* among indigenous peoples is today even more pronounced than in the U.S.: since the 1980s, the term First Nations has become common language not only among indigenous peoples but also in the political language of Canada. First Nations is now used for Canadian indigenous peoples with a common government and common languages, however not for Métis or Inuit peoples.

One of the strongest and best-known examples of what nationhood and sovereignty for American Indians respectively First Nations mean is provided by Haudenosaunee or Iroquois confederacy inhabiting the borderlands between the United States and Canada. Their territory stretches from upstate New York to the U.S. American border into modern-day Quebec and Ontario. The Haudenosaunee people use their own passports for international travel. I quote from the website of one of the Haudenosaunee nations, the Onondaga:

> Although physically situated within the territorial limits of the United States today, native nations like the Onondaga Nation and

the other members of the Haudenosaunee, or Six Nations Confederacy, retain their status as sovereign nations. Like the United
States, the Haudenosaunee is a union of sovereign nations joined
together for the common benefit of its citizens. Governed by a
Grand Council of Chiefs who deliberate and make decisions for
the people concerning issues both domestic and international,
the Haudenosaunee began as a confederacy of sovereign nations
aligned to deal with other native nations surrounding their lands
and, later, to negotiate with Europeans when the latter came into
their territories beginning in the early 1600's. [...] It is the contention of the Onondaga Nation, then, that it maintains and has
never relinquished either its national or collective sovereignty as
a member of the Haudenosaunee. [...] There has never been any
provision for transferring that sovereignty to any other entity, nor
have the traditional chiefs of the Haudenosaunee ever consented
to such a transfer. Like the individual states of the United States,
each member nation of the Haudenosaunee retains the authority to
govern its own internal affairs. Within the framework of the Great
Law and its own specific laws, each individual nation reserves the
right to adjudicate internal disputes, pass laws for the welfare of
their own community, assess fees, regulate trade and commerce,
control immigration and citizenship, oversee public works, approve
land use, and appoint officials to act on its behalf. Every member of
the Haudenosaunee has the authority to defend its citizens against
internal and external dangers and to advocate for the peaceful
resolution of conflict and the equitable distribution of collective
resources (Onondaga website).

From an U.S. American federal government perspective, American Indians are today – as scholars put it – in an in-between space: they are "ex-
traconstitutional," "domestic dependent nations," there is a "two-tiered
structure of Federal Indian Law" and "measured separatism" – which
Bruyneel interprets as a Third Space, with uncertainties but also room
to re-negotiate American Indian status in the U.S. (Bruyneel 2007, 5).

8.   Conclusions

This chapter has tried to show how Europeans developed colonial notions of nationhood and how these changed with the on-going process
of colonization in North America. In the "old colonial period" indigenous
peoples were practically treated as sovereign nations. In the later seventeenth and throughout the eighteenth century, Europeans still recognized Native American nations as allies and independent nations. In the
nineteenth century, the United States of America sought to turn American Indians, first, into dependent nations, then tribes and bands up to
the dissolution of any kind of collective indigenous nationhood and collective rights to self-government.

Throughout all phases of old and new colonialism, American Indians have tried to make use of European concepts of nationhood and
national sovereignty to uphold and make claims to self-government
and territories within the legal framework of the United States. With
adaptiveness and legal-political agency, Native Americans have used
the colonial master's arsenal of ambivalent semantics of nationhood to
defend sovereignty rights and to develop nationalisms that are more
than just strategic. Aware of the changing languages and semantics,
aware of historical change, Native Americans now trace their integrity as
sovereign nations not only to the beginning of the colonial period, when
this terminology was first introduced to them, but project their nationhood back into pre-Columbian times, thus adopting primordial notions
of nationhood. They thus borrow from early modern and modern European concepts and performances of nationhood and sovereignty, they
demonstrate the subversive power of language and semantics, which
can be reloaded to both assert and question the integrity and sovereignty
of political entities or the modern colonial state.

Works Cited

Banner, Stuart (2005) *How the Indians Lost Their Land. Law and Power on the Frontier*. Cambridge/Mass., London: The Belknap Press of Harvard University Press.

Bruyneel, Kevin (2007) *The Third Space of Sovereignty. The Postcolonial Politics of U.S.-Indigenous Relations*. Minneapolis, London: The University of Minnesota Press.

Calloway, Colin (2006) *The Scratch of a Pen. 1763 and the Transformation of North America*. New York, Oxford: Oxford University Press.

Cherokee Women and Nancy Ward, Petition to the Cherokee National Council, 30 June 1818 (2000). In: Kilcup, Karen L. (ed.) *Native American Women's Writing: An Anthology*. Oxford: Blackwell.

Deloria Jr., Vine (1988) *Custer Died for your Sins. An Indian Manifesto*. Austin: University of Texas Press.

Deloria Jr., Vine (1998) Intellectual Self-Determination and Sovereignty: Looking at the Windmills in our Mind. *Wizaco Sa Review* 13(1), 25–31.

Depkat, Volker and Susanne Lachenicht (2022) Nations, Nationalism, and Transnationalism Revisited. *Yearbook of Transnational History* 5, 1–39.

Gould, Eliga H. (2012) *Among the Powers of the Earth: The American Revolution and the Making of a New World Empire*. Cambridge: Harvard University Press.

Harring, Sidney L. (1995) *Crow Dog's Case: American Indian Sovereignty, Tribal Law, and United States Law in the Nineteenth Century*. Cambridge: Cambridge University Press.

Hoxie, Frederick E. (1994) Why treaties? In: Lindquist, Mark A. and Martin Zanger (eds.) *Buried Roots and Indestructable Seeds. The Survival of American Indian Life in Story, History, and Spirit*. Madison: University of Wisconsin Press.

Kelderman, Frank (2019) *Authorized Agents: Publication and Diplomacy in the Era of Indian Removal*. New York: SUNY Press.

Konkle, Maureen (2004) *Writing Indian Nations. Native Intellectuals and the Politics of Historiography, 1827–1863*. Chapel Hill, London : The University of North Carolina Press.

Labat, Jean-Baptiste (1722) *Nouveau voyage aux isles de l'Amérique*. Paris : Cavelier.

Lachenicht, Susanne (2018) Learning from past displacements? The History of Migrations between Historical Specificity, Presentism and Fractures Continuities. *Humanities* 7/36 (e-journal). Web: https://www.mdpi.com/2076-0787/7/2/36/htm.

Lachenicht, Susanne (2022) Early Modern Diasporas as Transnational Nations. *Yearbook of Transnational History* 5, 41–72.

Onondaga Nation Website: Web: https://www.onondaganation.org/government/sovereignty/.

Parkman, Francis (1905) *Montcalm, and Wolfe. The French and Indian War*. Boston : Little, Brown and Company.

Raynal, Thomas (1780) *Histoire philosophique et politique des établissemens et du commerce des Européens dans les deux Indes*. Geneva: Pellet, Jean-Léonard.

Richter, Daniel K. (2001) *Facing East from Indian Country. A Native History of Early America*. Cambridge : Harvard University Press.

Rochefort, Charles de (1681) *Histoire naturelle & morale des iles Antilles de l'Amérique*. Rotterdam: Leers, Arnould.

Smith, John (1612) A Map of Virginia. *With a Description of the Countrey, the Commodities, People, Government and Religion*. Oxford.

Snyder, Christina (2017) *Great Crossings. Indians, Settlers, and Slaves in the Age of Jackson*. Oxford : Oxford University Press.

Thevet, André (1558) *Singularitez de la France Antarctique*. Paris : Maurice de la Porte.

Tóth, György F. (2016) *From Wounded Knee to Checkpoint Charlie: The Alliance for Sovereignty Between American Indians and Central Europeans in the Late Cold War*. Albany: State University of New York.

Treaty of Dancing Rabbit Creek. Web: https://www.choctawnation.com/sites/default/files/2015/09/29/1830_Treaty_of_Dancing_Rabbit_Creek_original.pdf.

Treaty with the Delawares, 1778. Web: https://avalon.law.yale.edu/18th_century/del1778.asp.

Treaty with the Great Pawnee, 1818 (1904). In: Kappler, Charles J. (ed.) *Indian Affairs: Laws and Treaties*, vol. II. Washington D.C.: Government Printing Office, 156–157.

United Nations Charter. Web: https://www.un.org/en/about-us/un-charter/chapter-1.

United Nations Declaration on the Rights of Indigenous Peoples. Web: https://www.un.org/esa/socdev/unpfii/documents/DRIPS_en.pdf.

United Nations, Department of Economic and Social Affairs, Indigenous Peoples (UNDRIP) (2020). Web: https://www.un.org/development/desa/indigenouspeoples/news/2020/09/undrip13/.

White, Richard (2010) *The Middle Ground. Indians, Empires, and Republics in the Great Lakes Region*. Cambridge: Cambridge University Press.

Wunder, John (1994) *Retained by the People. A History of American Indians and the Bill of Rights*. Oxford: Oxford University Press.

Contributors

Michael Butter is Professor of American Studies at the University of Tübingen. He is the author of The Nature of Conspiracy Theories (Polity, 2020) and co-editor of Covid Conspiracy Theories in Global Perspective (Routledge, 2023). He is the Principal Investigator of the ERC-funded project "Populism and Conspiracy Theory" and one of the PIs of the CHANSE Project "Researching Europe, Digitilisation, and Conspiracy Theories," which seeks to produce a thick description of how the internet has affected conspiracy theories in different European regions and seeks to develop recommendations of stakeholders on the national and EU levels. In 2021 he was awarded the Tübingen Prize for Knowledge Communication.

Jörn Dosch holds the Chair of International Politics and Development Cooperation at the University of Rostock. He is also an Adjunct Professor at the Asia–Europe Institute, University of Malaya. Previous positions include Professor of International Relations at Monash University (Malaysia Campus) and Head of the Department of East Asian Studies, University of Leeds. His research focuses on politics and international relations in the Indo-Pacific region, the European Union's foreign relations, US foreign policy as well as migration and development theory and practice. Jörn also regularly works as a Consultant for the EU's development program and has evaluated several donor-funded projects in support of partner countries in Asia and Latin America. His publications include *The New Global Politics of the Asia Pacific*, 3rd edition, Routledge 2018 (with M. Connors and R. Davison).

Daniela Gottschlich was trained in political science and German literature. She is presently Professor for Sustainability and Social Design ("Gesellschaftsgestaltung") at the Hochschule für Gesellschaftsgestaltung (hfgg) in Koblenz. Her research and teaching interests are sustainable development from a critical-emancipatory perspective, new economies, right-wing populism and socio-ecological transformation, and ways of democratizing social relations with nature. Her transdisciplinary and collaborative work is informed by feminist economics and political ecology. Together with Christine Katz she published "Caring with Nature/s: Zur transformativen Bedeutung von Care in More Than Human Worlds" (in: *gender<ed> thoughts. New Perspectives in Gender Research*. Working Paper Series, vol. 3, 2019). Together with Sarah Hackfort, Tobias Schmitt, and Uta von Winterfeld she co-edited the first German-language handbook on political ecology, *Handbuch politische Ökologie* (open access, transcript, 2022).

Susanne Lachenicht is Professor of Early Modern History at Bayreuth University, Germany. She works on Europe and the Atlantic World with a special focus on diasporas and nationhood, religious migrations, knowledge transfer and transformation as well as temporalities in the early modern world. Her more recent publications include (as ed. with Charlotte Lerg and Michael Kimmage) *The TransAtlantic Reconsidered* (Manchester University Press 2018/paperback 2020), (as ed. with Mathilde Monge) *Nations et empires*, thematic issue of *Diasporas. Migrations, circulations, histoire* 34/2 (2019), (as ed. with Marianne Amar, Isabelle Lacoue-Labarthe, Mathilde Monge and Annelise Rodrigo) *Négocier l'accueil / Negotiating asylum and accommodation*, thematic issue of *Diasporas. Migrations, circulations, histoire* 35/2 (2020) and (as ed. with Guido Braun) *Spies, Espionage and Secret Diplomacy in the Early Modern Period* (Kohlhammer 2021).

Gesa Mackenthun is Professor of American Studies at Rostock University, Germany. She works on the coloniality of knowledge, particularly in US discourse. Her books include *Embattled Excavations. Colonial and Transcultural Constructions of the American Deep Past* (2021), the co-edited *'Prehistory'. Deep Time and Indigenous Knowledges in North America* (with Christen Mucher, 2021), and many edited volumes on the intersections between cultural encounters and scholarly/scientific discourses. She also did two books on oceans. More recently, she has published various critiques of the ideological uses of deep historical narratives, as well as on the sustainability of (future) stories. Her current research deals with representations of the transatlantic history of enclosures, evictions, and ecocide.

Hans-Jürgen Puhle is Professor (em.) of Political Science at Goethe Universität Frankfurt. He gained his PhD from Freie Universität Berlin (1965) and his Habilitation from the University of Münster (1973). He held appointments in history and political science at the universities of Münster and Bielefeld. He has also been visiting professor or fellow at Harvard, Oxford, Cornell, Stanford, Tel Aviv and other European, North and Latin American universities and research institutions. He has published extensively in the fields of European, North and Latin American social and political history, comparative politics, trajectories of modernization, political parties, movements, nationalism and populism, regime change, democratic (de-)consolidation and quality of democracy. Recent publications include *Protest, Parteien, Interventionsstaat. Organisierte Politik und Demokratieprobleme im Wandel* (Göttingen 2015) and "Populism and Democracy in the 21st Century" (SCRIPTS Working Paper Series No. 2, 2020). He is member of the Excellence Cluster "Contestations of the Liberal Script" (Freie Universität Berlin). He currently researches recent changes of the structures of political intermediation and communication.

Enrico Schlickeisen graduated with a degree in English and History from the University of Rostock in 2019. Between 2019 and 2022, he worked on a dissertation on "Ideological Continuities in Right-Wing

Literature" exploring the transatlantic connections of the Alt Right movement. As of May, 2023, he works as a primary school teacher in Berlin.

Christine Unrau is a Research Group Leader at the Centre for Global Cooperation Research, University of Duisburg-Essen. Her research focuses on the nexus of emotions, narratives and politics, especially in the context of migration, humanitarianism and right-wing populism, as well as alter- and anti-globalization movements. Her book *Erfahrung und Engagement. Motive, Formen und Ziele der Globalisierungskritik* (transcript 2018) focuses on the motivations, forms and aims of political commitment in the Global Justice Movement. She has published in *Sustainable Development*, the *Journal of International Political Theory*, *Zeitschrift für Politische Theorie* and *International Political Sociology*.

Aram Ziai studied sociology, history and English literature in Aachen and Trinity College, Dublin. He has held research or teaching positions at the universities of Amsterdam, Hamburg, Bonn, Accra, Vienna, and Tehran. He is Professor of Development and Postcolonial Studies at the University of Kassel and Head of the Exceed Center "Global Partnership Network" (GPN). He published widely on postcoloniality and development discourse, including *Development Discourse and Global History: From Colonialism to the Sustainable Development Goals* (Routledge, 2017) and *The Development Dictionary @25: Post-Development and its Consequences* (Routledge, 2020).

GPSR Authorized Representative: Easy Access System Europe, Mustamäe tee
50, 10621 Tallinn, Estonia, gpsr.requests@easproject.com

www.ingramcontent.com/pod-product-compliance
Lightning Source LLC
Chambersburg PA
CBHW070102030426
42335CB00016B/1979